DON'T FALL

Adventures in Love, Loss, and Lead Climbing

Sophie Smith

Cindy :)
We May not Be ~~in~~
named in the Book
But we are un ut
from Costa Rica
   to Italy
     and Even
        Belize + Barcelona
we were there in the
   Beginning .. ♡
      Happy Reading Kim

CONTENTS

AUTHOR'S NOTE

It's taken me a long time to figure out what this story is about. It's about travel, but it is by no means a travel guide (I don't recommend my itinerary, nor my general approach to travel to anyone sane). It's about love, even though that's the last thing I was looking for, and I did a very bad job of navigating it. It's about coming of age, and finding yourself, and overcoming loss, but honestly, all that happened much later (and I swear, it's not as cheesy as that makes it sound). Oh, and it's also about rock climbing, where the sole objective is to increase the vertical distance between oneself and the ground, through a combination of scrambling, pulling, balancing and jumping up a vertical or overhanging rock face. There's a metaphor in there somewhere. I should also point out that I'm in no way qualified to give climbing advice either, and the technical definitions in this book should not be taken as anything other than a literary device. I've written this story using the notes, letters, journals and photographs from the three months I spent in South America, and the eight months I spent travelling in Europe and Asia. I've changed the names of the people involved (they might have their own narratives to tell), but I've tried to be as accurate (and entertaining) as possible.

"It's a terrible thing, I think, in life, to wait until you're ready. I have this feeling now that actually no one is ever ready to do anything. There is almost no such thing as ready. There is only now. And you may as well do it now. Generally speaking, now is as good a time as any."

— *Hugh Laurie*

CHAPTER 1: SOUTH AND CENTRAL AMERICA

The Warm Up: the short or easy climb you start your session with, in order to warm up the mind and body for the real project.

"Gav, look, you can ride mountain bikes down the side of a volcano in Ecuador!"

I waved the massive tome of the *Lonely Planet Guide to South and Central America* tantalizingly under my little brother's nose. He glowered, and moved as far away from me as the tiny airline seat would allow.

My Dad leaned over from the seats in front of us.

"That sounds *muy divertido!*" he enthused, employing one of the fifteen or twenty Spanish phrases he had memorized, after weeks of lessons, in preparation for the trip. My Mum, who was pretending to be asleep in the seat beside him with an eye mask over her face, had attended the first two Spanish classes, and then refused to go back after she had decided that the teacher was useless. She insisted that she would be able to survive in South America for six months using "hand signals and charades".

I tried to match my Dad's energy, as I flipped through the guide book which had become my bible, showing him the various "adventure activities" that were available, as I fought the sinking feeling that had been threatening to draw me down for the past few weeks: that this grand adventure on which we were all embarking, at my suggestion, was going to be a fucking disaster.

I come from a far-flung family. Parents who wandered from England to South Africa to Australia. Cousins who drifted to America, Canada, and New Zealand (my dad's backpacking adventures through Africa, South East Asia and the Middle East in the seventies alone are worthy of their own memoir). Thanks to our worldly relatives, I could navigate a baggage check in and find my way through an international airport alone by the time I was ten. Travel was always just what we did as a family, and so it hadn't seemed strange that my parents (who were in their late fifties) had decided to piggyback onto my Grand South American Adventure. Not only that, but they'd somewhat eclipsed my own modest summer plans by selling most of their belongings, renting out our house, and finding a new home for the family dog so that they could backpack together *for a year*. I'm not saying it was a competition or anything, but they sure showed me who the real "adventurers" were. Mum had confided in me that she and Dad *really* needed this...but I hadn't been sure what that meant.

The four of us landed in Buenos Aires eight hours later, jet lagged and strained, and my brother immediately cloistered himself in one of the colonial-style four poster beds of our charming B&B, and attempted to go to sleep. I watched him, feeling equal parts guilt and frustration. I had roped him into coming on this trip with me, after two years of studying Spanish in University had left me with a burning desire to explore South America and practice with actual Spanish speakers. Gavin had just finished his high school exams, just got his first serious girlfriend, and as the date of our departure approached, had just decided that he did not want to spend his first summer out of high school on a foreign continent with his sister after all. Plane tickets were, however, already purchased, and since my parents had already rented out our family home for the duration of their own adventure, he'd been left with no choice but to come along.

People always commented on how similar my brother and I looked, with the same round face, round, hazel eyes, olive skin and curly brown hair, but he had grown a foot taller than me since I'd moved out of home three years earlier. This was going to be the first time since then that the two of us would be spending any length of time alone together, and at the moment, he wasn't talking to me.

My mum, Kathleen (shortened to Kath - *not* Kathy) started rifling through her behemoth of a backpack, convinced she had left some vital piece of equipment behind when she and my dad, Robert, had packed up all their worldly possessions in preparation for their "both our kids are legally adults" year abroad.
"I can't find the fucking head lamps!" She burst out, before sitting abruptly on one of the other beds, and groaning.
Even though people said my brother and I looked alike, they said my brother resembled our mum - perhaps in personality even more than appearance. She refused to dye the grey streaks in her short, thick, dark hair; never put on makeup; and was stubborn, compassionate and artistic. She had practiced law in England, raised two kids in Australia, studied art and photography, and worked as a special needs teacher.

My Dad was already off at the front desk, grilling the clerk on the best spots in the city for walking tours, tango shows, architectural landmarks, and cultural "must-sees". In a few minutes he would be back in the room, and start berating Mum and Gavin for the very idea of *sitting down* when there was a whole new city to explore. People always tell me I look like my dad, although I'd somehow managed to inherit neither his height nor his metabolism - he was tall and wiry, with round wire rimmed glasses, and short cropped grey hair. He had studied medicine in Liverpool before leaving home to backpack around the world for five years, and was a frustrated but determined guitarist and surfer.

And me? I was two years into an Arts Degree, and I had been working part time in a rock climbing gym since I moved out of home, tying ropes, cleaning toilets, and teaching annoying groups of children and their parents how to put on harnesses and belay safely. The best thing about that job was that it was flexible enough to allow me to cobble together this Summer trip as an alternative to spending a semester studying abroad, and lucrative enough for me to buy a random assortment of flights based on "places I'd heard of that sounded cool", but which didn't logically follow much of a path. Like most twenty one year olds, I was equal parts bravado and insecurity about my looks, my brain, my social skills, and my ability to hold it together around my family.

The plan, such as it was after six months of tinkering, was as follows. Gavin and I would be travelling together for three months, from Buenos Aires to Iguazu Falls, then north to Ecuador, up through Panama, Costa Rica and Nicaragua. My parents planned to travel together for a whole year (just like they had done when they first got married), starting in Argentina, then down through Patagonia, before taking a boat to Antarctica (my dad had managed to get hired as ship's doctor) and then north through Bolivia, Chile, Central America, Mexico, the United States, Canada, and then on to Europe and the UK to see their family. At that moment, in that hotel room, with my mother's belongings strewn on the floor, my brother curled up in bed, and my Dad's overly energetic footsteps approaching, I failed to see how any of us would survive the first night.

*****

Three days later, at around eleven pm, I sat on a bar stool beside my mother, as a ridiculously gorgeous Argentinian hipster mixed our fourth round of pisco sours. It's not possible to eat dinner before midnight in Buenos Aires, so we had resorted to filling our empty stomachs with cocktails while we waited for a table. Alcohol, it transpired, was key in dissipating the tension of traveling with your nearest and dearest. After the first day, and the first successful Skype session with his girlfriend back home, Gavin had either come around to the idea of travelling, or resigned himself to the fact that there was no alternative. Either way, he had reverted to his old, funny, affectionate self, and was at that moment deep in conversation with my Dad (who had calmed down to a more manageable level of enthusiasm) at the other end of the bar, unpacking the various pros and cons of our parents' upcoming adventure to Antarctica.

"So explain to me again," Mum was saying, "what's happening with you and Eli?"

Eli was the boyfriend I had left back in Sydney. We had been together nearly a year, and been friends for nearly three. He was gorgeous, kind, funny, with long, curly pirate hair, a twinkle in his eye and a loud, infectious laugh. We spent long afternoons lazing around the beaches, or going on weekend adventures to the river or the mountains, usually with a crowd of friends. We were good together, and my family all loved him, especially Mum.

"We're doing long distance," I told her. I was used to people being incredulous when I explained this, but I was confident we would be able to manage. Well, reasonably confident.

"He's going to miss you," Mum mused, sipping her drink, and giving the gorgeous bartender an appraising once over. "I wonder if you'll miss him? Maybe you'll get distracted by someone you meet here…"

"Mum!" I was appalled. "I can keep it in my pants for a few weeks, for God's sake! Besides, I'll be with Gavin the whole time, it's not like anyone is going to hit on me in front of my little brother."

"I was only teasing, darling," Mum placated me, "I'm sure you are very committed."

"We both are!" I pouted, although, if I were to be honest with myself, I didn't really know if that were true. It was an easy, relaxed, happy relationship, and for the most part we were on the same emotional level – happy to see where things went, not in any rush to make plans for the future.

I loved this new intimacy I had with Mum - playing girlfriends going for drinks, rather than mother and daughter. We had had a rough couple of years back when I'd been in high school, and hated everybody; but we had started to reconnect when I began training and entering climbing competitions, and she became my coach and chaperone. Since I'd moved to Sydney for university, we'd gotten into the habit of writing letters to one another, something she had been doing for her family back in England for years. I felt really close to her, and I was a bit sad that we were going to be going our separate ways the next day: Gavin and I heading North; she and Dad, South.

*****

After saying goodbye to Mum and Dad around 1.30am, Gav and I had gone out to explore the city after hours, or, in Argentinian terms, just as everyone was getting started. In the first bar, we latched onto a large, boisterous group of local students (several of whom were phenomenal dancers), and we followed them as the night wore on, going from bars to nightclubs, losing ourselves in the city's beating heart, emerging only after the sun had come up. Our ears still throbbing from the beat of the dance floor, our feet aching from the whole night spent trying to keep up with our new friends, our heads pounding from too much Argentinian wine, we crawled through the airport and onto an unnervingly tiny airplane, bound for Iguazu Falls. When I unpacked my bag a few hours later, I found a tiny, leather bound notebook packed on top of my clean underwear and sensible fleece jacket.

Mum's handwriting was scrawled on the first and second page, with one of her small, delicate sketches at the end, depicting a snowy mountain range.

> *Darling Sophie,*
>
> *I know these last few days have been kind of tricky, with everything so up in the air, and everyone feeling insecure and jetlagged. Thank you for being so positive and brave! I love that you were the one to get us all to go on this adventure - we needed it.*
> *I'm sure you and Eli will manage to make the distance work, and I think once we are out of the way, you and Gavin will have so much fun! Dad and I will always be only a matter of days out of contact, so keep in touch and we will help out however we can.*
>
> *All my love,*
> *Mum xxx*

I could hear Mum's soft voice as I read the letter, with her slight English accent (which persisted, despite the two and a half decades she had lived in Australia). I could picture her sitting up in bed in the B&B, wearing her rectangular reading glasses, and scribbling in her cramped, left-hand-writing, as she tried to reassure me (and herself) that everything was going to be ok.

*****

On a hot, January afternoon, Gavin and I disembarked the bus from Bocas Del Torro in the middle of San Jose, the grimy, crowded capital of Costa Rica. We had been travelling for a little over a month, flying from Iguazu Falls to Quito, then to Panama City, then catching buses north to Costa Rica. We had survived a freezing mountain bike ride down the side of volcano in Ecuador; white water rafting (and nearly drowning) on the Amazon river; a case of viral meningitis on a boat in the Galapagos (me); being attacked by bedbugs in Panama (also me); and a severe case of "travel panic", where we had decided that this whole trip was the worst, and tried (unsuccessfully) to change our flights to go home early. Although we had spent several days fighting and not speaking to one another, by the time we got to San Jose, we had reached a point where we felt comfortable with one another, and fairly confident that we were going to survive the rest of the trip.

The hostel where we were staying was familiar - all the hostels had started to merge together in a kind of montage of dodgy looking bunk beds (we had each brought our own sleeping sheets), lockers that didn't lock, and kitchens with the ubiquitous "free breakfast" (instant coffee, instant pancake mix and syrup). We had developed a routine whenever we arrived in one of these places: dump our bags, shower, and go see who was hanging out in the garden (there was almost always a garden), to ask if they were interested in a game of cards. In this particular hostel, we ended up with a loud group of Americans, who decided that we needed to go and buy more drinks before we could start a game.

In the supermarket, I rounded a corner to find Gavin being berated by one of our new friends over his choice of drink. In Gav's defense, he had only legally been allowed to buy alcohol in Australia for a year, where it was prohibitively expensive; and had grown up in a household where junk food of all kind was banned; so at that point he chose his beverages based on two criteria: low cost, and high sugar content. The American wrestled the four pack of Vodka Cruisers firmly from his protesting grasp. "You can't drink that!" he stage-whispered to my bewildered little brother.

"Why?"

"Because that's a girl's drink!"

He declared that Gavin had been spending too much time with his sister, and threw me a mock-disapproving glare. I couldn't help laughing at the whole exchange, even though, ethically speaking, I objected to the attribution of binary gender roles to inanimate beverages. Gavin sheepishly purchased his manly rum and coke, and the three of us headed back to the hostel with the group.

Sometime during the night, I mentioned to Gav's new mentor (whose name we discovered was David), that we were travelling up to the mountains the next morning, and suggested he join us. The invitation was genuine, but I was more than a little surprised when, at four am, he was waiting at the reception with his backpack, sunglasses and hangover. The bus trip was three hours of hot, bumpy torture. Gavin and I distracted ourselves with our recently acquired skill of macrame bracelet weaving (I never said we were cool). Our new friend sat beside us, slightly green about the gills, miserably questioning what the hell kind of people he had shackled himself to, as the bus lurched up along the ungraded mountain roads. We managed to make it to the beautiful mountain village of Monte Verde without anyone vomiting on anyone else, and we fell ravenously onto a huge plate of $2 tacos.

We spent the next week together in Monte Verde, and slowly got to know one another better. David looked like a very well brought up boy who had decided to embrace the backpacker look, letting his blonde hair grow extra-long and investing in an impressive collection of brightly coloured tank tops, which he paired with surfer shorts and sandals. He had a smattering of large, graphic tattoos on his chest and down one arm, and had taken to wearing a tangle of hemp and string bracelets, which he bought in each new town as he travelled. He had a loud, American arrogance, which I found both annoying and endearing, but he was also surprisingly easy to talk to, and pretty gorgeous to look at, although I chose to ignore that fact. He told me he had come traveling after breaking up with his last girlfriend, and quitting his corporate job, which he had hated; and I told him about my degree and my boyfriend and friends back home. We went zip-lining, which everyone loved, and canyoning, which everyone (except me) hated, and discovered a huge old tree that was completely hollow inside and most likely full of scorpions, something we only thought of after we had already climbed up inside it.

*****

We split up for a couple of weeks while Gavin and I travelled to Nicaragua, and David attempted to learn to surf in a little Pacific surf town called Malpais, which was where we found him, with three weeks left until our flight home. David had stumbled upon a fantastic, eclectic group of people: a tiny German girl called Stephi, who had been a professional gymnast, and quickly earned the nickname "little ninja"; another Australian called Tess, who had quit her corporate job after only six months and bought a one way plane ticket, and told the dirtiest jokes I'd ever heard; and a tall, bearded med-school dropout from Vancouver called Ryan, who took personal offense if anyone besides him tried to light the campfire. We all spent the next few days in the idyllic little beach town - really no more than a collection of laid back hostels, surfboard rental shops and bars, with dilapidated Internet cafe at the end of the single "main" street - surfing, practicing yoga on the beach, and cooking hot dogs and s'mores (at David's insistence) on campfires as the sun went down.

David and I got into the habit of walking down to the beach together after everyone else had gone to the bar or to bed, and having long conversations about our plans for the future. I had recently decided to go into a masters of teaching after I finished my degree - an idea I had briefly entertained in high school (to loud snorts of derision from my own dear teachers, as they peered out from behind mountains of essays, and clutched their cold cups of coffee).

"So why do you want to do it now?" David asked, as we gazed out over the silver waves. The moon was full, and the late afternoon rain storm had cleared to leave a starry sky in its wake.

I shrugged.

"Honestly? I don't really know. I think I would be good at working with people, rather than in some office job... I don't hate kids... I can't really think of a better idea..." I trailed off, glancing at him to gauge his reaction.

"Hey don't look at me - I'm about to start my first degree at twenty six. It's taken me this long to even think about what I want to do."

I loved these conversations. I never felt judged or pressured to say the right thing, and I always felt I could be honest. By the way, I had been wrong back in BuenosAires, when I'd told Mum that a) having a boyfriend and b) travelling with my brother would keep me from being "distracted" by guys. I'd stayed staunchly faithful to Eli, but I had also drunk a bottle of tequila in the jungle on Christmas Eve with a tall, Canadian raft guide; gone hiking to a "secret waterfall" with an incredibly cute local guide in Boquete; and salsa danced the night away with a devastating Brazilian in Bocas Del Toro. Gavin had accused me of leading these guys on, but I, perhaps naively, insisted that I was then free to drink, dance, and hike with them without it leading to anything, as long as I was honest from the start. The boys tended to take my brother's perspective rather than mine.

David was different. I don't mean that he'd taken my side on the whole "leading them on versus being friendly" debate, but he

19

had never once tried anything beyond the bounds of being completely platonic, and I felt comfortable with him.

Our much-anticipated return to Sydney was soon upon us, and just as it was time to leave, after weeks of homesickness and insecurity, I suddenly felt as if I could keep travelling indefinitely. On our last night in Costa Rica, David and I sat by the campfire and reminisced over how crazy the past few weeks had been - how different we felt, how much the experiences we'd had were changing us. He fell silent after a while, and we stared into the flames of the dwindling campfire, as the waves washed in from the Pacific: all the way from Australia, where my real life was waiting.
"Don't leave. Stay here with me".
He said it so quietly that I wasn't sure I had heard him, and so I pretended I hadn't. And then, the next morning, I left.

*****

We flew down to Santiago, Chile, where we were met by our weathered, wind-swept, wayward parents, fresh from the mountains of Patagonia, and looking happier than I had seen them in years. The four of us regaled one another with travel tales, swapping photographs, luggage and gifts, and warming ourselves in the palpable relief we all felt that we had made it this far. All the fears and insecurities and stress under which we had arrived in Buenos Aires had evaporated in the ten weeks we had spent apart. Gavin and I had survived this bizarre social experiment of a trip, somehow managing to keep our relationships back home intact over the three months we were away, and even more impressively, managing not to kill one another when we got on each other's nerves.

I sat on one of the tiny twin beds with the contents of my backpack spread out around me for the last time. The apartment we had rented for the two nights we were spending in Santiago was cramped and charmingly old fashioned. Mum appeared in the doorway, lugging her monstrous hiking pack over one shoulder. "Do you have room for a few more things in there?" she asked, dropping the pack to the floor with an audible thump.

"How the hell did you carry that up a mountain?" I asked incredulously. "It's bigger than you are!"

"Well, it was smaller before we got to La Paz. You know I hate shopping, but your Dad insisted we check out the markets, and I couldn't resist getting a few gifts for people."

She started pulling dusky-coloured woven wool rugs, shawls, hats and scarves out of her pack, and unravelling a collection of leather belts and colourful beaded necklaces, laying each one out on the bedspread with instructions as to who should receive it.

I heard Dad and Gavin returning from the shops, and they clomped into the room with a plastic bag hanging from each arm.

"We got stuff for a picnic lunch!" Dad announced, with the satisfied air of a philanthropist who has just bequeathed a million dollars to a charitable cause. "Apparently there's a fantastic view to be had from the top of San Cristobal Hill – it's about a two hour walk."

I saw Gavin roll his eyes behind Dad's back, and dump his bags on the counter.

"What's all this stuff?" he asked, indicating the mess on the bed.

"Ah! I think we've got something for you somewhere here!" Dad said, momentarily distracted from his grand plan.

He disappeared into their bedroom and emerged with a lumpy package in one hand, and a small, drawstring bag in the other, which he handed to me before pulling Gavin over to the other bed.

"We found this in La Paz, and I thought it could be something fun for you to learn, now that you are getting so good at guitar!"

"Oh yes, Gav's musical skills were very popular." I said, smirking at him. "He had to beat the girls off with a stick whenever we stayed somewhere that had a guitar to play."

"Shut up." Gavin groaned. "Besides, you were the one who kept nagging me to play so you could show off your singing."

"I was just looking out for you, little brother."

He rolled his eyes again, and opened the package, to reveal a small, handmade instrument that appeared to be a cross between a ukulele and a mandolin, but with far too many strings. He strummed it hesitantly, and it gave off an unpleasant twang. I burst out laughing.

"It just needs tuning!" Dad blustered, and busied himself tightening the strings at random while Gavin sidled back to the counter and began tearing apart pieces of bread and putting them in his mouth.

Mum nudged me. "Look at yours!"

I opened the little bag, and inside I found an exquisite pair of silver earrings, each shaped like a breaching whale's tail.

"We bought them in a little shop in Ushuaia." Mum said. "They're from the very last place on earth where you can get a cup of coffee."

"Yes, not too many cafes in Antarctica" Dad chimed in, abandoning the strange little instrument on the bed, and slapping Al's hand as he reached for his fourth piece of bread. "Let's finish this packing later. That hill won't climb itself!"

As we sat in the airport café the next morning, taking photographs of one another, Gavin and I moaning about the long flight ahead; none of us felt a shred of foreshadowing. The only apprehension in my mind was my nervousness at being reunited with my friends and boyfriend after ten weeks away, and having to return to work and university in just a few short days. I didn't know that the next time my family would all be together, everything would have changed.

*****

Two months later, half way through a remote and physically demanding horseback trek through Torres Del Paine National Park in Bolivia, Mum began to experience pain and swelling in her legs. At first she thought it was just fatigue and over-exertion, but despite being dutifully ignored (in the time-honoured manner of all doctors' families' illnesses), the discomfort worsened.

I was on the fourteenth floor of the library building at the University of New South Wales, researching an essay on the *conquistadors*. It was getting late, and the library was almost empty, except for a couple of other students from my Latin American History class who also, it seemed, had left the essay till the last minute.

I glanced at my phone to check the time and saw a call coming in on an unfamiliar number.
"Hello?" I whispered, craning my neck to make sure I wasn't within earshot of any of the library staff.
"Soph? It's dad."
The line was crackly and punctuated by blank spaces of sound.
"Dad? Where are you calling from?"
"We're in Santiago… can… hear me?"
"I can't quite…Santiago? I thought you were in Bolivia?"
"We had to fly back here… Mum… hospital."
"Mum's in hospital? Why? Is she ok?"
A litany of infectious, tropical diseases parades themselves through my brain, as I felt myself starting to panic.
"It's alright Love…she has a touch of DVT… she's getting some treatment…going to…home."
I had vague memories of my Dad arguing with his own mother years before, telling her that if she wasn't careful, she would get deep vein thrombosis (DVT) on her flight home. It seemed like a disease for old people, and Mum wasn't old. Something in Dad's voice sounded off, even though the patchy connection.
"Can I talk to Mum?"
"She's resting right now darling, but we'll call again tomorrow. We have to… the doctors approve Mum…travel."
After we hung up, I suddenly felt like I couldn't breathe. Some-

thing was wrong, something he wasn't telling me. I called Eli, and begged him to come and pick me up, then spent the next half hour frantically googling DVT. According to every source I read, there was no reason for Mum and Dad to come home if the treatment was successful. Mum would need a few weeks of rest, but then she should be completely fine...

*****

When the doctors in Santiago told my mother she had cancer - a large, inoperable tumor in her lung - she wrote in her diary that she didn't feel anything, only that she felt sorry for my dad. Then she wrote about going through preliminary treatments, and the struggle with the language barrier, and wanting to come home.

Then the pages are blank.

CHAPTER 2: AUSTRIA

*Belayer: the person who holds the rope for the climber, and
catches them if they fall. It's important to have a belayer
you can trust, since they are literally holding your life in
their hands...*

Here's a fun bit of trivia for you: when I was sixteen, I
qualified for the Australian Climbing Team, and travelled
to the Youth World Cup in Austria. This was something of a
shock to everyone (including me), because I'd never been the
sportiest child, but nevertheless, there was something about
rock climbing that appealed to me in a way that running fast,
or jumping high, or throwing things only to have them thrown
back at you, never quite did.

Competitive lead climbing takes place on artificial rock walls,
with climbing routes designed to demand maximum agility,
strength, endurance and skill from each climber. The climber
ascends, tied into one end of the rope, clipping it into the protection while the belayer on the ground endeavors to make
sure they don't die if they become detached from the rock. The
climbing routes are long and difficult, and points are awarded
for the highest hold the climber manages to control before falling. The goal, of course, is not to fall at all, but to make it to the
top, and get a grip on that final hold.

I loved climbing, but I hated falling.

When you fall on a lead climb, you drop as far as the last clip... and then that distance again (further, if your belayer has left the rope loose). I couldn't stand the utter loss of control, the drop in the pit of your stomach as you plummeted for half a second before being yanked to a halt by the rope. My coach would tear his hair out in frustration during training when, with only a few moves to go before the top, I would sometimes choose to simply let go, rather than attempting the move, missing, and taking the fall.

Somehow, despite my fear, I was on my way to "worlds" (as I nonchalantly referred to the single biggest event of my young life, in an effort to disguise my utter certainty that I in no way deserved to be there), accompanied by my Mum, who had been playing the part of chauffeur, cheerleader, and medic as I trained and competed.

The trip started off as a bit of a disaster: we arrived in Munich to discover that our bags had not yet made it, and were in fact sitting in a huge mountain of luggage from about thirty different international flights on a runway in Abu Dhabi, labelled simply 'Germany'. We stayed in Munich for two days with only carry-on luggage and one pair of undies each to sustain us, until our bags finally arrived. Luckily, we still had time to meet the team before the orientation session, provided we caught a specific express train from Munich to Salzburg which only ran twice a day. At the train station early the next morning, we became very quickly confused by the seemingly contradictory schedules and the lack of discernible platform numbers beside each track. The fact that everything was signposted in German didn't help.
"That's not our train," Mum insisted, indicating the one in front of us. "I'm sure we want the one after this".
"But this one has the number we want" I argued, as the doors

closed in front of me.

"Oh," said Mum, as the train pulled away from the platform without us, "you're right. That was the one we wanted."

The next train wasn't due for another eight hours, by which time we would have missed orientation with the team. It was at that moment that I had my first experience of the gut-wrenching fear that assails all travelers when all one's plans go terribly wrong due to some avoidable human error. I flopped down in my brand new, green and gold "Team Australia" track pants, on the bag with which I had been so recently reunited, and started to cry pathetically.

Travelling, I decided, was the fucking worst.

Mum was less than impressed.

"Get up! We're going to figure out a way to fix this."

Sniffing and glowering and lugging my huge bag behind me, I followed her down the stairs from the platform and out onto the street. The warm smell of the coffee shop where we had just had breakfast embraced us, as Mum swung the door open and hauled her bag inside, with me following forlornly behind.

The man behind the counter recognized her at once, and smiled. "Did you forget something?" He enquired, in clipped, accented English.

"No, no, nothing like that," Mum said, sighing and rolling her eyes melodramatically. "My daughter and I just missed our train, and we have to be in Salzburg by this afternoon. Do you know if there's a bus service or something that we can take?"

"This is a good day for you!" the man said, and for a moment I thought that we had just witnessed the first ever recorded incident of German sarcasm, until he indicated two young girls drinking lattes at the table by the window.

"Those girls are driving to Salzburg when they finish their coffee – we were speaking earlier – they are visiting friends for the weekend. I'm sure they would take you."

Without waiting to be introduced, Mum brushed back her short, shaggy curls with one hand, and marched over to their table.

"Excuse me, I'm terribly sorry to interrupt your coffee – do you speak English?"

One girl laughed, and the other nodded her head.

"Yes, a little. Can we help you?"

"Yes, I hope you can. It's just that my daughter and I are trying to get to Salzburg, and the gentleman behind the counter told me that you were planning on driving in that direction. Would you happen to have room in your car for the two of us to come along?"

The girls looked a little taken aback.

"Are you English?" asked the other girl.

"Yes. Well, English via Australia."

Both girls laughed this time, and spoke rapidly to one another in German while Mum and I stood awkwardly over them, trying not to look too desperate.

"Australians are always traveling – always hitchhiking!" the first girl explained, once she had recovered her composure. "But the ones you see here are usually, how do you say it? – the swimming boys!"

"The surfer boys!" her friend corrected, pinching her arm. "Of course you can come with us. We will just have to pay for our coffee and move some of our things."

Mum insisted on paying their bill, and we somehow managed to squeeze all four of us and our bags into their ancient little Morris Minor. As we sat squished together in the back seat, zooming along the highway towards Austria, Mum laid her head against the window and gazed out at the countryside as it flew past. I saw her close her eyes and massage one of her hands with the other, something she always did for me when I needed to relax. In that moment, I realized that when the train had pulled away and left us on the platform, she had probably wanted to sit down and cry right beside me.

Despite our initial setback, we made it in time for orientation. The teams were all being housed in the same gigantic hotel, which served absolutely disgusting food, cooked to mush and drowned in salt. The competition site was a fifteen-minute walk away, through corn fields and apple orchards - it was all *very* idyllic. Within hours of arrival, my more astute teammates observed that the legal drinking age in Austria was 16 (rather than 18 in Australia), and the whole team received a severe talking to about "professionalism" and "being competition-ready", after two of the boys were spotted downing beers on the second day of the competition. I myself, did not get in trouble for drinking, partly because I considered it an honor to represent my country, but mostly because I was quick enough to hide my glass when I realized our coach was looking for us.

From the first day of the competition, it became blatantly obvious that, despite having trained my arse off, I wasn't going to be able to keep up with the career athletes against whom I was competing. I was eliminated in the preliminary round, after making a half hearted attempt at a particularly difficult move and coming off low on the first climb. I had to sit through the next two days watching from the sidelines, feeling humiliated, embarrassed that I had thought I could hold my own at this level. It didn't make me feel better that all but one of my teammates had suffered a similar fate in the face of the indomitable competition.

"I should have paid more attention to my feet - it was such sloppy footwork" I muttered morosely, as we sat watching the finals. It was an excuse: I just didn't want to admit that I could have gotten higher if I hadn't been so afraid of falling.

"It was very impressive for you to have been here in the first place," Mum said, stroking my hair, as we watched a bionic looking Russian teenager do a one arm chin up from the final hold in victory. "I'm very proud of you."

I learned two important lessons on that trip: if you're going to travel, be prepared for shit to go wrong. And if you're going to climb, be prepared to fall.

CHAPTER 3:
AUSTRALIA

Off route: rock climbs follow a specific route of hand and foot holds, from the bottom to the top. If the climber is unfamiliar with the route, they may take a wrong turn, and find themselves scrambling for purchase on a smooth rock face, with nowhere to go.

When my parents got off the plane from Santiago in Sydney, Mum was almost unrecognizable. In January she had been fit, glowing and full of life. In April she was wheeled off the plane in a chair: tiny and frail and diluted. Seeing her was like being punched in the throat - once again I felt that I couldn't breathe, but I was determined to be brave, and hold it together.

Over the next week, we were given a grim picture: the cancer was wide-spread and very far advanced. Mum's previous levels of strength and fitness had meant that she hadn't felt unwell in the early stages, whereas someone less healthy might have sought a diagnosis before it had a chance to get this far. The irony of this, along with the irony of a staunch non smoker developing lung cancer, was less than comforting. We mentally prepared ourselves for the months of treatment we thought she was facing, and Gavin and I set about reorganising our lives (although he hadn't really had time to establish a life for himself since we had come home) so the four of us could be together as much as possible through the treatments. I remember going clothes shopping with her in the tacky shopping centre where I had hung out in high school. She had lost so much weight that her old clothes were hanging off her tiny frame. I picked out the most colourful, happy clothes I could find – a pair of bright leggings and an oversized orange cardigan, because she had been shivering, even in the late summer heat - and waited outside the change rooms as she tried them on.

They were both too big.

"Could I get these in an extra small please?" I asked the shop assistant, reluctant to step away from Mum even for a moment.

She fetched them and passed them over the door to Mum.

"Thank you." Mum said, with an attempt at brightness. She emerged, and we headed for the counter.

"Goodness, I wish I fit into an extra small! You're so lucky!" chirped the moronic shop assistant. I stared at her, with her rosy cheeks and shiny hair; and her curvy, healthy, cancer-free figure. I wanted to punch her right in her stupid face, but Mum only smiled tightly, and paid for her new clothes.

*****

My friends had huddled around me like warm blankets as I told them the news one by one. Eli was at my side, feeling helpless, yet desperate to help. After a while, I stopped crying every time I told someone new – it became as automatic as asking about their day.

"Mum has cancer."
"She has cancer."
"Mum's getting chemo."

Life, weirdly, continued as normal. I went to classes at uni. I spent the night at Eli's house. I went out. I went to work at the climbing gym. I talked to Mum every day on the phone, and she was always unfailingly optimistic, but it worried me how she tried to trivialize what was happening to her. One night, after this had been going on for about a month, I went to the movies with my friends, and somehow lost my phone, which was no great tragedy, because it had been old and cheap. The next day I was at work, giving a group of awkward teenagers a lesson on climbing safety, trying to make them laugh and relax. One of the other staff came over with the phone in his hand.

"Sophie, phone for you."

"I can call them back if you get the number?"

"It's your Dad– he says he needs to talk to you. Here, I'll finish this."

I gave the teenagers one last encouraging smile, and took the phone.

"Hi Dad, sorry I lost my phone last night. What's up?"

My supervisor found me by the lockers five minutes later, crouched on the concrete floor, holding the phone, sobbing uncontrollably. Mum had fallen asleep on the couch and had been unable to move when she woke up: they thought she'd had a stroke. I was waiting for Dad to call back – he was still trying to get in touch with my brother, so that the two of us could drive home together. My coworker, with whom I'd previously never discussed anything more sensitive than balancing the till at the end of the day, gingerly put his arm around me for a second, and then told me to take as long as I needed, and backed awkwardly out of the room. Minutes passed. The phone rang – but it was just a customer asking about our opening hours. I hung up on them. It rang again. My Dad had gotten through to Gavin, but he was in the process of moving out of his house, and had said something about waiting for his landlady to arrive so he could return the keys and get his security deposit back. I wrote his number down on my hand, and was dialling it when the phone rang again.

"Sophie?" It was my Mum's friend.

"I've called Tony" (her son, a close friend from high school) "he's going to leave uni now and come and pick you up, and he'll drive you and Gavin up here. I don't want either of you driving on the highway right now. Give me the address for your work and he'll be there in twenty minutes."

I gave her the address, stammered my thanks, and hung up. I called Gavin.

"Gav, Tony is coming to get us. Are you on your way here?"

"I'm still waiting for my landlady. She said she should be here in half an hour."

"Gav we have to go. We have to go now!"

"I have to give my keys back or I wont get my deposit. She said it had to be today."

I could feel my throat tightening.

"Leave the fucking keys under the fucking mat and have her mail you a cheque! We need to go now. Mum might not... she might not have much time."

My brother went silent. I realized Dad hadn't told him this. My heart felt as if it were being squeezed.

"I'll call the landlady now. I'll try to be there soon."

I paced the tiny, airless room, cluttered with bags and ropes, and waited.

Tony called a few minutes later to say he was on his way, but I still hadn't heard back from Gavin. I wiped my eyes with my sleeve and tried to comb my hair with my fingers, and went out to let my manager know what was going on. Everyone was horrified and supportive and told me to go, and not to worry, and to let them know if I needed anything. I waited for Tony out in the parking lot, and then the two of us waited for Gav, me huddling under Tony's arm for comfort, or safety, or something. Finally Gav's car pulled up, and we jumped in, Tony folding his lanky frame into the driver's seat, Gavin in the passenger, and me in the back. We didn't talk much - there wasn't anything to say. The next five hours of highway were the longest of my life. Every traffic light and slow zone and road works felt deliberate and unbearable.

It was dark by the time we arrived, and stepping over the threshold of the house, I felt as if I had entered a strange new country, whose language and customs were utterly unknown to me. The stroke had left Mum paralyzed on one side, and she could barely speak or move. The huge house pulsated with people, but the room where Mum lay was sequestered quietly away at the end of a long narrow corridor. I came to both love and dread that tunnel. On the one hand, when the influx of visitors, well wishers and dish-bearing friends became too much, we were able to contain them in the main part of the house, keeping Mum's room a quiet sanctuary. On the other hand, it meant that walking down that tunnel was an all-too-symbolic transition from the bustling, warm, noisy living area, to the quiet, cold, isolated room at the end of the rabbit hole, where "nothing could be what it is, because everything would be what it isn't. And contrary wise, what it is, wouldn't be, and what it wouldn't be, it would".

After the stroke, Mum was too weak to receive more chemotherapy, and over the next few days, it became obvious that this wasn't a fight she would win. Obvious to everyone, that is, except her. Lying in bed, unable to move, she made jokes about needing to eat more kale, and talked about starting alternative therapy, whilst at the other end of the rabbit hole, people were preparing resignedly for the worst. It became impossible to remember which end of the corridor was the dream, and which the reality.

After the first couple of days, she wasn't able to speak properly, and her strength was so far gone that even her right side was no longer any use. Once, I came into her room, and found her half hanging out of the bed, unable to roll herself back in. I couldn't sleep that night, thinking of how helpless she must have felt in the five minutes that she had been left alone like that.

Late on Friday night, a week after we had arrived, she started to die. It wasn't peaceful, and it wasn't quick. There was no soft closing of the eyes, or gentle sighing as her spirit left her body. She lay unconscious for four hours, her breathing becoming more and more ghoulish as her body fought desperately to carry on. My Dad called the hospital for more morphine, but it was too late. I would give anything to have kept my brother from sitting through those hours. After her harsh, gasping breaths finally slowed, and then stopped, the three of us sat beside her bed, unable to leave her alone, while the rest of her family, flown hastily in from England and America, slept, jet-lagged in the guest rooms. After a long while, I crawled back into bed, and fell into a deep sleep.

When I woke up, it was to the feeling that I had fallen, and was stuck down that rabbit hole, so deep in the ground that not even a speck of light remained to show me the way out.

*****

The one time Dad had been able to have a conversation with Mum about "the worst case scenario" (which everyone else had already decided was the inevitable one) she had requested two things: to be buried on our land; and that when our golden retriever died, that she be buried beside her. Not my Dad, but the dog. Who knows if she was serious or not, but it was all we had to go on in terms of "last wishes". It turned out that burying someone on private property is not that easy. Gone are the days of the family plot in the backyard, marked by mossy stones and crosses: now there needs to be council approval, planning, paperwork, red tape. Luckily for us, my friend's brother worked for the local council, and he hurried the process along as best he could.

I'll never forget the day we buried her – the memory is more vivid than her funeral, or the memorial ceremony they held for her at the school where she had worked with disabled students (I sat through both in a state of utter stillness and silence, staring at my shoes). My parents had built our family home thirty years earlier, on the end of a narrow ridge of bush land, which dropped off steeply on either side, overlooking shallow green valleys and – on a clear day – the ocean. The soil was primarily red clay and rock, and it was a testament to my mum's gardening skills that she had been able to coax a garden of natives to grow there. The entire perimeter had to be regularly cleared, raked, and monitored to protect the house from bushfires. We were told that Mum's grave had to be accessible from the public road for some reason (I suppose in order to allow other people to pay their respects), and Dad picked out a spot on top of a steep gulley of tree ferns, with one path leading back to the house and another to the road.

My parents had always been very eco-conscious people, and my Dad – far from being stingy – had objected to having a fancy coffin on the grounds that it was going straight into the ground, and should therefore at least be biodegradable. So we had ordered a plain cardboard coffin, and when it came, everyone who could hold a paintbrush had decorated it with pictures of wildflowers and native birds. The box was a work of art, and the tragedy of burying something so lovely made it easier to forget what was inside it. In direct contrast to the beauty of the box, the weather seemed determined to make everything else ugly. For the three days before the burial, it rained. The tractor that had been arranged to dig the hole got bogged down in the sticky scarlet mud, and, like some kind of children's rhyme, a bigger one was required to rescue it. Both were nearly lost down the slope as the tires skidded and slid on the impossible, scrubby incline. The hole itself, when it was finally excavated, was a deep, rectangular gash in the hillside, oozing mud, with three inches of rain water collecting at the bottom. It seemed ghoulish of us to put her down inside that earthy pit, but I didn't have the energy to be upset about it.

The day of the burial dawned behind grey clouds, and by the time we had made our way to the site with the coffin and a few close friends, the sky was dripping. In our rain boots and jackets, we skidded and squelched through the mire, carrying the brightly coloured box that carried the body that carried the cancer that had carried away my mother. Disaster was narrowly avoided when my Dad's friend slipped and nearly fell in while we were lowering the coffin. Angry red bull ants (the kind that bite and sting) swarmed over our boots when my brother accidentally knocked their nest, causing us to kick and stamp, like we were practicing some bizarre kind of bush jig. The mosquitoes were vicious and unrelenting, and still, it rained. After we had lowered the box safely down into the water-logged pit, we discovered that it was almost impossible to move the sodden clay, which had been piled beside the hole in the rain for two days, and was now too sticky and heavy to shovel. It took us two hours to fill in the grave, after which time it looked more like a construction site than a place of rest and peaceful reflection.

When we had finally put down our spades and mattocks, my grim faced little brother, taller than me by a full head, slung his arm around my shoulders. I leaned against him, exhausted, and looked over at my Dad, whose forehead had been smeared with red clay and sweat, and who was gazing at the muddy pile at his feet, perplexed by its stubborn ugliness.
"Dad."
"Hm?" He looked up at me, and tried a wobbly smile.
"I love you and all... but you are getting fucking cremated."
My brother snorted, and grinned at my Dad, who threw back his head and laughed. The sound reverberated around the clearing, previously silent but for our frustrated grunts, and the occasional squelch and splash of muddy earth.
"It's not been a very dignified day, I must say," Dad agreed, surveying the wrecked hillside. "Maybe when my time comes, just

strap me to my surfboard and give me a Viking burial."

"You must be joking," my brother said, straight faced. "Can you imagine the council approval process for a Viking burial?"

"Yeah, forget it Dad: it's cremation for you. If you wanted a fancy burial you should have died first."

Laughing, dirty, exhausted, and less than we had been before, we stood together in the rain as Dad's friend Jeff fetched a bottle of champagne from the car. The bubbles fizzed in my empty stomach, and the alcohol made my head rush, as we toasted the muddy, skid-marked mess that was my Mum's final resting place.

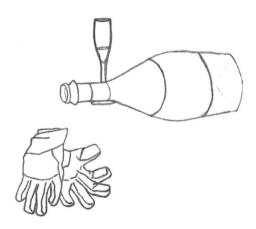

CHAPTER 4: LEAVING AUSTRALIA

Cranking: relying on brute strength (usually upper body) rather than balance or technique to make a difficult climbing move, sometimes with disastrous consequences (like the time I popped a tendon in my finger).

In the beginning, I would start every day on the verge of tears, convinced I was unable to function as an adult, wanting someone to just wrap me up and hold me, and make work and university and every other thing disappear. Over the next few months, I progressed from feeling this way every day, to every few days, once a week, two weeks, until I was able to go for weeks at a time without experiencing one of these episodes.

For a while I was relieved, but as time passed, I began to feel guilty about how normal my life had become. People stopped asking me how I was, I could study and work, and most days, I didn't feel sad. And then came one day in November, when I realized I could no longer picture Mum's face. I started frantically writing down memories – every memory I had of her that I could put into words. As the days passed, I realised that she was no longer part of my present: she only existed in my past. That was when the nightmares started. I would wake up in a cold sweat, having dreamt about my life in the distant future, one where every decision I had made had put more and more distance between myself and my memory of her. I began to develop an irrational fear of the future, and of making decisions. I began to try to think of ways of stalling. I wanted to go back in time to the weeks when Mum had been sick - if only so I could have more time to process what had happened. I wasn't ready to move on with my life yet – I didn't know how.

I dropped out of my Spanish language course after *la puta profesora* demanded to see Mum's death certificate (something none of my other professors required) before she would grant me an exception on my mid year exam, which had been on the same day as Mum's burial. I switched to Latin American film studies to complete the requirements for my minor, and, paired with my classes on American Literature, a trend began to emerge: in Latin American film, there was a common trope of the absent father. He was dead, or imprisoned, or just gone. In North American literature, it was the dead mother. We started the semester with Faulkner's "As I Lay Dying", then moved onto Cormac McCarthy, "The Road", then Hemingway's "A Farewell to Arms"... it was brutal: once I'd noticed the pattern, it was impossible to ignore. Dead mothers, and the things they motivate people to do in the wake of their death, seemed to be all these authors could talk about. Somehow, I managed to write a passable essay on the elements of the books not related to authorial matricide, and made an attempt to maintain a semblance of a social life, but I was a mess. A close friend in my Controversial Lit class had lost her grandmother to cancer in the same week as mum had died, and she and I would check in with one another before each class, bringing tea or cookies on bad days, but even this didn't make me feel better. It felt like shit, because a shitty thing had happened, and no amount of normalcy or sympathy made it less so.

After my final exams, I went back home for a few days to visit

Dad, and get a break from the city. In his usual, absent-minded way, he had forgotten to tell me that he had another visitor that weekend: a traveller named Derek, whom he and Mum had met on their hike in Patagonia. I found it very easy to talk to Derek, but even easier to listen: I loved his stories of travel and adventure. When I told him that I had been accepted into a Masters of Teaching degree for the next year, he asked why I wasn't taking a break.

"Why go back to doing the same thing straight away? Why not go and do something crazy?"

"Because I've already been accepted... and I have friends, and a boyfriend, and a life in Sydney. I'll have plenty of time to do other things once I finish."

"Sure, but you have time now. You are young now, and you don't know how your priorities could change. Go and do the things you may never get another chance to do. University can wait. Work can wait. Relationships can wait. You should do something crazy."

My Dad was less than thrilled when he discovered that his young guest had been filling his daughter's head with such things. I was, after all, very impressionable.

*****

When I returned to Sydney from my Dad's house, with a head full of half formed plans and ideas, for going very far away for a very long time, I knew I had to talk to Eli. I wasn't sure what to expect from him. I knew without a doubt neither of us wanted to do the long-distance relationship thing again – it hadn't been much fun the first time – and that had only been for three months. If I left, it would mean breaking up.

I have never been very good at emotional conversations. I tend to just blurt out what I want to say, usually without a lot of tact. "I think I need to go away next year...for a long time. If I stay here, I'll just keep moving down the path that's in front of me, and I'll never have a chance to stop and figure out what I really want."

Eli reached out and hugged me. His solution for everything in life was physical contact, so he was an excellent comfort-hugger.

"I think that sounds like the right thing for you. You need to go out and have some adventures, and if I stopped you from doing that, I would hate myself. I'll be here when you get back."

I could see he was struggling to keep his voice neutral, but I knew that the sentiment was genuine. We had always said that we didn't want our relationship to prevent either of us from having experiences that could help us grow, but until now it had been mostly theoretical.

"I don't want you to be sitting at home waiting for me to come back. If I go, there's absolutely no obligation on either of us."

"I completely agree. No obligations. But... will we still talk?"

"Of course we'll talk! But I don't think we should talk about, you know, *everything* we do while I'm gone. I think that stuff might be better left unsaid."

"If that's what you want then we will make that the rule. But my rule is that we stay honest with one another – even if there are things we don't talk about."

"And when I get back we will see where we are. But no promises from either of us – let's make this year about experiencing as much as we both can apart, and then see if we want to get back together at the end."

"Deal."

*****

I spent that summer preparing to leave. I bought a one-way ticket to Europe, got cold feet, almost cancelled it, then had a total change of heart, and changed it to one three months sooner. I declined my place at the university, rented out my room, sold things – or threw them away – and stored everything else in my Dad's second shed. I had to come up with a somewhat plausible story to give people when they asked what I planned to do with myself, since privately, I had no idea. I remembered a conversation I had had years ago with my Mum, who had been bemoaning the fact that my Dad always seemed to be going off and doing exciting things by himself while she stayed at home. She told me that the next time he went on one of his trips, she was going to go and live in Spain for six months, hole up in a little apartment somewhere, shop in the local mercado, and learn to speak Spanish. It seemed fitting that since I was paying for this trip with the money she had left me, I should go where she wanted to go. I told everyone I was going to go and live in Spain for a while, and explore some rock climbing areas around Europe.

In the back of my mind I was acutely aware that I was living the cliche of my American writers (tragic death of mother spurs massive life change for grieving protagonist), and I tried to ignore the anxiety that other people may be thinking the same thing, and judging me for it. To avoid any possible mention of my true motivations, I indulged in a paradox of long, cosy evenings with Eli; and wine-fuelled, giggling conversations with my girlfriends about the romantic trysts I might have with some mysterious, alluring Spaniard, who would no doubt write me beautiful poetry and shower me with adoration before we parted ways, never again to meet. Turns out, I was wrong about the poetry part, but more about that later...

It was clear in my mind that I wanted to have adventures: I wanted to climb, to explore, and to discover; but I also wanted to escape. I wanted to slow my life down and remember what I had lost, before I tried to figure out what I wanted to do next. And so I set out into the world alone: wide-eyed, optimistic and scared absolutely shitless.

CHAPTER 5: WALES

Trad Climbing: or traditional climbing, as the name suggests, is the original style of rock climbing, from a time when people didn't have fancy equipment like harnesses and carabiners. Trad climbing basically involves hauling yourself up the bare rock face by hook or by crook (or by knotted pieces of rope shoved into cracks and held in by prayers and friction), without the comfort of bolted titanium protection.

In early April, after a very bumpy and boring flight, I landed in Manchester, England, completely unprepared for the horizontal snow and two degrees celsius wind-chill factor which greeted me as I stepped out of the airport. I was going to spend a few days with family in England, giving myself a chance to recover from the inevitable jetlag that comes from traversing half the world's time zones in one day. I was enveloped in the welcoming arms of my aunt and uncle, and their cosy home in the Welsh countryside where I spent the Easter weekend.

On my third night there, my aunt and uncle invited some friends around for dinner – an old school-friend of my Dad's, his eldest son, and his son's friend. It soon became apparent that my Auntie, concerned perhaps at my complete lack of planning and forethought, had invited them around because the son's friend was a rock climber. When I discovered that his name was Alex, I chuckled to myself: for whatever reason, I have an uncommon and enduring affinity with people called Alex, and I wondered what connection I would have with this new member of the club...

In high school I was never very good at negotiating the plethora of rules and subtleties that seemed to govern the social inter-actions between the other girls my age. As a result, I bonded with a boy called Alex– one of the only boys who didn't care about cricket, soccer or rugby – and we spent most of our high school years laughing at jokes nobody else thought funny, and going off on adventures or to music festivals. He enjoyed an en-during and ruthless air of superiority over all the boys I dated (which, though justified, was very annoying). When school ended and I moved to the city, he stayed in our hometown for the year, but we still talked on the phone every day. He had been the first person I had called when we got the news about Mum's cancer, and he had gotten on a train for twelve hours from Mel-bourne (where he moved to study) when I told him she was dying. When he got a job in Alice Springs (in the very centre of the Australian desert, a 16-hour drive from the nearest major city), I flew down to Melbourne and we drove there together. We made our first mistake when we left Melbourne without look-ing at a map, but just heading in what we imagined to be "sort of the right direction". As a result, we spent the first day going in a long and scenic loop along the coast, before arriving – after eleven hours of driving – a mere two hours from where we had started. The rest of the trip was similarly haphazard, and took us four days. When we got sick of talking to one another, we turned on my camera and pretended we were talking to other people. It was a miracle we arrived in Alice Springs without one or other of us jumping out of the moving car along the way.

When I started climbing in competitions, I met another Alex, and developed an immediate and unrequited crush (unrequited apart from a very ill-advised week spent fooling around when we were both in between relationships). He spent most of the first few years of our friendship traveling: backpacking around Europe, working in a ski resort in France, climbing in Italy and Thailand. He was addicted to adventure, and pursued it with such blind fervour that when he finally stopped, his inertia sent him in precisely the opposite direction, instilling in him a desire for peace and tranquillity, rather than mobility. Our friendship had abruptly ended when his girlfriend found out about the aforementioned foolery, and gave him an ultimatum about being friends with girls who he had seen naked. I can't say I blamed her, but it sucked. We did reconcile, but not until years later.

In my first semester at university, I had joined the choir (because I was a rebellious spirit in those days) and stood next to a pretty girl in the soprano section who was, it transpired, called Alex. She and I moved in with another girl from my Spanish class a few months later, and together we rode the tumultuous rollercoaster of relationships, fights, parties, assignments, exams, borderline alcoholism and rental disputes that are par for the course in one's first year at university. We were our own gang, ready to leap blindly to each other's defence, ready to fight the world at the slightest provocation: be it the guy who overstayed his welcome after being invited up for tea (who was unceremoniously chased out with a broom); or the landlord who took us to court after we stopped paying rent when the kitchen shelves fell off the wall and nearly killed our housemate (unfortunately for him, her father was a lawyer, and he was ordered to repay us half of our rent plus damages). Years later, I was maid of honour at her wedding.

*****

So, suffice to say, I was curious to see how this new Alex would feature in my story. He was about my height, with sandy brown hair and brown eyes, and an incongruous smattering of freckles on his nose. I sat next to him at dinner: we chatted easily about climbing, and he asked if I'd like to go to a local gym with him the next day. When he and the others left, I felt comforted to know that my mysterious connection with Alexs was something that had followed me all the way from home.

I met Alex Number Four in Liverpool the next afternoon, and he took me to a huge cathedral that had been converted into a climbing wall. It was incredible – the stained glass was still in the windows, and the roof soared above us in a dignified arch, as climbers shouted encouragement and grunted their way through particularly difficult problems. We climbed for three hours, commiserating about our general lack of power and endurance. These shortcomings were thrown into sharp relief when we found ourselves climbing beside a girl who couldn't have been more than fourteen, and was obviously in the middle of an intense training session.

Watching her scale climb after climb, her headphones in, and her face intent, I remembered how it had felt to have a body that performed at that level. I remembered the immense satisfaction that comes from looking at a climb, setting your mind to it, and having your body follow, all the way to the anchors at the top. I rarely felt that satisfaction any more – over the past three years I had sacrificed my training sessions for time spent with friends, dates with my boyfriend, or desperately finishing assessments that always seemed to be overdue. I knew that it had been my decision to prioritize university and my social life over my training, but watching that young girl climb with such grace and ease made me regret it. I wondered if, at 22 years old, my best days as an athlete were already behind me.

"Shit, I wish I could still climb like that." I muttered to Alex.

"Well, aren't you taking a year off? Why don't you start training again?" There was no sarcasm in his tone: he asked the question with the earnest optimism that I was beginning to realise was his default setting. I had no answer for him. Over here, I had no friends, no boyfriend, no university assignments, no job. Maybe this was my chance to get my climbing strength back? Maybe this could be my purpose?

I enjoyed climbing with Alex so much that when the next morning dawned sunny and clear, we went to the wild hills of North Wales, where I got my first, extremely tame, taste of traditional climbing. A quick note about the different types of rock climbing (apologies to non-enthusiasts): the majority of the climbing I had done in my life up until this point had been single-pitch, indoor sport-climbing, where there is plenty of protection already in the wall, and you return to the ground after ascending for 20 or 30 meters, almost exclusively in the safety of the gym, on walls I have climbed a hundred times before. Any "real" climber would be disgusted with this curriculum vita. "Real" climbers place their own protection in whatever cracks and crevices the rock has to offer (a style favoured by certain Hollywood directors burdened with overactive imaginations, and a total lack of technical or physical knowledge. For a good laugh, see films such as *Cliffhanger* and *Vertical Limit*... unless you intend to climb anytime soon, in which case, don't). I did not have enough confidence (or a big enough collection of gear) to truly embrace trad climbing, but it was fun to try something new, and I was happy that I didn't embarrass myself too much.

Ok, I lied before when I said I didn't have any friends in the UK. I heard from a climbing friend of mine from home, Stuart, who'd moved to England for work. He invited me to come with him to Snowdonia National Park for a few days, to stay in his friend's family cottage, which he described as "traditional", and "rustic". Because coming up with a plan by myself was too daunting and enormous a task, I said yes.

And so I caught the train from the village near Golly Farm, through Snowdonia National Park to the unpronounceable town of Llandudno, where Stuart met me at the station. He had two other friends with him; and a slender, blue-haired Canadian girl called Heather, who was, like me, traveling alone; and a loud, cockney London friend called Adam, whose family owned the cottage. My overall impression of Wales as we drove through the countryside, was that it was wet, and it was green. We drove up winding, glistening roads; through dripping, dark pine forests and emerald green fields dotted with soggy sheep and puddles; through tiny little towns with only one street each; until finally we arrived. The cottage looked exactly like the houses you draw as a child: a single door in the middle with a square window on either side, a chimney perched on one end of the tiled, mossy roof; and a straggly tree growing over the other. It was only then that my host let us in on the minor detail that our accommodation had no running water or electricity, and the only shower was the frigid trickle of a waterfall in the field beside it. We deposited our bags in the two stuffy attic bedrooms, and arranged our paltry collection of blow up mattresses, camping mats and sleeping bags to look as comfortable as possible. The little windows in the attic were so grimy with soot from the chimney that what little watery light there was outside failed to penetrate, and I nearly broke my ankle tripping down the narrow ladder in the dark. Heather was clearly putting on a brave face, and even Adam seemed a bit taken aback at the state of the place, but I was secretly delighted. I'd gone through a long phase of reading Enid Blyton books as a child, and this seemed like the perfect setting for an adventure.

Stuart seemed to be thinking along the same lines as me.
"This place is fantastic!" he declared, after circumnavigating the garden and treading mud around the little kitchen. "Let's go and explore!"
It was impossible to resist his infectious energy.
The cottage had been built next to a little lake, surrounded by fir trees, with a small hill rising behind it. On the other side, the trees parted in a valley, through which flowed the tiny stream that served as our running water supply. We wandered around

the lakeshore, finding trees we could climb, and this developed into a twisted version of hide-and-seek, where Stuart and I tried - unsuccessfully – to ambush the others by dropping down on top of them from the trees. This in turn escalated into a kind of medieval battle, waged with pinecones and sticks, until we were all doubled over with stomach cramps from laughing so hard. It felt so freeing to behave like children in this story-book wilderness. I imagined this was how Adam and his family must have spent their time here when he was a boy.

"There used to be an old mine shaft up here somewhere," Adam told us, striding up the slope through the scree and shrubs. We followed him and soon came upon the entrance, which looked as though it had been boarded up many years before. I felt a terrified thrill when we saw, on closer inspection, that the lock had been knocked off, and several of the boards were missing.

"Well. There's clearly some kind of mine-monster loose in these woods now," said Stuart, matter-of-factly.

"Oh dear. I don't suppose the cottage has a lock on the door?" I asked.

"A lock won't save us – look what happened to the padlock here!" Adam picked up the useless piece of metal and chucked it to one side. Heather giggled nervously.

"It's probably out there somewhere right now, plotting our bloodthirsty deaths..." Stuart said in a ghoulish stage whisper. Right at that moment, a tree branch snapped with a loud crack, and the four of us yelled and began scrambling back down the slope to the lake, laughing and tripping over our own feet with the silliness of our own constructed terror. We ran all the way back to the little cottage and slammed the door, collapsing helplessly into the old chairs in the tiny living space. As night fell, we lit a fire in the tiny brick hearth and discovered that the chimney was so clogged with disuse that most of the smoke billowed back into the room. After several solutions to this problem were proposed and rejected, we were left with no other alternative than to keep the front door open to allow the smoke to escape, although the resulting draft rather cancelled out the warmth from the fire. We huddled in our coats, taking sips from the bottle of cheap whisky someone had brought, as our clothes and skin slowly infusing with the pungent smoke, and defiantly agreed that one did not need such new-fangled trappings of modernity as electricity and heated water to appreciate the wilderness. The troll from the mine prowled amongst the pine trees, claws and teeth glinting in the moonlight, as the fire dwindled, and sleep enveloped us like smoke, exhausted from our brief adventure back into childhood.

*****

The next day was classic Welsh weather (that's driving rain, for the uninitiated: not ideal for scaling rocks), but we were undeterred and decided to go for a walk. After stomping up through a steep bank of pine trees, we found ourselves at the apex of a soggy sheep field, and in our attempts to reach the road again, inadvertently invented a new sport: bog running. We gave up trying to keep dry and went hell-for-leather down the slope, which we soon discovered was more of a shallow lake, in the vague direction of the car. The same childlike thrill that had terrified us the day before now made this the most hilarious activity imaginable. It took us the best part of the afternoon, and all night to dry off, aided less by the stubborn little fire than by the impressive quantity of low quality scotch (we had bought another bottle) that we consumed between the four of us.

On our third morning, in spite of our fierce hangovers and still-soggy socks, we decided to tackle the forbidding Mount Snowdon: the highest peak in Wales and England. It was a beautiful, if challenging walk, given our various states of unfitness, tiredness and hung-over-ness from the night before. The path wound up through emerald green fields – some as boggy as the day before, others more boulders than grass. About an hour up the slope, I spotted an interesting looking outcrop of rock to the side of the path, and having judged it 'slabby' enough to be safe, Stuart and I scaled it in our hiking boots, racing one another to the top, before scrambling down the other side and scaring Heather on the path ahead. As we climbed higher, the clouds started to thicken, and Heather's 'hiking' boots began to chafe her feet in their damp socks. The green fields had been replaced with grey rocks and gravel; the path was little more than a vague scribble on the desolate hillside; and we hadn't passed another hiker in the last hour. I was steeling myself to voice the opinion that in bad weather, even such a small mountain as this might present a very real danger to such inexperienced adventurers as us, when suddenly we rounded a pile of boulders and came upon a huge, silver tram station, perched improbably on the very peak of the mountain. It turned out that there was actually a sort of light rail service that people could take to get to the top, and most people opted for this route, walking down if the weather was nice. It transpired that we were not, in fact, in such a wilderness as we had imagined, and as we sat sipping our hot drinks, looking out at the clouds, I must admit I felt a little let down. Without realizing it, I had been craving something wild, something challenging. A vague idea started to form in my mind, that maybe all I was really seeking by coming on this journey was a good rush of adrenaline.

Two hours later we were back at the foot of the mountain, and it was once again raining. By this point, much of the novelty of our rustic accommodation had worn off (although the smell of smoke had not), and I would have sold my laptop for a shower and some clean clothes. Thankfully it didn't come to that: on our way back to the cottage, Adam suddenly pulled a terrifying U-Turn, screeching to a halt outside the local YHA hostel. We sent Stuart in as our emissary, having voted him the most-charming-while-covered-in-his-own-filth, and within minutes he had convinced the little old Welshwoman at the front desk to let us use their showers.

Feeling much more human, we returned to our cottage and prepared massive plates of pasta, which we ate without pause for breath or conversation, before falling straight into bed. By the next morning, Heather had had enough. "My back is killing me, I didn't sleep, I'm cold and all my clothes smell. I'm out." We tried to coax her into staying another day, but to no avail. So we cleaned up the cottage as best we could, and bid it (and our as-yet-unconfirmed mine-troll) farewell. As I sat in the back of the car in my smoky clothes and muddy boots, staring out at the Welsh countryside, I realized that I might just have gotten back my taste for mountains... even the small ones.

CHAPTER 6: ROME

Problem: bouldering is a form of climbing short, difficult routes with a mat as protection, rather than a rope. Because they're short, boulders usually demand a precise sequence of difficult moves to complete, so instead of routes, boulder climbs are called "problems".

David (you remember him, the tattooed American from Costa Rica) and I had kept in touch over the year, which was a miracle, because I had collected barely any contacts from my travels. I knew he had kept traveling for a couple of months after Gavin and I had left, and then gone back home to the U.S. and started his degree. I knew he was coaching and playing basketball, and I vaguely remembered him mentioning an upcoming trip. Neither of us had mentioned the conversation we had had on our last night in Costa Rica.

A few months before I was due to leave Australia, I'd gotten a message from him, asking me when I was planning to be in Europe. I told him April. He replied that he was going to be studying in Rome for the semester, and wanted to go to a music festival in Spain in July. Did I want him to get me a ticket? I checked the line-up and told him "definitely yes". We talked some more, and I told him I had yet to make any concrete plans, only that I was heading in the general direction of Spain and was seeing where the wind blew me.

"Well, let me know if you ever want to come to Rome: I'm sharing an apartment with a couple of other guys, but there's a couch here you can crash on, and we're in a pretty cool part of town."

Over the next few weeks I tried on and discarded several different versions of my 'plan', and decided I would take him up on his offer, since I had never been to Rome, and hey, why not? I remember sitting with my brother at a friend's party two weeks before my flight, and telling him about the people I was going to meet up with in Europe.

"You're staying with David?"
"Yeah, in Rome."
"Uhuh. Well. No funny business, ok?"
"What? No. We're just friends."
"Yeah, well, he had a pretty big crush on you when we were traveling together last year."
I elbowed him. "Don't be stupid. Besides, I thought you liked him?"
Al made a face.
"Yeah.... in the hostel - and to drink with. I'm just saying he was a bit of a player."
I snorted.
"He was a single guy backpacking in Central America."
"I'm just saying..."

Suffice to say, I did not have my brother's blessing, but neither did I want it, since I had no intention of letting any "funny business" go down. This trip was about me, out in the world alone, finding myself, and reaffirming my... inner ... feminist ... stuff. Ok, so at that point I had absolutely no earthly clue what the point of this trip was, but I knew I had not deliberately terminated a long-term relationship with a perfectly lovely man just to fall into a more complicated one, especially not with someone who, from what I remembered, was not even my type.

*****

I said my farewells to my family in Wales, and made my way to the airport at 4am for a 6am flight to Roma, Italy. Upon arriving at security, I realised I had neglected to transfer a certain item from my handbag to my check in luggage...my engraved, beloved Leatherman knife, a birthday gift, and possibly the only practical thing I'd packed for the trip. Turns out, while you may get away with bringing a 200ml bottle of hand cream on board, a two-inch blade is definitely a no-no. What to do? It was too precious to let them throw it away, as they were threatening to do, but I couldn't afford the exorbitant fee Ryan air wanted to charge for a second check in bag (£150!) So, using all my powers of improvisation and breathing calmly and deeply, I raced upstairs; bought an envelope and stamps; found an Internet café; Googled my address in Rome; found a post-box and mailed the damn thing. I then dashed madly back through security *sans* my potentially lethal weapon, only to wait in line for 45 minutes at the gate before boarding. That same knife saved my butt many times during my next two months of camping and living 'rough' in Spain, and served me well, until I lost it at a friend's sister's apartment, a month before they emigrated to America. He promised to ask her to mail the knife back to me in Australia, but it was never recovered. Such is life: never travel with anything you cannot afford to lose.

I sped away from the airport in Rome, clinging on for dear life in the back seat of a taxi, as my driver, paying little to no attention to the road, gave me a lively and entertaining verbal tour of the city. We careened past the ancient Roman walls, and towards the Campo de' Fiori, where the students of the University of Washington Study Abroad program kept their rooms. In a similar vein to the Australian Gap Year, the infamous and time honoured American tradition of 'study abroad', designates a period of months wherein students tell their parents they're going to have an "authentic cultural experience", while in reality appear to major in such subjects as "aimless walking around 101", "advanced artsy Instagram photography", and "competitive pizza consumption"; whilst on weekends taking absurdly cheap flights and even more absurdly expensive trains to various exotic and exciting locations around Europe, where they can put their new skills into practice. Even more impressive is the fact that they complete all these tasks (including their cursory classes and examinations) while blind drunk on €2 bottles of wine. I was wholly unprepared for what awaited me in Rome, both culturally and emotionally.

Sitting at the small café at one end of the Campo de' Fiori that first morning in Rome, waiting for David to finish class, I savored the fact that I'd survived my first Roman taxi ride. The square was sunny, warm and bustling with people packing up after the morning market. I sipped my mineral water and gazed languidly around me, feeling every bit as sophisticated and elegant as Audrey Hepburn in *Roman Holiday* (minus the waif-like figure, the pixie-cut, and the Givenchy dress... but basically the same apart from that). Suddenly, there he was in front of me: grinning his big, American grin, and looking *completely* different to the last time I saw him. Gone was the scruffy backpacker hair and beard; gone were the tank top and board shorts in which he had lived his days in Costa Rica. Instead he wore a button up shirt and chinos, and his hair was short and styled (and clean). He looked... really good. Utterly unbidden, the phrase "the kind of boy you take home to meet your parents" came to mind. That is, until I took in the tattoos peeking out from under his rolled shirt sleeves, and the collection of woven *tica* bracelets clustered at his wrists (some hanging on by a mere thread), and I felt myself relax a little. He greeted me in his familiar, laconic tone, as if he might be teasing me with a secret joke. "Hey Aussie! Welcome to Rome..."

We instantly fell back into the easy, bantering conversation we had found so natural back in Costa Rica: exclaiming how weird it was to see each other out of the familiar Gringo-Trail context; talking about his trip so far, my trip so far; his utter refusal to try to learn Italian; my wavering determination to improve my Spanish; and hey, did I want to get pizza?

We dumped my bags in his high-ceilinged, studio apartment (whose old-world beauty was entirely unappreciated by the four boys staying there) and returned with pizza and two bottles of wine. His roommates - both 20, both very taken aback that David had a *girl* staying with him - drifted in and out as we ate and drank and caught up on one another's lives. At some point, we arrived at the topic of my new relationship status, and I gave the same explanation I'd been giving for over a month now:

"I wanted to do this trip on my own terms, and keep an open mind about where it took me, and I couldn't do that while trying to maintain a long-distance relationship. Long distance is the devil, and after a while it just eats away at the good things you have together, because you are trying so hard to hold onto them. It puts so much stress and pressure on the things that brought you together, because there is nothing new to keep it going. I defy anyone to make a long-distance relationship truly work, long term."

"Weren't you guys in a long distance relationship when you were in Costa Rica?"

"Yes, but that was a couple of months - I don't plan on going home till December at the earliest."

"Huh. And will you get back together when you get home?"

"I don't know. Maybe? No. I don't plan on... I don't know." Even though our feelings fro one another hadn't changed, Eli and I had agreed not to think of this as a 'break'. Our deal had been: no expectations, just see what happens. So, obviously, my feelings on this matter were crystal clear and not at all complicated.

"So you came halfway across the world, alone, to go traveling, alone, for... an indeterminate amount of months..." he said, with just a hint of a wine slur on the *indeterminate*. "Why?"

I was silent for a little while, sipping and trying to look pensive rather than tipsy. This was the million-dollar question. I had been getting quite good at fudging the answer to friends and family before I left: "I need space", "I want to experience life in another country", "I want to get out of my comfort zone"... While none of these were strictly wrong, none were completely truthful either. I decided, for once, to be totally honest.

"You know what? My mum died a year ago. I have no idea what I'm doing. I'm just trying to make sense of the world when I wake up every day."

We sat for a while, and it was, surprisingly, a comfortable silence. I stretched and got up to get some water.

"Let's play cards."

He grinned leant back in his chair.

"Sure you don't want to play 'Never Have I Ever'?"

Something in the way he smiled as he said this told me I had better keep my wits about me with this boy and his games...

****

The next morning when I woke up, David had already left for class, so I called Liz, one of my best friends from home, because she was Irish, and I needed confession.

"Liz? I've done something really stupid."

My friendship with Liz had, until I'd left Australia, been a contrast between my stable, monogamous existence, and her single, crazy, city-girl life. As such, this conversation was something of a role reversal for us, and she (not being one to miss the irony in a situation) howled with laughter as I recounted how my staunch resolve about *boundaries* had dissolved with startling rapidity the night before, and how this morning I had woken up, dishevelled, disorientated, and dismayed to find myself in his arms, the two of us fighting gravity to stay in his impossibly narrow single bed.

"For the record... for the record!" I said, trying to get a word in as she giggled with uncontrolled *schadenfreude*. "We did NOT have

sex."
"Oh, SURE!"
"No, I'm serious! We were sitting on the bed together, and I was telling him about all the places I wanted to visit on this trip..."
...He had been stroking my fingers with his, and I had been struggling to think of anything interesting to say...
"...and we had both had a lot to drink..."
...it had been hard to focus on his eyes when I looked at him, he was leaning in so close...
"...and out of nowhere, with no warning..."
...he had reached up and held my face in one hand...
"...we were making out on the bed!"
His chin had been rough with stubble, and he kissed me without the usual hesitation of a first kiss. For hours we had tangled and touched and tormented one another on the narrow bed, but I'd woken up with my clothes still on.
"But it was a one-time thing! And it's not going to happen again."
... The entire night had felt like a pretty clear promise that there would be more...
"If I'm going to get involved with anyone on this trip, it's going to be some alluring, mysterious Spaniard with dark eyes and a career as a Matador... not some random American guy who got my brother drunk last year and caught me off guard last night."
Liz smirked in a superior, big-sisterly way.
"You've been off the market way too long. You've forgotten how these things work. Call me tomorrow, and let me know how that goes. Also: you have a giant hickey on your neck. Goodbye!"

After applying a liberal layer of concealer, I spent the rest of the morning wandering the streets of Rome, warming myself in the sun and ticking the odd historical and artistic monument off my list. It was beautiful, and only slightly ruined by the fact that I had never in my life seen so many tourists! It was absurd – the pavements were choking with excursion groups, school tours, families and couples, making walking a delicate science of sidestepping and dodging. When I made my way back to the apartment in the afternoon, David was waiting. I had been dreading an awkward reunion, but he made no mention of the night before, (which was worse, in a way), but I consoled myself that it meant nothing more was likely to happen.

I must say (based on my observations of David's classmates in Rome), that every single Hollywood stereotype of American fraternity and sorority students that has made its way over the seas to our screens in Australia is pretty damn accurate. They're all loud, attractive, mostly drunk, with upsettingly perfect teeth, and they are always looking for the party. I had timed my visit so I could be there for David's 27th birthday, an event that set him apart from everyone else who was there for study-abroad, in that he had been legally allowed to drink in America before he left, and they had not. The ten of us made quite a spectacle when we all stumbled into the nice, quiet, family-restaurant, raising the volume from a murmur to a heady roar, more high-pitched towards the girls' end of the table. I noticed more than one table around us deciding to skip dessert. Everyone tried to outdo one another with stories of being inappropriate in another country (it's such a mystery why American tourists have such a bad reputation in Europe) and I successfully upheld four or five conversations at the same time, despite not remembering anyone's name.

The plan was for everyone to carry on to an American bar for beer pong and other such cultural experiences, but I had to go back and get my camera from the room, and with David following me, one thing led to another, and we never resurfaced.

*****

"Liz? It happened again."
I was sitting in David's bed, with the midday Italian sun streaming in through the window behind me, making sure I was at all times acutely aware of my hangover. Somehow (to this day I do not know how), David and the other boys had gotten up three hours earlier and gone to class, and were due back any minute.

Liz did her best to reassure me.

"Maybe he only fancies you when you're both drunk."

"Thanks. That makes me feel so much better."

"Well it's good news if you are worried about him having feel-ings for you! I doubt you have anything to worry about, get anyone drunk enough and they'll hop into bed with you. I don't mean "with *you*" I mean in general… hey! At least you're having fun!"

Liz was not very good at reassuring people, but I deferred to her superior level of experience in these matters.

"It is fun. He's fun. You're right; I'm not going to worry about it. I leave in a few days anyway. And thank goodness: I need the detox!"

"Yeah, you look shit. Talk to you soon!"

When he returned, David looked like death warmed up, which made me feel a little better, but despite appearances, he was eager to go and explore with me.

"I haven't done much here by myself. Or, you know, sober." He said, sheepishly. "I wouldn't mind having a wander around without the group."

We ended up at a Salvador Dali exhibition, and geeked out over his bizarre style and quirky subjects. Despite the fact that he was studying European history, it had never occurred to me that David would be an art enthusiast. Wandering around the cool, air-conditioned gallery together, it was easy to pretend that the last two nights hadn't happened, and that we were just two traveling friends hanging out together. 'This will be easy', I thought to myself. 'We can just go back to being friends, and in a few days I'll leave'.

That night at the apartment, I broached the subject of our sleep-ing arrangements.

"I think I'll sleep on the couch tonight. The bed is really tiny, and… yeah. I think I should sleep on the couch."

He didn't argue, but didn't agree either, just found me a pillow and blanket, and asked if I needed anything else.

I lay down on the lumpy couch and closed my eyes like a good girl, but couldn't shut off my brain.

Was I making too big a deal out of this?

Wasn't this year supposed to be about taking risks and having fun?

Was sleeping on the couch really giving me some kind of moral high ground? What was this, the 1900s? Didn't I owe it to *feminism* to sleep with whomever I damn well pleased?

I heard him roll out of bed and walk quietly over to stand over me in the dark.

"This is stupid. Come to bed with me."

I propped myself up on one elbow and looked him in the eye with what I hoped was an earnest and steady gaze

"You know I just broke up with someone, right?"

"So? I know that. I'm not asking for anything. You're here for the rest of the week, so let's just have fun. You were having fun before, weren't you?"

I had been having fun.

"You promise it's not going to turn into anything serious?"

"Promise. Now shut up and come to bed."

It really is surprising how well two people can fit into a single bed if they're willing to compromise on shared space.

The next day, David smuggled me into the Vatican.

His class was taking one of their rare, legitimately educational field trips, led by the affectionately nicknamed "Profé" - their long-suffering teacher and tour guide - who turned a blind eye to an imposter student joining their group. Profé was something of a comic genius, and kept up a witty commentary through our headsets as we took in the artistic wonders of the Vatican museums, the picture gallery, and the Sistine chapel, where stern faced Vatican guards insisted in loud voices that we "Shhhh!" and "No photo!"

I'd examined Michelangelo's masterpiece in Mum's art books as a kid, engrossed by the bright colors and story-book scenes. As we gazed up at the real thing, I felt David's fingers brush against my arm, and a faint warning bell went off in my subconscious.

That weekend, David, myself, and seven other wide-eyed students-of-the-world undertook the four-hour train ride up the coast to Cinque Tierre, or Five Towns, which is, as the name suggests, a cluster of five picturesque villages perched precariously along ten or twelve miles of rocky Mediterranean coast, north of Rome. You've probably seen pictures. The houses are all painted in complementary oranges, yellows and pinks, the ocean laps at the cliffs, and the hills are scored with tangled grape vines, whose ancient branches somehow convey a sense of days-gone-by simplicity. If you've seen these pictures, you probably had a fleeting impulse to jump on a flight and spend your days sitting on one of those wrought iron terraces, looking out over the ocean, sipping local wine and hearing the sounds of gentle merriment drift up from the restaurants below. For anyone who acted upon that impulse during the weekend we were there, I'm truly sorry.

We survived our four-hour train ride in the only way possible for a large group of young people with short attention spans and American dollars: by taking over two of the compartments and running our own casino. We had five decks of cards, seven bottles of sparkling wine (at €5 per bottle!), four cartons of orange juice, and a stack of stolen Mcdonalds cups with lids and straws (we were, after all, nothing if not discrete). We were all getting happily day-drunk, laughing and joking at a volume that was probably inappropriate for a train carriage (or a music festival), when all of a sudden someone pointed out that another person had entered our compartment. A large man, wearing a beige suit, was (somehow) dozing in the corner, and when he stirred and turned to the side, we were greeted with the sight of the sizable black handgun strapped to his hip. We were very, very well behaved after that, watching him uneasily as he snored against the door, until he awoke exactly thirty seconds before his stop, and left the carriage. To this day I have no idea why he had a gun. Very soon after he left (and we all breathed a collective sigh of relief), all nine of us caught our first glimpse of the sea from our window, and began pointing, shouting and crowding around the window. If there had been any doubt amongst the other passengers that we "weren't from 'round those parts", it was swiftly dismissed. Once again, we made our home countries proud.

We arrived at our station and found our lodgings for the weekend: one apartment for the boys and one for the girls, just like in Rome. When time came for us to check in to our rooms, one of the girls with whom I'd been chatting on the train wrapped her arm around me and asked whether I wanted a bunk bed or to share a double, since their apartment had both. I felt David take me firmly by the arm.
"She's staying with me."
There were several other couples amongst the group, and one pair who'd been dating since before the trip, but no one else was sharing a room for the weekend. I turned a little red as the girls raised their eyebrows, and the boys groaned, but David ignored them, and put our names down for a "private" double room.

The group all spent the afternoon out on the rocks, chatting, playing cards, taking pictures and watching the sun set over the waves of the Mediterranean. Eventually we got hungry, and went back into the town in search of somewhere to eat. We ended up seated at a long, wobbly table outside a miniscule, clifftop restaurant, whose grumpy proprietor was less than thrilled to be hosting such a rowdy bunch. We were curtly informed that there were only two items available, and the rest of the menu was "finished". We each ordered our preferred of the two choices, and then waited for over an hour as behind the double doors, the staff lounged against the counter, smoking cigarettes and doing very little in the way of cooking. When the food finally emerged, it was brought in two dishes, which were slammed down in the centre of the table, beside a stack of smaller plates. There were eight of us, and there was nowhere near enough food, but we distributed it as best we could while we waited for the owner to come back so we could ask for more. When he did return, some time later, it was to deliver the bill and tell us that the kitchen was closed and we needed to leave so he could go home. So much for Italian hospitality! Everyone grumbled and griped as we made our way back to the apartments, but I soon forgot about my empty stomach when David and I got back to our real, grown-up sized bed and locked the door behind us.

"I can't believe we just wasted the whole afternoon with all those other people around and all of your clothes on." He growled, whilst working to remedy the clothing situation.

"Yeah that was the worst. I hate other people. Let's just stay in this room for the weekend." I replied, fumbling to take off my shoes.

"I hate everyone except you. And let's stay in this room forever!" He said, pulling his shirt up over his head. I couldn't think of a good reason not to.

Inevitably, hunger, and a desire to shower, did force us out of the room, and all I can say was that those two days in Cinque Terre were like living in a postcard. We hiked along the coast and up through the steep (so, so steep) hilly vineyards to the furthest of the tiny towns. We sat down to pizza after being accosted by a man who insisted we call him Emmy, who possessed an attitude towards customer service that was a complete reversal of our host the night before. No accommodation was too much for his young guests. "No cover charge!" he insisted, as he gave us all his card, and invited us to stay in his home any time, while telling us the story of his ex-wife, who had recently left him, but still supplied the freshly baked bread for his restaurant from her new home across the street where she lived with her much younger lover, and their cocker spaniel. The hike back was not made easier by the amount of pizza we ate.

That evening we crowded out on the tiny balcony of the boys' apartment, drinking wine and playing cards as the sun set. Despite a brief moment of panic the next morning, when we learned that there had been a last-minute rail strike, we managed to get back to Rome on Sunday evening unscathed. As we rode away from the private sanctuary of our locked room, I thought to myself that this weekend had been the perfect travel-romance.

Disaster struck, however, when we tried to find our way back to the Campo de Fiori from the train station. David and I got separated from the rest of the group, and got on a bus which David was "pretty sure" would get us there. This might be a good moment to mention that David's sense of direction was famously awful. Crammed in with our bags and about thirty other standing passengers, I suddenly felt a hand at my thigh. I glanced over at David, but he was on the other side of an extraordinarily obese woman who was wearing a black, woollen shawl, despite the thirty-five degree heat. The hand was still there. Unable to turn around and face the person who was currently checking the length of my inseam, I aimed my elbow in their general direction, and the hand retreated for a minute, but then returned. Mustering my limited Italian, and a good breath of air, I struggled around to face the man I thought was responsible for this undignified intrusion, and growled "Basta!" giving him another elbow for good measure. David, his face like thunder, attempted to make his way around the obese woman's girth, but at that moment the bus ground to a halt and we (and my new friend) were pushed out onto the pavement, whereupon the man disappeared into the crowd.

"That asshole grabbed me." I said, scowling.
"I know. Did you see which way he went?" David muttered, still scanning the crowd.
"Never mind. How do we get back from here?" I looked around hopefully, trying to spot something familiar.
"Ummm... I actually have no idea where we are."

Even though he had been in the city nearly two months, David's bearings were restricted to the Campo de Fiori, and his Italian vocabulary was restricted to those words necessary to order pizza. I had been finding my way around by way of a tattered map which was currently lying on the floor in David's room, and neither of us had a working phone. At the thought of wandering the city for hours in the hot sun, small tendrils of panic began to unfurl in my gut... until I felt David grab my hand. This gesture of affection, almost childish in its simplicity, and so out of the character of our physical relationship so far, both surprised and soothed me. I had thought I'd been very clear about wanting to keep our fling as much about the sex and as little about anything else as possible –and I had been pretty sure he was on the same wavelength, but hand-holding as a means of comfort didn't seem very sexy...

Awkwardly avoiding making eye contact, we walked hand-in-hand like a pair of chaste middle-schoolers in what we thought was the right direction, until the buildings started to look familiar, and we emerged into the sunny Piazza. He let go of my hand only to unlock the door to the apartment.

My flight to Spain was booked for six the next morning (because that's when flights are cheapest, and I couldn't afford convenience), meaning I would have to leave for the airport at three thirty am. Just as he had in Costa Rica, David turned to me as I was packing, and said the same words.
"Don't leave."
I laughed.
"What, stay here in your tiny bed, in this apartment with your two roommates? What am I going to do here while you are in class all day?"
"I don't care. I just don't want you to go."
Realizing he was serious, I sat back on my heels, and regarded him in the pale street lamp glow that filtered through his window. He might not care, but I did: I might not have figured out

my purpose on this trip, but I knew I needed to be doing something – I needed to keep moving – I needed distraction.

"I thought we said this was just going to be fun."

"It is – but don't you want to keep having fun?"

"I have to go."

"No you don't."

"I have to go."

"No, you have to stay."

We didn't sleep that night, and he did his best to convince me to
stay (and I'm certain we kept his roommates awake in the process), but at three am, just like in Costa Rica, I left.

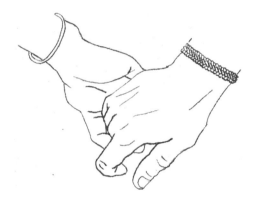

CHAPTER 7:
MONTSERRAT

Quickdraws and bolts: Quickdraws are essentially a strap with a clip on either end, one for the bolt, which has been driven into the rock and secured with glue or cement, and one for the rope. Bolts are usually spaced a meter and a half or (if the route is set by a sadist) up to three or four meters apart on the climb. In lead climbing, the gear is everything, since it will literally be keeping you alive if you slip and fall. Try not to think about that too hard when you're climbing.

I spent my first morning in Barcelona trudging around the streets and negotiating the metro line trying to find the cursed hostel I had booked. I was hot, sweaty and pissed off by the time I made it to the right address, and managed to force my bag into the unreasonably tiny locker in the unreasonably tiny dorm room. I showered, changed, and sat down in the kitchen to figure out what I was going to do next. After I'd made myself a cup of tea (taking advantage of the only thing not expired on the "Free Food" shelf) I messaged David to tell him I'd made it.

He wrote back immediately. "I miss you."

"Well I miss your room. Even with three other dudes sleeping there, at least it was big. The dorm here is freaking tiny."

"Will you still be there in a week?"

"In Barcelona? I have no idea. I haven't figured out the "plan" yet."

"I just found out this morning that some of the others are going over there for a DJ gig next weekend. You should be there too - I'll come and visit you."

"Visit me? I'm staying in a hostel."

"Well then get us a room... the kind with a lock, and a double bed. Like I said, I miss you."

I knew that I had sworn off this kind of making-plans-together-and-missing-one-another nonsense after leaving Sydney, and that I wasn't supposed to be getting mixed up in anything that would affect my freedom to travel, but I reasoned that I would probably have stayed in Barcelona for a week anyway, *and* I was still getting my bearings and... well... sex! Really good sex, if the previous few days had been anything to go by. So, I said I would find us a room. What's a girl to do?

****

I quickly discovered that privacy in Barcelona was an expensive commodity. In order to afford two nights in a private room the following weekend, I'd have to get out of the hostel. Before I'd left Australia, I'd planned to stay with friends wherever I could, and use my Couch Surfing profile to find places to stay the rest of the time, even though, when you think about it, Couch Surfing is pretty much exactly what your mother warned you not to do when you started using the internet. Under no circumstances should you ever meet up with a stranger with whom you be-came friends online, especially not at their house! And if you do, you would have to be absolutely mental to do it alone! Like-wise, only the truly naive would let a travelling foreigner sleep in their house, even give them a spare key, on the strength of a smiling profile picture, and expect to come home and still own a TV and computer. And yet, I had done, and intended to continue to do both. I loved the sense of community and all-for-one camaraderie you got from staying with someone who was temporarily stuck in one spot while you were in the process of moving. More importantly, it was a free bed.

Back in Sydney, I had joined Couch Surfing as a host, so I could get some traffic on my profile before traveling, and get an idea of how the system worked. Luckily, my housemates at the time were cool with having randoms sleep on their couch, and we managed to communicate well enough to avoid any nasty "what are you doing in my house get out or I'll call the police" incidents. Before I had left for my trip, I had mentioned my new network to a guy I knew, and he had smirked unpleasantly.
"I hosted for a year when I lived in New Zealand" he told me, "I've never had more sex in my life. The girls feel indebted to you, you know?"
Yep, charming. Form an orderly line ladies, I believe he's still single!

This unpleasant revaluation, while not enough to put me off, did give me a healthy respect for the fact that not everyone on Couch Surfing is a peace-loving, harmless hippie out to pay it forward: there are plenty of creeps there too. I knew that no matter how strong and independent I felt, there was no getting away from the fact that there are very real risks for a girl traveling alone who depends on the kindness of strangers. I quickly devised my own "stay-safe-and-don't-get-drugged-or-locked-in someone's-basement" formula for choosing a host. Firstly, I refused to stay with anyone who was new to the website. They might have been wonderful, and yes, it's hard to get started in a community based on peer reviews, but I didn't want to be the one to find out if they were creepy or not – let the three big German lads traveling together figure that one out. I also avoided people who didn't have any Couch Surfing 'friends'. 'Friending' on Couch Surfing is different to Facebook: by making someone your friend you are vouching for their trustworthiness. While in Rome, I had sent out a million charming couch requests, and got lucky with a response from a very sweet and quiet Swedish guy, who had moved to Barcelona fifteen years ago, and had been getting lovely reviews from everyone he hosted. I decided to bend my "only stay with women and couples" rule, since literally no one else wanted to host me. He gave me a key to the flat and told me "mi casa su casa" and I did, sleeping on his couch for well over the accepted length of "three days or less", suggested on the website. He didn't seem to mind, and never once gave me the creeps. To be honest, we barely interacted after he gave me his key - he was always working or out meeting friends, and so I was left to my own devices.

I caught the train through unfamiliar suburbs into the city, to meet up with a guy who described himself on Couch Surfing as a 'climbing nomad from New Zealand', and had been in Barcelona for a week already. When I first laid eyes on Tim and his two local hosts, Joaquin and Andreas, I was sceptical. Tim seemed normal enough, and friendly; but his two friends were scruffy, strolling, skateboard-clutching street kids, who could have been seventeen or thirty, and didn't seem to talk much. Joaquin wore his Rasta beanie as if it had been knitted directly into his skin (I never found out whether he even had hair or not), and Andreas had a black eye, a ponytail and a permanent scowl. In low, monotonous mumbles, they offered to walk me around the city and introduce me to some friends of theirs, who had room where I could stay if I needed to. I thought to myself that I would have to be sleeping at a bus stop in sub-zero temperatures before I would consider it necessary to accept such an offer, but followed them cautiously on my very first unofficial walking tour of Barcelona's old town.

We wound through zigzagging alleyways and out onto crowded boulevards, in and out of shops, stopping to buy massive baguettes stuffed with potato fries and cheese, and finally up a steep staircase in a dingy block of apartments. When the door was opened by yet another scruffy Barcelonan, I was overpowered by a strong whiff of incense, and the immediate conviction that it had been calculated to cover up the equally strong smell of the two dozen marijuana plants growing in their living room. It turned out we'd arrived earlier than expected, and the tenants of the apartment were busy relocating their crop from the living room to the box room. Rolls of reflective insulation sheeting were scattered over the floor and several heat lamps were lined up on the table. Squeezing my way through this impressive horticultural operation, I sat down (as there was no couch) on the bed. Tim's friends started to relax a little once we were inside, and began asking me questions about my life back in Australia. The three other boys who lived in the apartment all spoke excellent English, and of course all played guitar, and we ended up having a little jam session, jammed as we were in amongst their makeshift greenhouse. I realized that even though I would need to be cautious of the people I trusted, I would also have to be careful not to judge them too quickly: I have rarely felt safer or more welcome than I did amongst this unlikely band of drug dealers.

My host had suggested I take an actual walking tour run by one of the hostels. The tour started in the gothic quarter, in the shadow of one of the towering churches that hide around so many of the cobblestone corners of Barcelona's rambling streets. Myself and about ten other backpackers were led and entertained by a very funny English lad who had come to Spain to study four years previously, and had never left (I was starting to notice a pattern here). He showed us a city whose history was, quite literally, written on the very walls: in shrapnel damage to the side of churches; in Hebrew scriptures written on headstones that were stolen and repurposed to build palaces; in street signs which had been re-carved as they were changed from Catalan to Castilian, and back to Catalan, after the language was banned under Franco's regime. The Cathedral Del Mar was bracketed by two immense Roman towers, the only two left of the thirty that once encircled the city like a rune. There were splotches of bright paint on the buildings and streets from a recent protest for Catalan independence, eerily reminiscent of the blood, which was split between the anarchists, socialists and conservative classes throughout the 19th and 20th centuries. I could see so much conflict and tension and drama and romance and energy in this place, and I began to love it.

As I explored the city, I realised I still had no idea what I was going to do with myself after the weekend. What I really craved at that point was momentum, something to keep me busy and keep my mind from dwelling too much on my lack of purpose. I met up with Tim in a small, alley café, to brainstorm ideas over stale cheese baguettes (for some reason the bread in Barcelona was always stale, no matter the time of day. It's possible that it was supposed to be that way).

Tim's trip had been even longer and more poorly planned than mine – he had left New Zealand eight months before we met, and was making his merry way around the world, stopping whenever he ran out of money or found somewhere fun. He hadn't been climbing for a few months, and as we chewed, our crusty sandwiches with some discomfort, he told me he had heard about some amazing climbing in the area. A plan started to form, involving me, Tim, and as many rock faces as we could find. Tim seemed like a decent guy: he was about my height, with floppy blonde hair that he was constantly pushing off his face when he talked. His skin looked like it would normally be tanned and weathered, but was curiously pale when I first met him, an anomaly, he explained, resulting from the last few months spent in the European winter, and too much time in the pub rather than outdoors. He was boyish, slightly shy and quiet, but he had these arresting blue eyes, and a dreamy habit of gazing off at some point over your shoulder when he was speaking. I didn't find him particularly attractive, but he seemed sweet. It would probably do me good to spend some time around a person I *wasn't* attracted to. Maybe I'd take that vow of celibacy and focus on my climbing...after the weekend with David anyway.

*****

That night, Tim and I met up with his stoner/skater/music maker friends, and after eating some delicious Argentinian food at their flat (much more spacious, now that the greenery had been successfully relocated) we went out to a tiny underground bar, where two handfuls of people were crammed in with a piano, speakers, drums, a microphone and €1 cans of beer. There was a guy with impressive mutton chop moustaches who looked about fifty, wailing on the harmonica; another guy with elaborately beaded dreads playing the box drum; and a general feeling that everyone would be dancing if only there were room. I stayed there for three hours, as the music changed with strange fluidity; now and then someone would start playing a trumpet, the drummer switched with his friend, two African men alternated vocals on the microphone, someone played a few chords on the piano, the harmonica player returned, left and returned, to loud cheers. The audience flowed into the band and the band spilled over into the audience, and I felt myself begin to slowly unwind as I was jostled this way and that. This was my kind of place.

Back home in Sydney, my group of mutual friends with Eli had been largely of the musical persuasion. I had learned piano for a few years in high school, and sung in various choirs and ensembles, but I never considered myself to be particularly talented. My musical experiences had always been ones of community – I was addicted to the amazing rush of serotonin that you get from being a part of some beautiful sound creation. A few years earlier, Eli had gotten involved in a small group of friends who held a drumming circle every month in a (slightly spooky) storage building near the beach. Thanks to his ability to get people excited about pretty much anything, the event grew to epic pro-portions: people brought didgeridoos, guitars, flutes, trumpets, and of course, there were the big, heavy wooden hand drums that everyone seemed to own. My mum had bought one once, after attending an African drumming workshop, but it had lain forgotten in a corner somewhere for years. I brought it down to Sydney and it made its (slightly out-of-tune) debut at one of the circles. The sessions usually started with slow singing or meditation, and the energy would build from there, as the drum beats became impossibly fast and people started dancing in the middle of the circle. For Eli, drumming was a kind of dance – a physical way of expressing his feelings and wielding his energy. I loved feeling and hearing and making and moving to the music all at the same time, with so many other people who were hear-ing and feeling and making and moving to the same rhythm. I was so happy to have found this same kind of space so far away from home.

*****

The next morning, Tim and I (and a bag containing a borrowed climbing rope) hitched a ride out of Barcelona, through olive fields and small, rustic villages to the imposing monolith that is Montserrat, a towering, rocky outcrop in the middle of a flat plain. The distinctly Mediterranean vista spread out behind us, dotted with yellow-and-orange villages and orchards. Com-pared to the wild bushland and haphazard fields you could see while climbing in the Blue Mountains, it looked like a carefully rendered oil painting.

As we got our bearings and tried to settle on a good first climb, two short, dark-haired Spaniards stumbled down the path to-wards us, chatting loudly, their ropes looped about their shoul-ders and their gear clinking from their harnesses. I went over to ask them about the grades for the wall in front of us, and real-ized with a shock that I recognized them! I'd been introduced to them when I had been climbing in Thailand four years earlier, by a free-spirited, dreadlocked solo traveller called Helen, with whom they had both been infatuated. I remembered the seriousness and devotion with which the two had pursued Helen, a pursuit somehow devoid of competition or jealousy. I also remembered with some embarrassment how, at nineteen years of age, I had felt insulted that they had not been similarly infatuated with me. The three of us greeted one another, and exclaimed over the coincidence of meeting up like this after such a long time. Of course, they asked me if I was still in touch with Helen, and I felt a pang of regret that I had not made the effort to write to her since leaving the beach. They too had lost touch with her, and it was as if the three of us for a moment managed to conjure into being the presence of someone who, but for this chance meeting, would have been forgotten. When the moment passed, we really had no more to talk about. I asked them to recommend the best climb in the area; they politely explained; and then just as politely said their goodbyes and left. This meeting was not so remarkable – the climbing world is a very small and mobile one – but I relished the coincidence, and wondered what else the world would throw at me, now that the floodgates of possibility had been pushed open.

After climbing all morning, we decided to try some traditional Catalan food, and we went to a picturesque, ranch style restaurant just down the road. The food was delicious, abundant and fresh. We were confused when they brought out the wine – it was served in a jug with a long, thin spout, like a watering can. You were supposed to drink it directly from the spout, and it quickly became a competition to see who could pour it from the greatest height with the greatest accuracy. The bread was rubbed with raw tomato and garlic, then sprinkled with olive oil and salt, and we demolished the basket in five minutes, and vowed that we would never eat bread any other way for as long as we lived. On our way back to the city, Tim and I agreed that for the moment, the only place we wanted to be was on the rock, so we made plans to head to Siurana, the place I'd heard the most about since talking to Catalan climbers. The only problem was going to be how we should get there: it was a few hours out of the city, and we didn't have a car. Tim suggested hitchhiking, which I'd always been open to in theory, but hadn't had the need nor opportunity to try until then. We agreed to meet up the following Monday (I did, after all, have plans for the weekend), and somehow make our way to the famous climbing haven of Siurana.

CHAPTER 8:
BARCELONA

The Catch: when a climber falls, the belayer's job is to "catch" them, by activating the break on the belay device. Some belayers do this gently, gracefully, absorbing the shock of the fall by jumping slightly so that the climber bounces without jarring. If the climber falls without warning, or the belayer is inexperienced, the catch can be sharp and painful, as the unexpected weight yanks on both harnesses and throws the belayer off balance.

I looked forward (with increasing anxiety) to my reunion with David. After searching for about the length of time it takes to complete a medical qualification, I had managed to find an affordable place for us to stay (everything costs more on the weekend in Barcelona), luxuriously decked out with a balcony, hot water, and kitchen. I washed all my dirty clothes and draped them, somewhat indecorously, over the balcony railing to dry. I showered, shaved everything, and shoved my backpack under the bed. That still left me with around seven hours until David's flight landed. Seven hours is a long time to sit, and wait, and overthink everything. This whole "keep it simple" relationship approach seemed to be hanging by a very tenuous thread, considering how nervous I was feeling at the prospect of seeing David again. I decided to take myself out shopping (even though my long-term budget was not intended to cater for such frivolities), but I just ended up trying to find an outfit to wear to the airport. I tried and discarded a thousand dresses, shorts and skirts, in a desperate quest to find an outfit that would say "come here and rip this off my body" but simultaneously convey that I didn't need him to do so in order to remain perfectly secure and self-assured. Basically I needed an outfit which could lie for me. In the end, I bought a short, floral patterned summer dress from H&M, and in my anxious state, convinced myself that I looked childish as best, and at worst, fat and unappealing, and so decided to compensate by not eating for the day (always a good choice when you're feeling nervous).

A few hours later, with my self-esteem and blood sugar levels at a record low, I made my way out of Barcelona city to the airport. Considering our adventures in the streets of Rome, and the fact that David could get lost in a single aisle supermarket, I thought it might be a bad idea to let him loose on the Barcelona subway system alone. As I waited for him to come out of the gate, I was experiencing more emotions than I was comfortable with, but the second I saw him, I could tell he was just as nervous as I was, and I was swamped with a rush of relief. I ran up and hugged him, and he lifted me up and kissed me, making me regret the shortness of my dress, as the entire terminal caught a flash of my knickers. I scrambled down and readjusted myself, smiling like an idiot, and started chattering away about all the places we could go to eat, and go out to drink, and what did he want to do first?
"All I want," he said slowly and calmly, as if speaking to an overexcited child, "is to get back to the room with you as fast as we can. I don't care about food. I don't care about doing anything exciting or Spanish. I just want you."
In Tokyo, they have trains that run at 320kmph. The train from the airport back to our apartment felt like it was traveling at

about 3. By the time we finally got inside and locked the door behind us, we could have been in any city in the world: all either of us could see was each other.

We stayed in the room until 3 am, and then went out to meet some of David's study-abroad/alcoholics anonymous mates at a club, where we all danced awkwardly to house music, until the crush of sweaty bodies became too much to handle, and we escaped outside. The club opened out onto the beach, where one could get some distance from the vacantly staring, vigorously drinking, vacuously flirting, vibrating crowd and sprawl upon the cold sand, listening to the bassline wash back and forth in time with the surf. We stayed there just long enough to be polite, before sneaking back to the apartment with the double bed and the door that locked.

We returned to the same beach the next morning, and foolishly ignored the fact that although there was a cool breeze blowing, our skin was getting slowly fried by the Spanish sun, because, well, there was a cool breeze blowing, and we were very comfortable. This being Barcelona, the beach during the daytime was populated by the same, very attractive, very young crowd as the night before, except now they were all topless. Not being one to disregard local traditions (and also wanting David to think of me as the kind of girl who didn't flinch at going topless on what was clearly a topless beach) I flung my bikini top to the wayside. What followed was a rather painful 48 hours of sunburn, requiring an entire bottle of after-sun aloe vera lotion and the regular application of ice and cold cloths (all of which David selflessly administered back in the privacy of our apartment). Wandering back from the beach, as yet unaware of how badly we were burnt, we found ourselves in a tiny cobblestone square, nestled in the shade of the cathedral, where two musicians were jamming together, as passing tourists took photographs without stopping, no doubt in a hurry to see some "authentic" city attractions. They played facing inwards, watching each other for changing chords, improvising melodies. The square emptied, and it was just the two musicians and the two of us. I tugged David's hands – "dance with me!" – but he refused, and retreated to watch from the wall, as I stuck out my tongue at him, and began to spin and sway in time with the music. The musicians paid me no attention, and for the space of a few songs, I danced alone in that cool, secluded courtyard, while David took pictures, and laughed as I spun in a circle beside him, unable to wipe the smile off my face. We spoke with the musicians for a minute when the song finished, then they continued to play, and the sound followed us through the empty narrow streets back to the busy thoroughfares and marketplaces.

I wore that same smile for most of the weekend, as we continued to stumble across the best bits of Barcelona - the light show at the 'Magic Fountain'; amazing musicians performing in tiny, underground bars; cheap *tapas* and wine in hole-in-the-wall cafes. From the moment he arrived, I don't think David and I were out of physical contact for more than five seconds for the entire weekend. We explored Barcelona attached at the hips, the hand, the mouth, and anywhere else we could possibly touch. We made out in the middle of the street, oblivious to the people milling around us. We were swiftly becoming the kind of spectacle that makes involuntary spectators mutter darkly "God, get a room", but we couldn't help it. I was completely disgusted with myself, but ridiculously happy as well. I couldn't believe that this person, who until very recently had been such a miniscule part of my life as to be of no consequence, was now making me feel this way. We found ourselves talking long into the night about traveling together through Europe when his course ended, a future that seemed impossibly far away. We decided we should both go somewhere neither of us had been before, and settled on Greece (as the future plans alarm bells tolled dully in the back of my mind).

On his last night in Barcelona, I joked about making him miss his flight so he could stay with me, and, whether through some Freudian twist of fate or mechanical malfunction, his three am alarm failed to go off. He woke up at four, and immediately realized what had happened, prompting a frenzied ten minutes of phone calls to various taxi companies in my slurred, just-woken-up Spanish, until he told me to forget it. He booked himself a different flight, emailed his excuses to his professors, and we both went out to the tiny balcony and sat wrapped in blankets, watching the city slowly waking up, talking about everything, and nothing. I messaged Tim and begged him to wait another day – I wasn't quite up to the idea of hitchhiking halfway across the country by myself just yet. He agreed reluctantly – he was clearly itching to climb.

David and I had grown so comfortable with one another, that when it came time for him to leave for the airport (for the second time) I was shocked when he kissed me brusquely on the cheek and strode off without looking back. I watched him walk away, feeling confused, and hurt. Thanks to my indomitable instincts of self-preservation, I told myself to forget how I'd been feeling, and concluded that it must have been all in my head. I felt slightly disgusted at myself, and gave my inner romantic a stern talking to: if he had only been playing around when he talked about making plans together, this suited me just fine – I didn't need things to get too complicated. I was just surprised he hadn't said anything sooner... I told myself to put it out of my mind, and focus on climbing. I checked out of the apartment, and went to meet Tim.

It wasn't until that evening, unpacking my bag in Siurana, that I discovered I'd left all my underwear (including the lacy pair I'd purchased specially for that weekend) hanging out on the balcony of the apartment.

CHAPTER 9: SIURANA

"Pies De Gato": *the rather charming Spanish term for climbing shoes, literally "cat's feet". Climbing shoes are designed to hug your foot like a glove (or crush it like a vice, depending on your school of thought), and the soles are made of hard, grippy rubber to help you get traction on the rock.*

It took us eight hours, and four different lifts on the highway, but Tim and I made it to Siurana! However, we arrived at the campsite with no rope, no cooking equipment, no guidebook, and no car (long hours were spent fantasizing about the kind if van we would buy, and how it would be kitted out, if only we had the money - I was clearly comfortable making and with people with whom I felt no chemistry). Within hours of our arrival, we had not only borrowed a guidebook, but had also been gifted a rope by a couple seeking to lighten their bags for the flight home. We spent the first evening bemoaning the rice, soup, eggs and hot drinks that sat uselessly in our bags, as the camping ground had no kitchen, and we had no tools for cooking. Hungry, grumpy, and tired, we retreated to bed to read and beat ourselves up for our lack of preparation, and the impossibility of existing on raw eggs and rice.

That night, I had a message from David. It said simply:

"I'm an idiot. I should have kissed you goodbye."

After my frustrating travel day, I was in no mood for games, and told him so.

"What's going on?" I asked. "We were having so much fun and then you just flounced off. If I did something to piss you off, you could have had the courtesy to tell me what it was."

"You didn't do anything."

I waited for a better explanation.

"It was... a lot harder to say goodbye to you this time, and it took me by surprise, that's all."

"So, where does that leave us?"

He took a long time to answer. I bit the skin around my nails, since I had already cut the nails themselves too short to bite, and was halfway through typing a reply telling him not to worry about it, when he responded.

"It leaves us with six very long weeks until my course finishes and we can go to Greece."

*****

After three days in Siurana (or as I came to think of it, heaven-on-earth), I was bruised, skinned, and happier than ever. It was a place like no other I had ever seen. Hidden about two hours from the coast, with more than sixty climbing crags crammed into the cliffs below a tiny medieval village, which sat over-looking a river and lake; too remote from the city and coast to be touristy, mostly seen only by climbers and mountain bikers. I soon learned that the average climber here is much stronger than the average Australian climber – for them, the sport was a lifestyle, and an obsession. While this was a highly contagious attitude, I couldn't hope to reach the impossibly high bar set by the other climbers we met there. It was the perfect distraction from the dilemma of my "status" with David. We were now sending messages every day, and the tone was flirty but casual. I was determined to keep it that way.

Tim and I had run across the kind of good luck which doesn't really seem fair. The weather had been perfect - chilly and clear - and the climbs and the accommodation were wonderful, but it was the people there who really made an impression on me. On the first morning, we went out to explore the cliffs, and decided to hitch a lift back to the campsite as the heat rose with the sun. A brightly painted campervan – exactly like the one I'd built in my eternal nomad fantasy – slowed and pulled up beside us. Inside was an Italian couple who, I could tell just by looking, were stronger climbers that I could ever hope to be. The girl was short and slight, and her boyfriend drove with calloused and grazed hands on the wheel. Both had the wiry limbs and tanned faces of truly fanatical climbers, and their van was tidily packed to the roof and walls with gear. In the ten minutes it took to drive us back to the campsite, the four of us had become such good friends that the girl jumped out with us, and rustled around in the back of the van, emerging with a pot, lid, camp-stove and cutlery.

"Here," she said, and handed us this impressive booty. "We stay at this campsite for the next five days, and we have spare. You can borrow for now, and we will find you before we leave."

Tim and I almost stumbled over one another in our effusive thanks, promising to pay them back by cooking them a meal after we had gotten settled, but although the campsite was relatively small, we never saw them again. We kept our eyes out for the bright van, but after a week had passed and we had seen no sign of them, we presumed that they had moved on to another climbing spot. I kept the stove and pot with me for the rest of my trip.

I found it very easy to talk to Tim. He was a very simple guy, in the sense that he gave off the impression that he was very easily satisfied in the moment. I quickly discovered that if he had something to challenge him (mostly climbing), he could work at it all day every day for weeks on end, without getting bored, or worrying that he should be doing something else with his time. He didn't second-guess himself or his decisions; he was the epitome of going with the flow. I envied him that happy security. We talked about our travels, and I spoke about my life back home, so recent in my memory, yet so far away. I didn't talk to him about David, because I didn't know what I would say. When one night he tried to kiss me, I told him there was someone else, and he accepted that as an explanation without further questions, and for the most part, we had the easy, uncomplicated friendship between climbing partners that I'd been hoping for.

*****

On our third or fourth morning in the camp, a slender Polish girl dressed in baggy climbing pants and a ripped Heineken singlet sought me out. She introduced herself as Mila, and asked if I could help her.
"My friend tell me you speak English?"
"Yes."
"And you speak Spanish also?"
"Um, a little? What's the matter?"
She showed me a strange and painful rash on her hands that had appeared the night before, most likely from brushing up against a poisonous plant while walking back from the crag. She spoke no Spanish, and she needed someone to translate for her at the doctor's surgery down in the village. I agreed immediately, and told Tim I would meet him later in the day. I was sorry that she was in such obvious discomfort (for which the doctor prescribed a topical cream), but I was very happy that my limited talents were of help to someone. Mila and her dark, silent, Slavic boyfriend, Ivan, found us by the campfire when we returned from our afternoon climb later that evening, and she pressed a gigantic block of chocolate into my lap with a bandaged hand.
"How long will you be off the rock?" I asked, tearing open the packet, and handing it around the little group.
"Only one or two days" she replied. "I needed some rest day any-

way. He pushes me very hard."

She nudged her boyfriend, who had refused the chocolate, but managed a small, tight smile.

"He is training to climb an 9a while we are here" she said, by way of explanation, naming a grade that was so far out of my reach I could not even comprehend it. Tim also looked impressed.

"Which line are you working on?" He asked enthusiastically, with a mouth full of chocolate, pieces of which flecked his lips and chin. Ivan looked faintly disgusted.

"We are trying some of the lines in the cave on the Morning Crag" (it seemed that Mila always spoke for Ivan) "I am not strong enough for many of them, but I like to try some moves. You should come too – my hands will be better soon."

The prospect of more non-conversation with the unsmiling Ivan was daunting, but I was very much enjoying Mila's company.

As we chewed the chocolate and poured mugs of tea, two scruffy dogs wandered up to us and flopped down beside the fire. We'd seen plenty of these strays since we'd arrived: Spain is rife with dogs wandering the streets, un-collared and un-accounted for... or so we had previously thought.

One of the dogs was old and grizzled, with white eyebrows and a white moustache, but the other was no more than a puppy – a big, lanky, affectionate mutt, with a dirty brindle coat and soft, German shepherd ears. He snuggled up to Mila, then to me, before settling himself beside Ivan, who absent-mindedly stroked his head with one hand. Not five minutes later, a van pulled into the campsite in the gathering darkness, and three men in uniforms got out. Two set off towards the other end of the campsite, where another two dogs could be seen sleeping in the dirt by someone's tent; the third walked over to us. Through his broken English, and my Spanish, we established that they were the dogcatchers for the area, and, if these weren't our dogs, would we mind handing them over.

"What happens to them?" Mila asked.

"If they are not microchipped, they get put down" I translated, as the man explained. The old dog who had been sleeping by the fire, but had woken when the man came over, stood calmly while the collar slipped over his neck, as if to say, "that's fair, I've had a good run", and followed him quietly to the van. When the man returned with a collar for the pup, however, Ivan spoke for the first time.

"He is no stray. He is with us."

Mila looked a little taken aback, but didn't argue. Ivan gazed steadily at the man, who shrugged and strode off to help his friends with the two other dogs they'd managed to round up, who were putting up quite a fight.

I was impressed by the impromptu heroics, but told Ivan:

"He's just going to get him next time he comes here you know."

"No. We will take him with us. We are driving, and he will fit in the car when we leave."

Mila was sceptical, and they were still debating in rapid Polish as they walked back to their tents, with the pup trotting along beside them, gazing adoringly up at Ivan. I reflected that it was strange how animals could see through the facade we present to the world, in a way people sometimes can't. I had written Ivan off as a frosty and unaffectionate type; had even wondered if Mila was stuck in an unloving partnership; but the pup had chosen him out of our group, and been rewarded with another chance.

Two days later we went to watch Ivan as he worked on his 9a project in the cave. 9a is, I should add, a freaking ridiculous grade to climb. You're basically holding your entire body weight by your fingertips and making enormous, lunging moves the entire time. As Mila shouted encouragement up at his ascending form, all tendons and sweaty skin, Tim and I sat beside the pup, who had been given a name – Kofi – on a bed made of an old bouldering mat. We lounged in the shade and watched Kofi's rescuer crimp and scramble his way up the overhanging cliff face, while the warm breeze blew in our faces. When he finally pulled the last move, and hung from that final, elusive hold, he gave one short shout of triumph, and then returned to the ground in silence. Mila hugged him, and Kofi jumped up to lick his sweaty chin, and both received that small, tight smile.

"Well done!" I gushed, "That was amazing!"

"Thank you." He said, brushing the chalk off his hands, one of which was bleeding.

"So, what's next?" Tim asked, eagerly.

"9b."

*****

On one of our rest days (the limestone rock was tortuous on our poor fingers), Tim and I trekked down the mountain and up along the riverbank through scraggy trees and thorny bushes, until we came across a huge, dilapidated old house, whose roof and floors had mostly caved in, we supposed from a flash flood. It must have been beautiful many years ago: overlooking the river, hidden away amongst the trees, with a courtyard in the centre, and high ceilings, but now it was overgrown with weeds and moss. I wondered briefly who had lived there, and whether they had escaped the flood. Walking back down stream we came upon more and more beautiful pools, where the water became an intense, bright turquoise. Even though it was a cloudy day (the first since we'd been there), we stripped to our underwear and dove in, under the freezing mountain water, coming up screaming, skin and muscles awake and alive and tingling. As I floated in the pool, I reflected that this remote place had sharpened my appreciation for the tranquillity of being in nature; and the unexpected, unselfish kindnesses we humans are capable of bestowing upon complete strangers... be they human or canine. I felt innately connected to both humanity and nature, and utterly at peace.

Tim chose this moment to dunk me underwater and I nearly drowned trying to get him back. He wasn't big on moments of silent contemplation.

The climbing in Siurana continued to entertain, amaze, challenge and, well, skin me, for the rest of the week. Tim was climbing stronger than ever, and grinning like a happy puppy with each new conquest. I threw myself at harder and harder climbs, pushing myself till my old injuries started to play up and I was in agony every time I tried to grip a hold. I was so frustrated! Tim, a seasoned climber and therefore no stranger to perennial injuries, was sympathetic, but firm:

"Just rest" he told me. "Listen to your body. It'll scream before it breaks".

Quote of the trip so far.

My tendons calmed down after a day of rest and icing, and a little crew of climbers started to form, with Tim and I at the centre. There were two young guys from Texas, and a Canadian couple with a small baby, who had given us a ride up the mountain during our first week. Chrystal and Alex were an inspiration. Both in their early 30s, both strong climbers, they came to Spain for a two-month trip while Chrystal was on maternity leave with their four-month-old baby, Loik. All the guys were somewhat in awe of Alex, perhaps because he could come down from a climb three grades harder than anything any of us could finish, walk over, take the baby, and sit there cooing at him for two hours. I was in awe of Chrystal. She was a strong and determined climber; she absolutely adored her baby; she made every situation hilariously funny; she loved her husband; and she talked and talked and talked, with genuine interest, to anyone, on any topic. When I watched her with her baby and husband, the three of them on a climbing holiday in Spain, living it up with a ragamuffin group like us, I thought for the first time that what they had together might possibly be something that I wanted for myself one day.

My mother had always loved my brother and I – and had never been reticent in telling us – but she had never been one of those people who went about saying that parenthood had been the best decision she ever made, or that her children were the most important things in her life. I had never had the chance to have a proper conversation with her about her feelings on mother-hood, but I had cultivated the idea that it had been just one part of a life, which was rich and full of other things. I never found out if I was right or not. She and my Dad had lost a baby – my older brother – when he was only a week old, and born with a faulty heart. They had spent the next three years trying for me, and after they had almost given up on the idea of a family, a homeopathy practitioner friend of theirs had prescribed Mum with a tablet, the principal ingredient of which was squid ink. Two months later, Mum was pregnant with me, and three years after that, with my brother. We rarely talked about the fact that I should have been a younger, rather than an older sister, and the detail that I had focused on for most of my young life was that my parents were older than other parents we knew. I had been brought up on the stories of the places they had lived and worked, the relationships they had had, and the travels they had experienced, all before they had decided to have children. My resulting philosophy had been a vaguely feminist idea that I would be letting my mother down if the most important thing that I did with my life was get married and have children.

She had never spoken to me about her desire for grandchildren, much less her desire to see me settled and married – in fact she had bluntly stated the opposite on several occasions – never, that is, until we were staring down the barrel of the loaded gun that was her first and only round of chemo. She and I had been standing alone in the kitchen one morning, and an uneasy si-lence had fallen, as both of us contemplated what it was that lay ahead. She stared into the dark swirls of her bitter herbal tea (all my life she had drunk chai tea with a splash of skim milk, a fa-miliar ritual that she had given up, along with all caffeine, sugar, alcohol, dairy, and red meat, as soon as she had been diagnosed) when she spoke, her voice barely audible:
"I'm going to be fine. The doctors are always pessimistic – that's

their job. I know your Dad has this doom and gloom attitude to the whole thing, but I'm going to make it."

I had no response. It was true that my Dad, when he could be pressed to discuss what was happening, had painted a very grim picture: "months, not years". But this was my mother – she had always been this indomitable powerhouse of energy and life – I couldn't imagine her being defeated by anything.
The kitchen table stood between us, like all that was being left unsaid.
"I am going to beat this because I want to… because I want to be there on the day that you graduate." Her voice cracked, but she kept going, staring into my eyes as if I was the person who would give her permission to live.
"I want to stand there and watch you walk down the aisle, and have somebody hand me tissues because I'll be crying so much. I want…" she stopped to inhale deeply, but there were tears in her eyes and on her cheeks as she said "…I want to read *The Very Hungry Caterpillar* to your children. I want to be the one who spoils them and tells them how much they are loved."

I reached for her and she stumbled around the table, and I held her as tightly as I could because there was less of her than there had ever been, and in that moment it felt like every tear that fell was draining a reservoir whose source had dried up, and causing her to disappear. It wasn't the moment that my Dad told me "months not years". It wasn't the moment I saw her being wheeled off the plain from Santiago, gaunt and fragile. The first time she ever spoke to me about my children was the moment that I knew: even if I wanted to have them, she wasn't going to be there to meet them.

CHAPTER 10:
MALLORCA

Deep Water Soloing: *a peculiar variation of the climbing sport, known locally as 'psicobloch' – literally psycho bouldering – where the water below the cliff acts as your protection. No ropes. No mats. For a climb to be viable for DWS, it needs to overhang a deep enough body of water, so that if you slip and fall, you take a plunge and then get back on without hurting yourself.*

M other's day had come and gone without much to mark it, since we had been so far away from civilization; but the first anniversary snuck up behind me without warning, and hit me over the head like a mugger in a dark alley. I was not ready for the emotions that came with this day. I had not prepared for what it would mean to be spending this day with virtual strangers, no matter how sweet and kind they were. I was no-where near anyone who had ever met my mother, or even knew her name, or that she had existed. There were messages of love and support in my inbox from friends and family, but I couldn't bring myself to read them. I briefly Skyped with my brother, but it made me feel worse rather than better, because he told me that he and my Dad had fought over something to do with my

Dad's new girlfriend (whom I had yet to meet). I listened to him vent and fume, but neither of us mentioned how we felt about the date. After we said goodbye, I wondered if he felt like I had abandoned him. I felt helpless, halfway around the world, but I couldn't convince myself that I would be of any more help to him had I stayed in Sydney. I told the others I felt sick, and just sat in the campsite while they set off to conquer new heights. I could feel myself getting duller, and less excited about everything: a slow, creeping lethargy that I remembered from the first few months after it had happened. I needed to shake things up.

Luckily, while I had been moping around the empty campsite, Tim and the others had come up with an exciting new plan, which they couldn't wait to tell me when they came back that evening: we should all get the ferry over to Mallorca!

Mallorca is to climbers, what Ibiza is to pill poppers and ravers: paradise. The entire island is ringed by cliffs of varying height and cragginess, up which climbers can scramble without the irritation of ropes and harnesses, falling - if they fail - into the deep blue water below. Chris Sharma made this island famous with his video "King Lines," and now climbers were swamping the island and probably pissing off the local tourist industry by refusing to stay in the resorts or spend their money in the casinos or clubs like normal tourists.

Chrystal and Alex gave the four of us (Tim, me, and the boys of Team Texas) a ride to Barcelona, and we all jumped on the overnight ferry. We arrived in Palma, the only city on the island, just after sunrise. The four of us rented a tiny clown car, and spent the day driving along gorgeous winding cliff tops, around endless hairpin turns, stopping to spend the night in a deserted car park on a tiny mariner, where we watched the sun set over the Mediterranean and avoided the mangy sea-faring cats, which were there in their scruffy abundance. The next morning, after a breakfast of oatmeal and peanut butter (Tim and I had fallen into something of a competition to see how little we could spend on food each day – the record was €2 each for three days in a row), we reached our destination: the beautiful beach (and limestone sea cliffs) of Cala Barques. The only way to get to the narrow bay by land was down a long, dusty dirt road, scattered with potholes; and then down a winding, rocky path on foot.

For the next week and a half, we felt like the lost boys (and girl) living in Never-Never Land. Climbing solo above water, every wrong move precluding a screaming fall into the ocean, and a soggy return to the rocks... repeat ad infinitum and you have a recipe for some amazing days at the beach. It didn't hurt that the ocean around the island was gorgeous: warm, clear, blue and calm, and the beaches were postcard white and soft (although, as I discovered, not so soft when you sleep there without a mat). Free camping (the kind preferred by thrifty climbers) was technically forbidden, but we soon discovered that the woods around the beach were full of discretely equipped havens, where surreptitious meals were cooked and eaten, and tents sat camouflaged by spiky shrubbery.

On our first day at the beach, our group expanded to include Jim, Andrew and Joe, three more Americans who had recently finished their study abroad programs (do Americans do anything else?) and had been sleeping on the beach for the past month. The three of them were straight out of a cover-shoot for *Vagabond* magazine: threadbare fisherman's pants; sunburned brown skin; hair badly in need of a cut; and three sets of wide blue eyes and wide white smiles. Together, the seven of us found a routine; waking up late in the day, lazing on the beach, going through endless bottles of sunscreen and jars of peanut butter, yelling encouragement at each other as we ascended the cliffs above the waves, playing music and drinking the traditional €1 wine.

The biggest threat here, surprisingly, was not the police coming after us renegade campers, but the cows: the evil, godless, unexpected cows. We quickly learned that it was essential to store all food and food related items in a bag at the top of a tree, or the cows would tear into your tent, knock over your shelter, and rip through your bag to get to it. The biggest culprit was particularly detestable beast named (by whom it was never clear) Francesca. Yelling, arm waving and even rock throwing seem not to bother this dastardly destructress, and many a tasty treat was lost to her tramplings and snufflings. One morning, Tim and I walked down to the beach before sunrise, just in time to witness Francesca sniffing (possibly with a view to munching) Andrew's scruffy blonde hair, as he and Joe lay blissfully snoring in their sleeping bags. Before we could shout out to warn them, a slurp of bovine drool wrenched Andrew from his slumber. He very rapidly assessed the situation, and just as rapidly scrambled out from underfoot as the beast beat a hasty retreat. Tim and I were helpless with laughter, more than anything at the aghast expressions of total bewilderment on the poor lads' faces - how many of us can say we have been woken up by the kiss of a megalomaniac cow named Francesca?

After we had recovered, we walked up the rocks to explore a ruined cottage, which was perched on the headland. I found myself wondering what had motivated someone to build a house in such a remote location, hundreds of years ago. Was it the same idea of visual beauty that was holding us captive here on these warm, lazy days? Did they see the world back then as we do now? Did they have that luxury? Or was it the strategic position close to water, hidden from the open ocean, but with a clear view across the bay? I can't believe that anyone who saw this place could fail to be touched by its rough perfection.

As if to prove my point, boatloads of tourists are shunted into the tiny bay every few hours. Mallorca has always been a tourist hot spot, but Cala Barques used to be only for the locals and climbers. A few years ago, the tourists discovered it, and now it is not uncommon to be halfway through a cave climb, look over your shoulder, and find yourself the subject of infinity iPhone pictures from the decks of a behemoth boat, with announce-ments in English saying "This is Cala Barques, Cala Barques". The passengers never actually got off the boats to swim or lie on the sand, they just took pictures from the deck, sipping their drinks and staring.

One day, all seven of us made the pilgrimage to The Arch: a per-fect half 'M' sticking out of the ocean off the coast, which Chris Sharma, god of the climbing world, made famous in the video *King Lines*. We scrambled down the rocks from the tourist look-out and flung ourselves into the choppy ocean to touch the rock that Sharma touched. None of us even attempted the ridicu-lously difficult line he had climbed up the inside of the arch, opting instead to crawl over the top and take pictures 20 meters above the waves. Then, one by one, we jumped, screaming, into the water. When we returned to our camp, happy and buzzing from our brush with climbing fame, we found a stranger sit-ting beside the tents. For a crazy minute, we thought he was Chris Sharma – he had the same tousled hair and wiry physique, tanned and tall, and good looking in a very *European* kind of way. Then caution took over and we worried that he was some kind of beach policeman, waiting to fine us for illegal camping. He was, it transpired, neither of the two.

"Hi! There were some kids playing around near here and I was worried they were going to go through your things when every-one left, so I decided to wait here and make sure they didn't steal anything. My name's Matthias."

He spoke in a German accent, and waved his hands a lot as he talked. We instantly liked him, not only because he had saved us from possible robbery (and almost certain Bovine Sabotage), but also because of his easy smile, and the chalk bag and climb-ing shoes clipped casually to his belt: here was some kindred climbing spirit.

He told us he lived about twenty minutes away in one of the small, coastal towns, and that he often came out here to climb. "This was the first time I'd ever seen tents, but no climbers!"

We told him about our excursion to the Shrine of Sharma, and he nodded sagely.

"I was here when he shot that video. What a legend of a man!"

Of course, we invited Matthias to eat dinner with us, and I noticed throughout the meal that he kept looking over at me while we ate. After a little while he snapped his fingers and grinned cartoonishly.

"I DO know you!" he exclaimed.

"You do?" I was certain I had never seen him before.

"I recognize you from your photo. You put out a Couch Surfing request a week ago, and I invited you to stay, but you never wrote back!" Here, he clutched his chest in mock anguish. "I was heartbroken!"

I laughed.

"I don't know if you've noticed, but we aren't exactly hi-tech out here! My laptop died days ago."

We laughed at the coincidence, and I told the rest of the boys about my failed plan to Couchsurf my way through Europe.

"The problem is, either nobody gets back to you, or nobody has any room!"

"Well, when you get sick of roughing it, you are all welcome to come and stay with me – I have plenty of space!"

This announcement was met with raucous cheers.

Each morning in Cala Barques, I was woken from my uncomfortable sleep by our daily avian alarm call. What the island birds lack in physical size, they compensate for in considerable numbers, and in the early mornings, they made their presence well known. Lying in my sleeping bag, listening to the chorus of tiny voices, I would wake my stiff muscles in the smallest possible increments of movement: feeling them stretch and complain beneath my scratched and sunburnt skin. Everything hurt, but somehow I didn't care.

Sometimes when I climbed I was petrified of falling, sometimes

I could lose myself in the problem facing me and forget my fears. For the most part, fear held me back from what I was sure my body could accomplish if only I could relax and focus my mind. In Siurana it frustrated me to tears, that a climb I could complete easily when the rope was above me, protecting me from a fall, became utterly impossible once I tried it on lead. As soon as there was the possibility I might miss a hold and fall, no matter how certain I was that the rope would catch me, that my belayer was watching, that I could do the move in front of me... I couldn't get control over my fear. But in Cala Barques, surrounded by these encouraging, fearless, flawed friends, I was beginning to chip away at that fear.

Deep water soloing defies every instinct of self-preservation within you. You want to go for the next hold, but every move takes you higher above the water: every triumph makes failure all the more terrifying. Your mind, like a mother to a tree climbing child, screams "Why are you going HIGHER?! Get down from there right this instant!" For the first few days, this voice was almost constant, and I refused to attempt moves I was not absolutely certain I could reach - I was getting more and more frustrated because I wasn't challenging myself - physically or mentally - I was stuck in the safety zone. I should point out here that it is very unlikely and uncommon for climbers to injure themselves falling into deep water, hence the popularity of the sport. There is the thrill, but very little actual bodily harm to be had. The biggest barrier is the fear.

In the afternoons we always ended up in the far cave, where there was a flat expanse of rock from which to view the climbers as they ascended above the enticing blue water. There was one particular climb we had all been trying as a group: a climb that, were I on a rope or above a boulder mat, would be a matter of one or two attempts. Six meters above water however, I found myself unable to grasp this knowledge. But the more I went back to that one climb, the more I started going for the moves rather than backing off, and taking the falls when I missed, and the feeling was intoxicating! The day I made the final move, I forced myself to jump from the top of the cliff when I topped out, higher than I had jumped before, and I grasped onto the realisation that I was ok, that I could do these things, that I could control my body and my mind.

In the spirit of wild abandon and adrenaline, I hailed a couple of guys who were fooling around in the bay on a jet ski, and asked if I could have a go (having, not two hours ago, heard the noise on the water and grumbled to Tim about these oversized toys and their pollution). The tanned, middle-aged Spanish guy who was driving, was eager to show off what his 'toy' was capable of, and we sped across the ocean, doing figure eights and hairpin turns, bouncing over waves, with me laughing and clinging on for dear life. His friends called out to him from the beach, and, distracted, he suddenly lost balance, released his grip on the handlebars, and toppled over into the water, while I nearly died with laughter. We both returned to the shore, unharmed, save for his wounded pride.

*****

After we had been living at the beach for over a week, and my hair had come to resemble a particularly untended bird nest, I decided I needed some basic human comforts. Matthias had been coming to climb with us nearly every day, and Tim and I asked if we could go back to his place and stay there for a couple of nights, before I made my way back to Barcelona, and then on to a new climbing area I'd heard about from one of the other climbers at Cala Barques. Small luxuries like hot running water, cutlery, and the desire for a mattress can become all-consuming after a week of sleeping on bare, cold sand or in the back seat of a tiny car, and washing one's clothes, hair and face in the sea every day. When we arrived at his house, we discovered that Matthias was a talented woodwork artist, and his small, colourful, airy casa was filled with beautifully framed mirrors, tables and pictures. We all but collapsed onto the sofas for a nap, but not before serendipity once again dipped her toe into my fortune....

While in the town earlier that day, Tim and I had gone looking for hammocks, which seemed the perfect travel sleeping solution (especially after the cold, hard reality of sleeping on cold hard sand). The only hammock store in Palma had some beautiful, comfortable looking setups, but they were all way outside my price range. When we arrived at Mattias' house, we asked if he knew of anywhere we could buy a hammock more cheaply, not expecting a yes.

"Sure!" He replied, with his trademark grin. "My next door neighbour sells them, I think she'll have some in her house."

He walked out onto his balcony and called up to the neighbouring house, until a curvy, dishevelled looking woman with curly, auburn hair, appeared on the balcony wearing a brightly coloured sarong, obviously woken up from her siesta. Nonetheless she invited us in and produced a box of – oh perfection! – travel hammocks, made of bright orange and purple parachute material, and each weighing about as much as a sweater. Tim and I bought one each, and I practiced my Spanish for a while, asking the woman (whose name was Rosa) about her artwork, before we returned to Matthias' house for a nap.

That night, Rosa came over to the house, and the fours of us cooked the most luxurious feast – burritos with beans and salsa, mango salad, and freshly made chocolate cake for dessert. It may not sound like much, but after nearly two weeks on our "2 euro a day" diet, this was manna from heaven. We felt quite civilised, eating at a table for once! Matthias and Rosa made wonderful company, and we regaled one another with tales of climbs we wanted to finish, places we wanted to see, and languages we wanted to learn (both Matthias and Rosa were already multilingual, but Tim spoke only English, and my Spanish was still a work in progress).

After all the food was gone and the plates had been piled in the kitchen, Rosa said goodnight to everyone, and though Matthias pursued her to the door and tried to convince her, in hushed tones, to stay, she returned to her house. I curled up on the mattress Matthias had laid out for us, but before long, it became apparent that Tim had had too much wine, and intended to make one last effort to break out of the 'friend zone' I thought we had firmly established. After lots of awkward nudging and wriggling, I gave up trying to be tactful and retreated to the couch. Life was complicated enough with the prospect of seeing David in a few weeks, without having to deal with the consequences of too much Spanish wine.

The next morning when I was due to leave, Tim told me he had decided to stay on Mallorca for a while longer, but didn't ask me to stay with him. I realized we had been traveling together for over a month, and (even though I was keen to avoid a repeat of the night before, or any discussion thereof) it was strange to say goodbye. Matthias gave me a huge hug, a box of cookies and an orange from his tree, and told me to stay in touch.
"Let me know where you will be climbing this summer! I need a holiday – maybe I'll come and meet you."
I said my goodbyes and got into our tiny clown car, which didn't feel so tiny now it contained only me. Once again, I was on my own. But not for long....

CHAPTER 11: GREECE

Rest Day: ok, this one is kind of self-explanatory. A rest day is a day in which you do not climb. It seems fairly simple, but when you're on a roll with a project, or trying to manage an injury, but feeling good, it can be really frustrating to make yourself take a rest day. However, since climbing spots are usually in pretty spectacular places, it doesn't totally suck to take a break and enjoy the view once in a while.

T he flight from Palma to Rome was delayed, and I felt nervous and frustrated when I finally got the Campo. I shoved money at the taxi driver, convinced he had taken me for a ride I hadn't asked for, and shouldered my stupid bags, before pressing hard on the doorbell. I was hot and pissed off, and tired. And yet, inexplicably, when I saw him coming down the stairs, there was my goofy grin, plastered across my face. It was just as well this boy was going back to America soon, I thought to myself. Once he leaves I can stop acting like such a fool and get back to figuring out why the hell I'd felt compelled to travel halfway around the world...but for now, I'm going to kiss him and not worry about it. Kissing, and not worrying about much else, was basically what he had planned for that evening.

When we woke up in the empty apartment the next day (his

friends had left for their own adventures the day before) he turned to me with an innocent look on his face.

"Hey. What do you think we should do today?"

"Hmm, gosh, I don't know" I said, playing along.

"Do you think we should... go to Greece?"

I laughed.

"Why not!"

And so we got on a plane from Rome to Greece - my seventh flight in two months. It was a short, daytime flight, but it had been weeks since we had seen one another, and it was difficult to sit so close together with all our clothes on, and there were hardly any passengers. So, we contrived to sneak one after the other into the minuscule bathroom and, um, submit our application for the Mile High Club. After about five minutes my leg started cramping from being jammed against the door, and the captain asked everyone to take their seats for landing, so we reshuffled and snuck back out again but still, an "A" for effort.

Of course, neither of us had actually done any research about WHERE we should go in Greece. We had just assumed that the entire country was made up of charming little hamlets clinging to picturesque cliff tops, painted bright blue and white. As it turned out, this is not the case: Thessaloniki, the city where we landed, was modern, dirty, and only vaguely Mediterranean in any discernible sense. We caught a musky smelling cab from the airport to our lodgings; the wooden beaded seat covers leaving weird patterns on the backs of my bare legs. The city looked, frankly, nothing like a postcard. Even though this was not the Greece of the travel brochures, it didn't matter: we were too giddy with the fact that we were travelling alone together for the first time. After we dropped off our bags in the old-fashioned, minimally furnished room that David had rented us for the night, (and christened the creaky, four poster bed), we went out to explore the waterfront, which reminded me of Darling Harbour or Circular Quay in Sydney, with its wooden boardwalk, overpriced restaurants, and street vendors. It was all charmingly kitsch, and better suited to families than back-packers. All of a sudden, a man dressed as a pirate jumped out to stand in our path.

"Aarrr me hearties!" he growled, in an appallingly bad pirate accent, "Join us on the Black Pearl! Free harbour cruise!"

We were sceptical, wondering if this wasn't a poorly disguised people-smuggling racket, until we ascertained that 'free' meant 'free if you have a drink in your hand at all times', which seemed like a more viable business venture. We boarded the vessel, which had been decked out in full Halloween-pirate regalia, and were treated to an absolutely stunning view of the city from the water. We toasted our new adventure on the roof under the stars, as the boat slowly made its way across the dark, Mediterranean waters, back to the dock.

David had stumbled upon a review of a campsite outside of Thessaloniki, at the tip of one of the three peninsulas that form the northern Greek coast. According to the review, the campsite was well equipped, cheap, beautiful, and a great place to party with other backpackers. Other than that he hadn't been able to find much information, but we knew which bus to catch from the city, and we had nothing but time on our hands, so off we went. Sitting on the bus sharing a pair of earphones, we snuggled, we kissed, we held hands, we gazed, we murmured. If I had seen myself, I would have given my soppy face a good slap. After a while it dawned on us that this seemed to be taking rather a long time. We knew the name of our stop, and the three stops before it, just in case, but we hadn't heard any of them. After a brief charades session with the bus driver, who spoke only four words of English, it turned out that this little jaunt on the bus was going to be five and a half hours long! A small setback, but never mind, we said, settling in still further, rose colored glasses perched jauntily on our noses. It'll be worth it when we get there.

We didn't get there.

The bus stopped after four hours and the driver called out "last stop!" This was not where we needed to be. It was not even one of the three stops before it. We stepped off the bus into the sunshine, with absolutely no idea where we were. After a few unsuccessful attempts to ask for directions, we found two middle-aged men who spoke English, sunning themselves and smoking cigarettes on a bench outside of a milk bar. They explained to us that the bus didn't go all the way to the campsite anymore, and we would have to get a taxi.

"But of course, the taxi driver is in the next town."

"There's one taxi driver? For the whole peninsula?"

"No, no, just for the next twenty kilometers."

We retreated to the shade of an ice cream shop to discuss our options. We could stay here for the night, and catch the taxi to the campsite tomorrow, but given our luck that day, I pointed out that anyone else trying to get to the campsite would have encountered the same setbacks as we did, and was it possible that this place might not even be open…or indeed exist? We decided to find a bed for the night, and make plans in the morning. The men on the bench pointed us in the direction of a guesthouse, where we were given a beautiful room with large French windows, and seashells scattered along the walls and windowsills. We considered staying there for the rest of the week, but at 30€ a night, it was more than we could afford. I had budgeted roughly 1000 euros a month for my whole trip, although at that point I had no idea what shape it would take or how long it would be, since I still had no return ticket.

So we got back on the bus the next morning, and after about twenty minutes, we found ourselves a smaller, more private campsite, with trees to hang the hammock; a tiny beach, and only two other people staying there. We paid 5€ a night, and made campfires on the sand, and ate the delicious local food and did absolutely nothing for four days. Laying in the hammock, with only books and music and each other to entertain us, we developed a game where we would each listen through one headphone, and take turns to challenge the other to find the perfect song "for when you wake up... for when you are waiting at the airport and your flight is delayed... for when you just got really good news... for when you want to cheer up a friend... for when you want to get excited to go out..."

"The perfect song to describe us right now" I said, earnestly gazing into his eyes as we rocked gently in the sea breeze.

Keeping a completely straight face, David scrolled down the list, hit play, and rap lyrics flowed through the headphones:

"You ain't gotta say too much
From the look in your eyes
I can tell you want to f**k"

I yelped in protest and hit him on the shoulder, my face turning bright red. We both tumbled out of the hammock onto the ground as I did my best to beat him to death. He scrambled up and I chased him around the campsite and into the water, where he grabbed me in his arms and kissed me, as I almost suffocated from laughter.

With so much time on our hands, there was a lot of time to talk, but there was a lot that we didn't say. Naively, I had assumed that David was as resigned as I to the fact that this could only be a summer fling, and would have to end when he went back to America. I loved spending time with him, he was so interesting and easy to talk to, but he could also be sullen and silent for hours, and I knew that those times were when he was thinking about everything that wasn't being said. Some people would tell me I was leading him on, and playing with his emotions, but the reality was that I was being myself, and behaving the only way I knew how to with someone whose company I liked. I have never been good at being coy, or playing down my own happiness. I didn't think that two people should compete to be the least emotionally invested in the other, or that liking someone equated to anything more than the fact that you enjoyed their company. I didn't believe there was anything to lose by enjoying this time we had together to the fullest, and I didn't think it was worth anything less because it was going to be brief. Since leaving high school, I'd had two fairly long relationships and three shorter ones, and although I had felt strong feelings for each person (which I had labelled love, mostly out of a lack of alternative vocabulary) and had been faithful, I had never been asked to give up anything I wasn't already willing to relinquish. None of my relationships had ever encroached on my ability to do pretty much whatever I wanted, when I wanted, and so I saw no risk in being myself around David: that is, being affectionate and happy and enjoying myself. I must reiterate at this point, I was twenty two, and stupid to think I knew what I was doing.

After Greece, David's plan was to meet up with his Mum back in Italy for two weeks, and I was going back to England to spend some time with my family and see my Dad, who was coming over for his Medical School reunion. We still had tickets to the festival in Spain, a month away from now, and we had made vague plans to meet up beforehand and travel together, but we hadn't discussed them in detail. I was happy to leave it at that, and let things unfold naturally. However, that option was taken off the table when I woke up on our last morning at the campsite, and saw David sitting beside the hammock, holding a small bunch of wild flowers.
"Are those for me?" I said, sleepily, smiling and rubbing my eyes. He didn't smile back, but handed me the flowers and cleared his throat.
"I've decided to go back to the States after the festival." His voice was even and calm, and he was looking straight at me as he spoke, searching my face for a reaction. I felt something small but strong twisting at the pit of my stomach. I fought to keep my face neutral.
"Ok."
"I want you to come with me."
"I... what?"
"Come back to the U.S. with me."

"I can't just come to America with you! I have to go back to school in Sydney next year."

"So, come with me for a few months, and then we can figure it out from there."

"Figure WHAT out? What about my trip? I still haven't even decided what I want to do."

"You could travel in America – we have great climbing in Washington. And we can always come back to Europe another time and travel here together."

"I don't... I don't know. I can't think about this right now. We've only spent 16 days together! Can we not talk about it right now?"

Like it said, I lacked much in the way of an emotional vocabulary.

We were silent as we waited for the bus to go back north. We had another night booked in the same hotel in Thessaloniki, but when we arrived there that night, it seemed to have lost its kitschy charm, and just seemed cold and dingy. We fell into an exhausted sleep, too tired to have the conversation we so clearly needed to have. When my alarm went off the next morning, he had already gone.

CHAPTER 12:
SCOTLAND

Beta: advice from another climber which can help you get through a difficult section of a climb, or make sure you take the right sequence so you don't go off route. When giving beta, a climber might warn you about a bad bit of rock, or a dodgy hold, or show you a better way to do a move. Unfortunately, sometimes another climber's beta is just wrong for you, and causes you to completely fuck up the climb.

After David and I parted in Greece, I flew to England, which was just as grey and wet as it had been when I left it. I met my Dad at the airport, and he hugged me tight, looking tired after his twenty-something hour flight from Sydney. I chatted vaguely about my trip so far as we drove towards my Aunt and Uncle's house, but my mind kept wandering back to the day before, wondering what I should do.

It was then that I did something very stupid: I confided in my dad about my love life.

"So there's this American guy that I've been seeing, and he's really cool – covered in tattoos – and I've been having a lot of fun with him, but he just told me he wants me to come live with him in America, and I don't know what to do."

I blurted all this out very quickly and without preamble.

Dad's knuckles whitened on the steering wheel, and his voice suddenly got very high pitched.

"What?!"

"I mean, he's completely different from anyone else I've ever been with, on paper we are pretty much opposites, but he's really smart and funny, and nice... I just don't know if I am ready to cut my trip short, or commit to something as serious as moving to another country..."

I babbled on, as Dad fumed beside me, interjecting every now and again with huffs of disbelief.

I love my Dad, but I should have known better than to ask him for relationship advice, especially where there were tattooed, American strangers involved, wanting to steal me away to the other side of the world. With my Dad's palpable disapproval to egg me on, I began to effectively talk myself into a corner. I felt panicky at the thought that this person wanted to make me give up my plans - my independence! I hadn't come on this trip to get a boyfriend, I had left a perfectly good one back in Sydney, and I was here to find myself as a woman! What would people think if I came home with some random guy beside me? How was I ever going to get anywhere in life if I had never spent any time alone, but had just skipped from one relationship to the next, always having the safety net of stability to catch me? How could I even CONSIDER what he was asking of me??

By this point I was a little hysterical, and it was all I could do when we arrived at my aunt and uncle's house to say polite hellos and answer a few cursory questions, before I locked myself upstairs and called David. It was not a long, nor a pleasant conversation.

"I can't see you again. I'm sorry. I just can't. This is over."

Once he realized I was being serious, he turned cold, accused me of leading him on, of lying to him. I defended myself, reminding him that I had told him from the beginning I didn't want any-

thing serious, even though I knew we were well beyond that. His words were all the more hurtful when cut apart by the poor connection, his face flickering in and out of focus on the screen. "If you want to be alone: fine. But you are making a giant mistake, and you know it. I can't believe I let myself fall for you, but I did, and you won't even admit that it was all real."
I was so frustrated that he saw it this way.
"The fact that I'm ending this doesn't mean that it's been a lie: real things end. Real things die. Just because I couldn't give you everything doesn't mean what we had you was fake."
He stared at me, and for a moment I thought the screen had frozen, so steady was his gaze.
"It doesn't fucking matter. Whether it was real or not, if it's over, then it never fucking mattered in the first place."
He disconnected, and I was left staring at my own reflection in the blank screen.

*****

I told myself that everything would feel better once I'd slept on it, and when I woke up and it became clear that it didn't feel better, and in fact I felt as though I had been punched repeatedly in the stomach, I told myself that this was good. It was a clean start, a chance to re-evaluate what I wanted to achieve – I was just feeling nervous and excited at the prospect of what was coming next. I refused to let myself dwell on what had happened, or how much I wanted to call him back and hear his voice.

I focused on spending time with my Dad, who I had hardly seen in the months leading up to my trip. Dad had come back to England for various reasons - his sister's birthday, to catch up with me, his 40 year college reunion, and to spend time with his mum who, at 95, was finding it more and more difficult to live alone, and yet refused to move out of her cottage.

Living halfway across the world from their families can't have been easy for Mum and Dad – especially for Mum when my brother and I were small. Whenever we returned to England, and were enveloped into the warm, crowded, chattering nest of cousins, half-cousins, second cousins, aunts, uncles, grandmothers and siblings, I wondered what it would have been like to be fully integrated into this many armed octopus when we were growing up. As it was, we remained, for the most part, detached.

My Aunt's birthday party was a bright, crowded, warm, gluttonous affair, overwhelming after the relative solitude of the Mediterranean beaches. A multitude of Very British Relatives congregated in the cozy farmhouse to eat, drink, and be merry. Late in the evening, when most had left, we played charades, and prepared for the highlight of the evening: the bonfire. We all rugged up, wrapped garbage bags around our shoes and headed out into the field at midnight, where we gathered around a sizable pile of sticks, old ladders, broken chairs and crates. My uncle promptly doused the pile in petrol, and proceeded to light the whole contraption in a very innovative fashion: he set up a firework inside a plastic pipe, aimed it at the bonfire and lit it, shooting it directly into the wood and igniting the whole thing with a great bang! The whole night was a lovely distraction, but as soon as I went to bed, the David of it all came rushing back.

The next day, Dad and I set off on the seven hour drive to my Mum's sister's house in Scotland, making our way up the west coast towards Glasgow. Nearing the Scottish border, we passed a small town called Gretna Green where, years ago, young English couples would frequently elope. The marriage laws in Scotland were somewhat more lenient than those in England, and young couples would get as far as Gretna Green, where they would marry in the registry before returning to face their disgruntled families. Beyond Gretna Green, and past Glasgow, the landscape became sparer, the road lined with felled trees and blue-green grass. When you look at the map of Scotland, the roads are abundant as far as Glasgow, but then to the north and to the west the main roads wind through a few tiny townships and around silvery, glassy lochs, until only a single road remains, running through complete and total wilderness. No towns. No roads. Just the moors and the lochs and the sea.

My Dad and I had always been very good at talking about a lot of interesting things without saying very much. That is, we loved conversation, but were adept at skating over anything that we were feeling, and avoiding conflict. When Mum had gotten sick, I don't remember us ever sitting down and having an honest discussion about the diagnosis, or the treatment, or any of it. I remember bits and pieces of conversation gathered from different people, but I don't remember my Dad and I talking about it face to face. About three hours into the drive, we got onto the topic of our semi-annual family ski trip, which we had planned to take in January the following year. He was telling me how much the plane tickets had cost, and I was astonished.
"For three tickets??"
"Well, four."
"Wait, why four? You, Gavin and me - who's the fourth?" I asked, my heart skipping a beat.
"Well, Mary is coming along with us."
"She is. Well. You didn't mention that before."
My dad's face was all innocent surprise. "Didn't I?"
Suddenly I didn't have to try and distract myself from thinking about David: I felt sick for a whole new reason.

The story behind my Dad and his new girlfriend was actually a very sweet one. When he first graduated from Medical School, my Dad had travelled through the Middle East and South East Asia, before arriving in Australia, and staying to work there for a year. While he had been working in a hospital Sydney, he had met Mary, and they had dated for a while. In a very parallel story to the mess I was in at that point, they had fought over where the relationship was going: my Dad wanted to keep traveling, and Mary wanted them to stay in Australia. My Dad, being the stubborn person he is, ended up going on to Canada and finally, after five years of traveling, returning to England, where he met my mother. He and Mary had had no contact with one another since then, until the month after Mum passed away, when he looked her up through mutual friends, and asked if she wanted to catch up. At the time, I was very happy for him: I liked the idea that he wasn't lonely, and I thought it was sweet that he had found someone from his past to reunite with. But I had never met her, and the thought of her coming with us on a family holiday was very different to the idea of her merely existing somewhere out in the world as his girlfriend.

After I had sat in silence for about twenty minutes, fuming, I burst out:

"Dad, that's not ok. You can't just spring something like that on me without discussing it first! Why didn't you ask me how I felt about it? No wait, don't answer that: you knew exactly how I'd feel about it and you did it anyway! That's not fair!"

This was a rare thing for my Dad and I: an actual, legitimate conflict. Growing up, I had been eternally frustrated by his attitude to argument, which had always been along the lines of "this is silly, I'm the adult here, so let's just drop it". But I now realized that we were both adults, and this wasn't something that I could not just drop.

"I'm sure Mary is lovely, and I'm happy that you have someone, but if you want there to be even the slightest possibility of a good relationship between her and I, you can't force us to go on a holiday together as a family! I'm fine with her being your girlfriend; I'm not ready for her to be part of the family."

My Dad looked for a moment as if he might cry, and even though I'd managed to keep myself calm until now, I suddenly started crying myself. He pulled the car over, and we sat there, both staring straight out of the windshield, tears pouring down my face, and a wretched expression on his.

"I'm so sorry, love. It wasn't fair of me to do that to you. But the tickets are booked now, do you think you could just make it work and see how things go?"

I didn't know what to say. I felt like I had made my point so clearly, and he was just as clearly missing it. I said nothing as he started the car, and we rejoined the freeway, driving the rest of the way in silence.

We arrived late afternoon at my Aunt and Uncle's beautiful new house near Achohoish (don't worry, I had no idea where it was or how to pronounce it either) and went for a walk: walking being one of the two options for killing time, the other being sailing. As usual, in the UK, it was raining, but that never stopped anyone going out to "enjoy the countryside". I quite liked the rain: everything was cool and green, and the weather kept the sand flies, which bred during summer in their millions – at bay. My Uncle showed us down a narrow green pathway beside a brook, which flowed down to a beautiful little waterfall, past a six-foot tall standing stone, which had been partially obscured by bright green moss. I stood in that dripping glade and regarded the ancient stone. There are monuments like these scattered all over Britain – it isn't just Stonehenge – but no one can say for certain why they were erected in the first place, only that it happened many thousands of years ago. I felt the chill wind gusting over the lock and winding its way through the trees into the sheltered glade, and shivered. I couldn't imagine living in this desolate place when the only shelters were caves, and the only heat was fire.

We left the waterfall glade, and walked further along the loch shore, away from the house, wrapping out jackets tightly about us against the chilling, salty wind. Turning off the road, we made our way through dripping ferns and over mossy boughs to Saint Columba's cave – a narrow rock fissure, which supposedly sheltered the saint after he was shipwrecked during a storm. Inside, the cave was shadowed and damp, and someone had constructed a small shrine, and left behind a pile of candles and a tin box of matches. I caught a fleeting memory of visiting St Peter's Basilica in Venice, with Mum warning Gavin and I to stay silent, as we watched a black-clad old woman lighting thin spires of wax, and adding them to the already dripping, misshapen candle holder. I'd been fourteen, and I hadn't understood why Mum had stared so reverently at the flame as it flickered in the shadows. Her own mother had died a few months before, and she'd flown home to England for the funeral, without getting the chance to say goodbye. I inhaled the dank air of the cave, and the image of the cathedral, with its grand stained glass and polished stone, vanished. I took a match from the box, and a candle, but the match would not light. I went through all the matches in the box, but the damp had seeped inside, and they hadn't any fire left.

On that same family trip when I was fourteen, we spent Christmas with my aunt and uncle, back when they had lived in England (before they moved to the edge of civilization in Scotland). Before we were allowed to enjoy our Christmas presents and stuff ourselves with Christmas food, Mum and her sister decided that it would be fun for us all to take a little stroll. Up a mountain. In the rain. The hike took the whole morning, all of us bundled up in our rain gear, hiking boots and woollen socks: my brother and I whining and complaining with every step. I remembered my Mum and Aunt tramping up the hill ahead of us, their curly heads bent towards one another, as they whispered sisterly secrets, oblivious to the mud and driving rain. I thought of my muddy walks in Wales only a few months before, and wondered when it was that I'd made the transition from the whiny child bringing up the rear, to the walker in dirty boots who might have Alt my head beside hers, and leant into the same wind on some other mountain, in some other lifetime.

******

"Dad?" I pushed open the door to the guest room and stood there awkwardly, as my Dad stuck his shaving-soap-clad face out from the bathroom.

"What's up?"

I sat down on the bed and waited for him to finish shaving, trying to figure out how I was going to say this without sounding like a brat. Outside the window, the rain had morphed from a sodden drizzle to a pelting storm, and you could no longer see the bay on the other side of the garden. Dad emerged, wiping his face, and sat on the bed next to me.

"I'm really happy you've got someone to spend time with. I'm not just saying that, I promise. But if Mary goes skiing, I can't go. I'm sorry. I'm still not ready to see you with someone else. I miss Mum, and it's not Mary's fault, but she shouldn't have agreed to come, and you shouldn't have asked her. It's still too soon. It's still too sad."

My Dad sighed. "Ooookay. I suppose you are right. I just thought it would be fun for us, that's all, but I should have thought it through. I'll call her tonight and let her know."

"Thanks Dad. And", I paused, "...can you please *ask* me about stuff like this? Things aren't going to work the way they used to. We need to figure out how to talk...we don't have Mum to translate any more."

"Ok, love. I'll try."

*****

I had been avoiding social media since the horrible conversation with David, but back in England, I caved, and checked. There were no messages from David. I was equal parts relieved and devastated. I didn't know what I would have done if he had sent me an angry email (as he probably had a right to do). I also didn't know what I would have done if he had sent a pleading, reconciliatory one. But total silence left me with the ball in my court, and I decided to let it lay on the ground. I had been the one to break it off. I had been the one to decide. And as shitty as it felt, I needed to stick to my decision.

That did not solve the problem of what I was going to do next. I still had my return flight back to Barcelona, but the next thing I had planned after that was tickets to a music festival in July...with David...for which I had already paid...and was going to leave to Future Sophie to figure it out. So, I had a flight to Barcelona.

That was the problem with climbing as an activity: it was much easier if you had a partner. But who could I entice to come to Spain and go climbing with me on a moment's notice?

******

"A climbing road trip through northern Spain?? Absolutely. When?"
I couldn't help grinning at Stuart's message when I woke up. We had had so much fun in Wales, he climbed, and I knew his work schedule was flexible, so I had messaged him late the night before, after completely failing to come up with a climbing plan that I could pull off by myself.
"As soon as possible" I wrote back. "I have a flight back to Barcelona in two days."
"Hm, that's going to be a bit of a tall order. Let me see if I can move things around a bit and get back to you?"
That was to be expected. He did, after all, have a job, like a responsible adult. I tried to distract myself by researching places to go in Northern Spain. Everyone raved about San Sebastian, and I didn't hate the idea of a few days at the beach. I'd been told about an amazing climbing spot between Barcelona and San Sebastian: Rodellar; and a second one kept coming up: Riglos. After having so much trouble in Siurana with injuries, and after my small victory in Mallorca with heights, I decided I was looking for something that was a little less technically difficult than Siurana, but a little more mentally challenging than Mallorca. Rodellar was described as a "lactic factory" - meaning the climbs were steep and required a lot of muscle endurance to

overcome lactic acid buildup. This was going to be challenging for me since I had spent the majority of my time in England overindulging in chocolate biscuits with my tea and wine with my meals and not so much exercising as sitting in cars and sleeping. I'd justified it all by telling myself that I had been through a breakup, and living on 5€ a day, and that I was with my family... but the truth was, I was going to pay for the last couple of weeks once I got back on the rock.

The last destination was Riglos. I took one look at the photographs of the looming cliffs, and glanced at the description of the height of each climb, and clicked the tab closed. There was no way. No way in hell. Rodellar and San Sebastian would be just fine.

A reply from Stuart pinged on my screen.
"So I can get away for ten days starting Saturday!"

Saturday. That left me with three days in Barcelona. I didn't feel like spending three days in Barcelona. I did some quick calculations. Rodellar was about three hours drive from Barcelona - I should be able to get there ok on my own.

"Want to meet me at the first climbing spot? I'll make my way there and we can meet up once you fly in."

I sent him the websites on Rodellar, and we debated different car hire companies and itineraries for a while longer, before he had to go to work (at a job which apparently allowed him to take ten days off on a week's notice).

For my last night in England, my grandmother took my aunt, uncle, Dad and I to dinner at a charming little pub in the village, with a huge garden, lovely food, and walls adorned with antique photographs, medals and newspaper clippings. It was all terribly quaint and quintessentially *English.* As I sipped my glass of prosecco and picked at my salad (like a freaking saint) I recalled the beery, smelly, pokey pubs of country Australia, or worse, the nouveau poshe places in the Northern Beaches, with their tacky decor and overpriced potato chips, and quietly bemoaned the fact that Australia just doesn't get pubs. The English may have appalling weather, a lack of anything resembling a beach, and catastrophically over-cooked vegetables, but my goodness, they know how to do a good pub. Perhaps because the appalling weather is more than usually conducive to a dedicated drinking culture.

When I said goodbye to my family the next day, and boarded yet another Barcelona-bound, budget flight, I was shouldering a significantly heavier bag than when I arrived. Although I had purged my pack of "city wear" (anything not made from Gore Tex, Merino wool, or lightweight cotton) in preparation for my next adventure, Dad and I had taken a trip into Liverpool to go shopping. Now usually, Dad loathed shopping, shops, crowds, cities, and basically anything more cramped than a deserted beach, but the one thing guaranteed to get him excited was the opportunity to visit a "gear shop" and purchase large quantities of outdoor equipment. I was the one planning to spend the next few months backpacking, hiking, climbing and generally living outdoors, and so I purchased new hiking boots; woolen socks; a pair of hiking pants; a thin, woolen shirt; a sleeping mat (no more sleeping on the sand for me thank you very much); a tarpaulin to go over my hammock; a rope; quickdraws; new climbing shoes; and (at Dad's insistence) a hat which made me look like a fourth grader. Dad (who was going back to work, and had no plans for traveling in the immediate future) bought a tent, a sleeping bag, a waterproof jacket, a pair of approach shoes, a merino vest, and a head torch, (which he ended up giving to me, and for which I would be very grateful in the coming weeks), and a duffel bag to carry everything back on his return flight. It helped that the sales assistant was about my age, and flirted shamelessly with him the entire time we were in the store. I hope she got a decent commission.

Even though I had just spent the equivalent of a plane ticket to

Greece and back (that's a lie, the ticket to Greece had cost about a quarter of what I spent) I felt elated. Call it shopping endorphins, call it peer pressure, call it post-break-up retail-therapy: regardless, I was no longer going to be the girl who showed up at the campsite and was forced to scrounge off strangers for room and board; nor was I going to be the girl who relied on other people to make her plans.

No more distractions, no more excuses: this next chapter was going to be serious.
This next chapter was going to be about climbing.

CHAPTER 13:
RODELLAR

Run Out: in sport climbing, you are only as protected as the last bolt you clipped, or rather, if you fall, you will descend as far as the last bolt you clipped, and then that distance again. For this reason, bolts are usually fairly close together (a couple of meters at most). When a climb is run out, the bolts are spaced further apart, either to account for the topography of the rock, or because the route setter couldn't afford many bolts, and was trying to save money. To "run out" the rope is to deliberately skip a bolt, if you don't think you can pause long enough to clip it, and try to make it to the next bolt without falling.

G etting from Barcelona to Rodellar proved very interesting indeed. I had honed my hitchhiking skills getting to and from Siurana with Tim, but Rodellar was much farther north, about three or four hours drive from the city, and an hour off the major highway. I caught the overnight bus to a town called Huesca – about halfway between Barcelona and San Sebastian. Standing on the road out of Huesca (pointing in what I hoped was the right direction for Rodellar), brushing the sleep from my eyes, I stuck my thumb out purposefully, and waited.

And waited. Four cars passed by before one stopped, but they weren't going anywhere near the climbing area. An hour later another car stopped, but with the same story. I checked the map again, and a ridiculous idea popped into my head: if I could get as far as the highway turn off to Rodellar, it was only about a six hour walk to the climbing site. "Never mind that I'm on my own, with a heavy pack and no emergency phone", scolded the sarcastic little voice of reason in my head. "What could possibly go wrong?"

It only took about ten minutes to successfully repress the little voice, and I turned back to the little roadside convenience store to stock up on water and snacks. I hailed a car with a relatively normal looking couple in the front seats, and asked if they could drop me off on the highway. As we drove, I cheerfully explained my plan, and their expressions became more and more stern as they listened. They started conversing in rapid Spanish.
The man turned in his seat to face me, with a concerned expression.
"We have decided that you are either very stupid, or otherwise very crazy, Australian girl. But either way, we cannot let you do this stupid thing. We will drive you to your campsite."
I protested and insisted that I was fine, and that they didn't need to do this, but they ignored me, and began telling me about their children, who were studying in Germany.
I sat back in my seat, feeling secretly relieved that my insane plan had been thwarted.

As we drove into the campsite, we passed two people jogging, despite the midday heat, and I was momentarily daunted at how fit they looked. After two weeks in the UK, and a week in Greece, I wasn't exactly in the best shape. I wistfully thought back to how strong I'd felt in Mallorca, and wondered if I should take up jogging...

I thanked the couple who had given me the ride, and offered them money, which they refused.

"Be careful!" they called after me, as they drove away.

I found myself a camping spot, and set up my little Mallorcan hammock and tarpaulin, feeling smug at how prepared I now was, in comparison to when I arrived in Cala Barques. When I came back from the showers, I realised I was set up right next to the joggers, who were now stretching on yoga mats they had unrolled under the trees.

"Hi! Where are you guys from?"

"Australia - you?"

"Me too!"

"Nice!"

Jogger Girl had frizzy, light brown hair, wide eyes, and a pixie-ish face, and she introduced herself as Trish. She was skinny (bordering on skeletal), but clearly very strong, with broad shoulders for her small frame. Jogger Guy (AKA Nick) was lanky and sinewy, and ridiculously tanned. He had long blonde hair that flopped over his eyes, and a wide, toothy smile. Trish had been traveling by herself for the past two months, after having gone to England to compete in a climbing competition, and Nick had joined her the week before - they knew each other from the gym back in Australia. We chatted about climbing and competing, and realized I realized that I'd met Trish before, in a competition in Queensland, back when I'd competed in high school. Climbing really is a small world!

The sun wouldn't set until after nine, but Trish and Nick wanted to eat and get an early night, so we drank the bottle of wine I had bought at the tiny camping store, and cooked what Trish and Nick called "climbing food", which was essentially devoid of any calories or taste (thus revealing the secret to their utter lack of body fat). After dinner, Trish did 200 sit ups, while Nick washed the pots and plates. He then laced up his shoes to go for another run. I was way out of my league here...

I spent the next couple of days climbing with Trish and Nick, both of whom were, as previously indicated, far stronger and fitter than I. As I'd seen in my cursory research of the place, Rodellar was full of long, exposed, overhanging, lumpy climbs, which left your arms feeling like jelly, and your head in a spin. Your shoulders, laterals and trapezius muscles take the bulk of your weight as the wall slopes backwards, and you have to focus and tense your core to keep your feet on the rock. These faces are mentally challenging too, viewed from a negative 45-degree angle, with a devastating (if in fact perfectly safe) drop of empty space below you. Despite all this, these have always been my favourite types of climb. I love the feeling of springing up and backwards towards a hold; I love that if you keep your arms straight you can swing through the moves like a monkey. I love the feeling of cutting loose – feet hanging in space, as you stretch out to regroup.

Nevertheless, it had been over three weeks since I'd left Mallorca, and boy could I feel it: this stuff was pure lactic torture. My first day was … unimpressive. I failed to finish even the warm up climbs that Trish and Nick were getting on. After the first few moves, my forearms would begin to burn with the strain of holding my body at an angle, and I could feel myself being pulled back to the ground by the weight of my ass (although technically it was the weight of my whole body, I was painfully aware of my increased center of gravity). I felt humiliated that I couldn't make it to the top of these (objectively, pretty challenging) routes, when my new friends were able to fly up them with no apparent effort. Nevertheless, we made a good team, shouting encouragement and advice to one another, craning our necks backwards against the steep gradient of the cliff lines. On day two, I had minor success on some easy climbs, and in a moment of euphoric optimism, set my sights on a project: *El Delfin*; a climb so ridiculously beyond my reach (literally) that I could barely make it up the first four moves.

After a rest day on day three (and the increased power-to-weight ratio which resulted from eating nothing but "climbing food" for 72 hours), my sense of self-worth was somewhat restored when I managed to complete a difficult route that I'd failed on the first day. That afternoon, I got on another, new climb, and on-sighted it. On-sighting– completing the climb on the first try with no rests or falls - is considerably harder than working a climb bit by bit, since you are essentially making the moves blind, and if you go in the wrong direction, you lose precious strength to get back on track. These climbs weren't as difficult as El Delfin, but they were something. I was feeling good, and so, naturally, I was unable to get past the first move on everything I tried for the rest of the day. Chastened, and sulking, I hauled my rope and bag of equipment back up the steep path to the campsite.

That night, Nick and Trish left me alone, after trying briefly to remind me that I had actually climbed well, and that it was only my third day, and that it would take time to get my strength back. I wasn't interested in listening to reason, self-loathing was much more comforting. I was a failure and would never be a decent climber. I may as well quit and take up cross-stitch.
The next day, I on-sighted two seemingly impossible climbs, one after another.

It is bizarre how strength works. Sometimes you have it, and you know you have it. Sometimes you don't have it, and you know you don't have it. Sometimes you think you have it, and it fails you. And then there are times when you discover you are stronger than you ever thought possible.

Mum had thought that she was strong enough to beat cancer. Right up until the day she could no longer speak, she told us that she was going to beat it. Despite what everyone was telling her, she thought she knew her own strength. She had always been stronger than anyone else I knew. Maybe if she had been weaker, there would have been more pain, and they could have detected the cancer early enough to cure it. Or maybe it would just have killed her sooner.

*****

Stuart arrived from Barcelona, as planned, on Saturday night, driving a tiny, impractical hire car. He wasted no time in becoming best friends with everyone in the campsite. He was one of those people who had a permanently (and at times exasperatingly) sunny outlook on life and everyone he encountered. It helped that he was charming, and attractive, but I chose not to dwell on those qualities: all I wanted at that moment was a climbing partner. Even though he was a climber, Stuart's true love was canyoning. Luckily, Rodellar was famous for its canyons, and we made our plans to go out the very next day, after dragging The Joggers away from their project climbs to join us. We had bought a guidebook, but it turned out to be useless when it came to important details like locating the starting point. We had been assured that this canyon was popular, and fairly straight-forward to complete: just park the car in the car park, follow the trail to the river and start working your way down stream.

Ha.

With no reliable map, and no useful directions from the guidebook, we ended up bashing our way through not-un-spiky bushes, up, down, up and around the mountains for a good three hours, trying to find the trail that would take us down to the river. The terrain was steep, rocky and unreliable, and we spent most of our energy trying not to knock loose rocks over the cliffs onto the unsuspecting helmeted heads of the canyoneers below, who had taken the sensible option, paid the 75€, and gone with a guide. We looked like some odd kind of reality TV show, something called "Ill Equipped" (ironic, given my recent shopping expedition), in which a group of enthusiastic youngsters are given all the necessary equipment for a certain outdoor activity, (say canyoning), and then sent off to do something completely different (in this case, hiking around a mountain in the full sun), while carrying their now useless equipment with them.

Decked out as we were in canyoning shoes and wetsuits, with Trish and I wearing only our bikini tops, we must have looked very strange. The thorny bushes and crumbling rocks made walking very unpleasant, and we there was a very real threat of heat stroke. Every now and again we would glimpse the river a few hundred feet below us, with only a vertical cliff face in our way. We were just about to give up hope, when we stumbled, quite by accident, upon the right trail. The rest of the day ran smoothly, even though we had prepared for a five-hour canyon and ended up staying out for close to eight hours, without food.

Canyoning is like an adventure smorgasbord: you may have to swim through pools or float down rapids; you may be required to abseil down cliffs or crawl through caves; or you might end up just walking through a ravine, you just don't know! There's something for everyone – and that's part of the excitement. This canyon was punctuated with gigantic boulders, worn smooth by the water, and deep, turquoise swimming holes that seemed to go down forever. The sound of the river and the birds was soothing and almost other-worldly. We managed to stay far enough behind and ahead of the other groups that we had the place to ourselves for most of the day. At one point, we were floating through water so deep it was almost black, barely moving, as the walls of the canyon narrowed and formed a sort of corridor. It was utterly calm, and secluded, and out of no-where, I was struck by the image of the corridor that had led to the room where Mum had died in the night, and the knowledge that there was literally no way out of this canyon but by going forward, through the narrow passage. I fought down the panic, forcing myself not to say anything or try to swim faster, just to lay on my back and let the river bare me along. It seemed we were in that ravine for a year, but finally, the mouth of the canyon opened out into a wide reservoir, dotted with picnicking families and splashing children. We looked rather bizarre in our wetsuits, soggy shoes and helmets, as we tramped back along the road towards the car. After a blissfully hot shower and some clean dry clothes, when we had all gorged ourselves on rice and beans, Nick announced (while examining his collection of scrapes and scratches) that he thought he would probably stick to climbing from now on.

The next day, after seven frustrating, draining attempts, I admitted defeat on *El Delfin*, with very bad grace. Stuart wanted to head north, and even though it was frustrating to leave Rodellar without completing it, I had promised him a road trip, and we only had a few days.

We took a detour off the highway towards Riglos, "just to have a look", Stuart said. We could see the cliffs for about fifteen minutes in the distance before we arrived, but it wasn't until we parked the car and stood staring up at them that their enormity truly sank in, and I felt a little faint. Rising ominously out of the scrubby desert plain, like the spines of some long-slumbering dragon, were six, giant, semi-elliptical towers of dark red rock, stretching some 320 metres into the air. Some of the climbs at Riglos were more nearly 400 metres long, winding up and across the overhanging cliff faces in white snakes of chalk.

Stuart looked like a five-year-old on Christmas day.
"That. Looks. AWESOME!! Let's do it!"
"Are you mental? I'm not climbing that!" I said, aghast.
"Why not? It's gorgeous! Look at those lines."
I was looking. I was looking at the overhanging, exposed, seemingly never-ending lines of chalk which snaked up the face, and all I was thinking was "Hell, no."
We argued. Then we went and sat in the pub, where Stuart magically produced a copy of the Riglos climbing guide, and argued some more. I was resolute. I would climb single-pitch climbs (I'll explain the difference later), but I wasn't going to get onto an exposed cliff face and climb 400 meters of a climb

which would be difficult even if you were doing it in one go.

Begrudgingly, Stuart gave in, but he kept shooting resentful looks at me for the rest of the day as we drove north to Pamplona, and his consolation prize. I had been able to convince him that we weren't going to climb Riglos, only because today was the final day of the San Fermin festival in Pamplona, otherwise known as The Running of the Bulls.

What had once been a religious festival was now a recognized destination for adrenaline seeking backpackers, out to prove their metal (with the help of a few solid hours of drinking). The whole city was decorated in white and red, to match the crowd around us, who were dressed in white with red scarves and sashes. It was twilight, and the whole town (and that many people again) were out on the streets, drunk, loud and alive. We danced and stumbled from terrace to ale-house to street, till early morning, eventually making our way to the arena to get our seats to watch the bulls run. I managed to dissuade Stuart from joining in the chase, but only because I threatened to call his mother if he did. Had I not been there, he would have been at the front of the pack.

At 8am, the three hundred or so people who had chosen to run took their marks, and we watched on the screens inside the arena as they formed a great, nervous mass, squeezing into the narrow, cobblestone streets. Some jogged, nervously in place; some were focused and crouched; and many were obviously still drunk, and possibly had no idea where they were. It didn't seem *safe* exactly. Thirty seconds later, the bulls were released, and then, no matter how drunk they were, they ran. Some were lifted up and carried by the sheer mass of people running, some decided to bail after all, and scrambled up the barriers, helped by onlookers and police.

All of a sudden, the first runners came stumbling into the arena, and we looked down from the screens as they swarmed through the entrance, and fanned out to fill the space. A few seconds later, hot on their heels, the bulls burst into view. As the runners flattened themselves against the barriers, the bulls' handlers herded them, one by one, out of an exit. Then the real game began. The bulls were released, one at a time, back into the arena, where they cut a swathe through the milling, disorientated runners. Most kept their backs pressed firmly against the barriers, but the braver (or more inebriated) ones tried to touch and even jump over the bulls, and a few unlucky ones were tossed bodily to the ground by the bull's padded horns. I was happy to see that if any of the runners tried to injure the bull at all, handlers would appear and give the offender a hefty smack with their sticks. More than once, a man (nearly all the runners were young men) was frog-marched from the arena by the police, for trying to cause one of the animals harm. Even so, the whole thing had a distinctly barbaric feel to it, and I felt uncomfortable watching. I had no intention of waiting around for the real bull-fights that evening: I doubted there would be the same consideration then for the safety of the bull.

After falling asleep for a few hours in the shade of a large tree beside our parked car, we drove from Pamplona to San Sebastian, a tiny town on the northern coast, wedged into the corner where the French and Spanish borders meet. It was strange and exciting, seeing road signs saying "Pamplona, San Sebastian, Francia", all within fifty kilometres. The idea that we were on the border of two countries was hard for my Australian-grown, island brain to grasp, and I had to fight the urge to detour over the French border and back, just for the hell of it. I felt like a real, wide-eyed tourist. San Sebastian is a truly beautiful little city. I fell hopelessly in love with the quaint little balconies and flower boxes - all so very "European" - and the two beautiful beaches we spotted from the car - one sheltered and turquoise, the other with half decent surf. The water was cold, and beautifully refreshing after the cramped and stuffy car trip, and I loved the taste of salt water after my short stint inland.

Since we hadn't arranged anywhere to stay, we dried and dressed ourselves in the car park, and wandered into the town in search of food. At the first bar we came to, people were standing outside around tall tables, drinking watered down beer and wine, and picking at tiny plates of food. It took as a moment to understand the system for eating out in the region: bar snacks were served for one or two euros, always with a beverage, and eaten while standing. If you wanted a full "meal" you went to a proper, sit-down restaurant, but that seemed far too dull. We happily grazed as we flitted from bar to bar, trying to sample as many of these delicious (and unpronounceable) "pintxos" as possible. It turned out that San Sebastian was having its own festivities that week, and we found ourselves amid a cacophony of live music, street performers, colorful parades and people in pirate costumes. We watched a spectacular firework display over the harbour, danced in the street to the music of a delightfully cheesy nineties/Beatles cover band in front of the cathedral, and drank Tinto de Verano in the alleyway with a crush of young locals, dolefully discussing "el crisis".

True to form, Stuart had no problem going up to every person, male or female (well, mostly female), and just starting up a conversation, or asking for a cigarette, or for directions. It didn't matter that we were in Spain. "G'day! Can you tell me where/what/how...." he barked at his new 'friends', who for the most part, stared back in a state of total incomprehension, not speaking a word of English.

"It's more fun when you don't speak the language" he explained, a huge, unflappable grin on his face. It was a totally endearing attitude, and I must say that for the most part, his indefatigable optimism and friendliness paid off in our favour. He asked a young Spanish family if he could have some of their chips, and they told us where the best surf and climbing spots were. He chatted up a pretty Spanish girl in the street, and she offered us her spare room for the night. He impressed an Australian girl with his drumming skills, and she told us which nightclub the hostel had recommended. He was the perfect travelling partner: never grumpy, never anti-social, never tired.

There was one incident however, when speaking a few words in Spanish, or perhaps being a tad less enthusiastic, may have helped. At around four am, we had left the dance floor, and were in a small bar, where the bar staff almost outnumbered the clients. I was asking one of the barmen about the best surfing spots to visit and camp, when I realised Stuart was nowhere to be seen. I went in search, and found him sitting at a table with a very drunk Spanish couple, having a conversation comprised of them speaking to him in excited, rapid Spanish, and him replying in slurred English, with neither party understanding a word the other had said. When I sat down he said "Sophie! You gotta talk to these guys, they seem really nice - they keep buying me drinks. I think they're brother and sister."
It took me four minutes to discover that they were not, in fact, related, and that their intentions with my unsuspecting friend were far from honourable.
"They want you to go home with them" I translated, trying to keep a straight face. "They think you're *muy guapo.*"
The look on his face was priceless.
We decided to call it a night after that, and went gratefully back to the spare room we had been offered earlier that night. Stuart fell instantly asleep, face down on the bed, so I made myself comfortable on the floor with my new sleeping mat and a blanket, and drifted off to the sounds of the party continuing in full swing in the street below us.

The sunlight cut through the curtains the next day with more force than seemed necessary, given the severity of our respective hangovers. The best hangover cure, I've always found, is a swim in the ocean, and so we made our way, post haste, to the beach. After splashing around in the surf for a bit, I felt sufficiently revived to suggest we try stand up paddle boarding.

Given that neither of us had ever tried it (and given how compromised our balance was from the night before), it was disastrous, but funny as anything. It was so difficult to balance on those boards; any time one of us made the tentative effort to get to our feet, we would begin to pitch from side to side, and end up diving head first into the water. I managed to catch one wave on my knees, but the second I attempted to stand, I landed in the white water, and had to scramble to retrieve my board before it decapitated an unsuspecting swimmer. We gave up after about an hour, and lay on our backs beyond the breakers, enjoying the sun.

Stuart had been texting someone all morning, and just when I was about to ask him what he felt like doing next, he gave me a sly grin.

"So, you know Sam?"

I smiled, and nodded. "You mean the guy who introduced us? Yeah, I know him."

"Well, he is free this weekend, and he found some super cheap flights, and he is *dying* to climb Riglos."

"Is he now." I grimaced, thinking of the towering cliff faces of Riglos. I thought of the possibility of falling at that height, and dangling over nothingness. I thought of making a dickhead of myself half-way up a rock monolith and crying in front of Sam, and Stuart, who was looking at me expectantly.

"When is he coming in?"

"He can fly into Madrid tomorrow night, if we can go pick him up."

"Bloody hell, that's a lot of driving. And then back to Riglos?"

"Nah, it's not that bad! Come on, Sam's done heaps of climbing, he has all the gear, it'll be great!"

"Hmm. I'm fine with picking him up, but isn't there somewhere else we could climb? Somewhere less... fall-to-our-inevitable-death-ish?"

Stuart shoved my shoulder in a big brotherly way, which made me feel like a five-year-old asking to be carried because she was tired. What kind of a weak-ass climber was I that I was too scared to climb?

"It'll be fine! We'll look after you, don't worry!"

I was worried.

Our San Sebastian host had kindly told us we could stay another night if we wanted, and we insisted on buying her dinner. When I got out of the shower to get ready to go out, I saw the small number 1 on the messenger icon on my screen

It was from David. One word: "Hi."

I was so relieved to have heard from him, that I didn't bother to analyse the best way to respond, or whether I should respond at all.

"How are you?" I typed back, because I really wanted to know.

"Miserable. My Mom keeps asking me what's wrong. We're back in Cinque Tierre and all I can think about is you."

I laughed in spite of myself. Having never met his mum, the only thing I could picture was his sullen expression and his monosyllabic responses – I felt sorry for her for coming all that way to find him like that.

"I know. I feel like so much has happened that I've wanted to tell you about, but I couldn't. And now I'm travelling with someone who has a death wish and wants me to go climb the highest rocks in the world with them."

"Gross. You shouldn't do that."

I smiled at that. I remembered his fear of heights from when we had been canyoning in Costa Rica.

"Yeah, but I don't really have any other plans."

"I still have your festival ticket. I didn't know whether I should sell it or not."

I didn't know either, so I just responded: "I know."

There was a long pause.

"I miss you."

I stared at the last message. Suddenly I felt the strongest urge to do something wild.

"Come and meet me in Spain."

This time there was no pause, just: "Where?"

"I'll be in Madrid tomorrow night?"

Five minutes passed with no response. I wondered if he had left. Then he replied.

"I can be in Madrid tomorrow night by seven thirty. I'll have to catch the train back to Rome and then fly to Paris. Find us a hotel, and I'll meet you there."

I felt like I was standing off to the side of myself, watching in disbelief: how did I think this was ever going to end well?? I literally *just* broke up with this boy, and now I was asking him to come and meet me?

Somehow, all I wrote was: "I'll see you tomorrow..."

I should be honest: there was a tiny part of me that was thrilled to have an excuse to bail on Stuart and Sam's Riglos adventure. I'd "mentioned" David to Stuart over the last few days, so it wasn't totally out of nowhere when I said I was ditching him in Madrid to meet up with him. When I broke the news to him a few hours later, Stuart took it with his usual sunny enthusiasm.

"That's awesome! Good for you for giving it another go!"

He raised his glass and clinked it against mine. We had taken Laia (our host) out to one of the quieter, nicer restaurants in the old part of town, and she was thoroughly confused by the whole conversation.

"I don't understand. Are you two breaking up? She is leaving you for this other man and you are happy??"

There was a beat, and then Stuart burst out laughing.

"No!! No, no, no, we aren't together. We're just friends!" I said, trying not to make it seem like I was too happy about this – I didn't want to be insulting.

"But you are travelling together in that tiny car. Don't you get annoyed with each other?"

Stuart grinned. "I'm a very tolerant person."

I punched him affectionately on the shoulder. I had no idea Laia had thought we were a couple.

I explained the David story to her properly (the shorter version), and she politely said that it was always a good idea to give someone another chance (even though in this case, David was the one giving me the chance). Even so, I thought she seemed a little sceptical. I couldn't blame her.

I noticed that as the night wore on, she and Stuart were inching closer and closer together, and when he put his arm around her shoulders and suggested another bar, I took my cue and asked for the keys so I could "have an early night", and leave them to it.

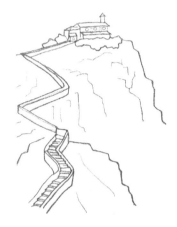

CHAPTER 14:
MADRID

Figure Eight Knot: I had learned to tie into the rope using a figure eight, so called because you make the shape of the number eight with the rope, and then tie the end back into itself by retracing the same shape, until you have two identical "8s" intertwined. It's the strongest, safest knot to use, but it has one downside: there's no quick release. If you take a fall on a figure eight, the knot can pull so tight around itself that it's almost impossible to undo.

I waited nervously in the hotel room in Madrid, as the clock ticked steadily past the half hour, then past seven forty-five, and then past eight, with no sign of him. I had no working phone, he wasn't online, and although the website said his flight had been delayed; I began to wonder if I had been stood-up. As it got later and later, I became convinced that he had planned this ruse to get his revenge for being dumped out of the blue over Skype, after such a magical week together in Greece. Part of me, begrudgingly, admired such a gutsy and definitive 'last word'. Most of me was wondering how long it would take me to get to Italy, find him, and punch him in the throat. I curled up miserably on the bed, and tried to get to sleep. At ten, there was a knock on the door, and the short, balding man from the front desk stuck his head inside.

"Señorita, your friend is here…"

David didn't say a word. He closed the door behind him, grabbed me, and kissed me like he was never going to stop.

I had heard that Madrid was a beautiful city, with lush gardens and a lively cultural scene, but we didn't see any of it. For the next three days, we stayed in the hotel, going out occasionally to eat and bring supplies back to the room, the rest of the time laying curled up together on the bed with the curtains drawn, watching stupid movies and talking about stupid things, and wholly uninterested in what was happening in the rest of the world. Whenever one of us seemed in danger of examining our situation too closely, the other would just start taking off their clothes. We both knew that it wasn't sustainable, but neither of us wanted to think (or talk) about the reality of what we were doing. It worked better that way.

The festival wasn't for another two weeks, and David had arranged to meet Carly, a friend of his from home, in France a few days before, then travel down with her. This 'friend' prompted the closest we came to having an actual conversation. He had mentioned that she would be coming when we bought the tickets, six months ago, before any of this other stuff had happened. After David and I had become more than "just friends", I'd done a little social media stalking (something I'd always looked down on my girlfriends for doing) and was strongly convinced that she had bought her ticket less because of the festival line-up, and more because of David. She was pretty, with red hair and fair skin, and I couldn't help reminding myself of the time David had casually mentioned his fondness for redheads. I couldn't help myself – I needed to find out if my hunch was accurate. I'd never thought of myself as a jealous person. I'd never felt the need to question someone's friendships, or ask for reassurance of their commitment to me. But this was a whole different game: we weren't committed to one another. I'd made it quite clear that commitment was the last thing I wanted – so logically I needed to make sure that he wasn't planning to sleep with anyone else.

We were laying in bed on the second day, googling options for our next few days of travel, and I saw a message from Carly on his profile. I adopted what I hoped was an uninterested tone of voice, and without making eye contact, asked David "so have you and Carly ever slept together?"
I could feel him leaning back to look at me, but I kept scrolling through a list of campsites, acting *super* casual.
"We might have. I've known her for a long time."
"I see. Don't you think she might be a bit annoyed to fly all this way and find you with someone else?"
I was trying to find out if he had mentioned me at all, not sure which would be worse: whether he had or he hadn't.
"We're not dating. We didn't date. I'm sure she's seen pictures of us together by now, and she knew you were coming to the festival."
So that was a no, then. I suddenly didn't want to talk about it anymore.
"Are you jealous?" he asked, and I could hear the smirk in his voice. It pissed me off, and I felt the urge to start a fight.
"I'm just worried she'll feel short changed after coming all this way. You seem very popular."
I expected him to rise to the bait and tell me I had no right to be jealous or insecure, since I had dumped him only days ago. Instead, I felt him wrap his arms around me, and nuzzle his face into my hair.
"You're a giant pain in the ass, do you know that?"
"Shut up." I said, my voice muffled by his sleeves. He kissed the top of my head.
"You're an idiot to think that I want anyone but you."

*****

Neither of us had figured out what we were going to do until the festival (or in David's case, until he met up with Carly). I was still itching to climb, especially since I had bailed on the Riglos "adventure", and David was supposed to be meeting up with friends of his in Mallorca, (a last-minute plan he'd made after I had unceremoniously broken up with him over Skype like the nice girl I was), but after three days in Madrid, he hadn't been able to get his credit card to work to book the flight there. I'd suggested he get the ferry, but he turned green at the idea, and told me he had terrible motion sickness.

While David had been getting frustrated at his credit card company, I'd been researching car rentals, and found that I could actually afford to rent a (tiny) car for the next few days. I briefly considered looking for new climbing areas, but reasoned that since I already knew the area, only had a few days, and had unfinished business (my project climb) in Rodellar, I should just go back there.

When David still hadn't made any progress with his flights by the time it was cool enough to go outside and eat (to be fair, his efforts had been interrupted several times when one or other of us had had the sudden need see the other one naked), I asked him if he would want to come to the mountains with me.

I had debated long and hard about asking him to come with me because a) he wasn't a climber; b) there wasn't much else to do in Rodellar but climb; c) we still hadn't discussed "us" and what "this" was; and d) I'd broken up with him to travel alone. On the other hand, I really, *really* loved being with him. It wasn't just the fact that I wanted to spend all day naked in bed (even though I did, and we had); he was just so much fun to be around. He could be goofy and silly one minute, and then get into an indepth discussion of some serious, high minded topic the next. I still hadn't been able to figure out what all this added up to, for me or for him, and I knew I was putting off the inevitable "discussion" we would have to have.

But despite all this, I told him I was going to the mountains, and asked him if he wanted to come with me. I told him the campsite was beautiful, and cheap. I told him there were lovely hiking trails, and a river. I told him there would be lots of cool people there to hang out with. And I told him that I was going there to climb, and to try and finish my project.

"So, I would just be waiting in the campsite for you to come home after climbing every day?"
I faltered. I couldn't tell if he was serious or not.
"No, there's hiking and stuff..."
"Basically cleaning the tent and making dinner for you while you're off gallivanting with your climbing buddies? A kept man?"
I started laughing. "Well, when you put it that way..."
"Just admit it. You want me to be your travel bitch."
He was grinning now, and he hugged me close as we turned the corner to the narrow street of restaurants where we had eaten each night.
"It's not that at all." I said, poking him in the side with my elbow as we walked.
"I know it's not that." He murmured, nuzzling my hair. Then he sighed dramatically. "You just don't want to be without me for a minute, and you need me with you to be happy."
I mumbled something about him being a big idiot, and blushed, although I was deeply offended. I knew he was only teasing, but it grated on the "strong independent woman who don't need no man" vibe that I'd been building up in my head.

We ate fried chorizo and *patas bravas* (a small part of me panicking that I wasn't going to be able to pull myself up the wall at all at this rate), and shared a bottle of red wine, and by the end of the meal my indignation had vanished, and I was left feeling warm, and wanted, and looking forward to what I now thought of as "our adventure" in Rodellar.

*****

Rodellar was a disaster.

David had no camping gear to speak of, but decided he would rather save the money than buy a sleeping mat. This was the first mistake. I had a tent, a mat and a sleeping bag, all of which we attempted to share, but it's impossible to overstate the difference between sleeping on even the cheapest, shittiest, foam mat; and sleeping with nothing between you and the dirt. It's also difficult to overstate the impact a poor night's sleep will have on a person's mood the next day.

The first day was kind of magical. We hiked down into the canyon, and found a Ald in the river where a collection of fig trees, a cliff face, and a clear rock pool formed a perfect secret corner to hang the hammock. We gave the water a cursory dip and lay in the sun to dry off, then spent the rest of the day in the hammock. A room would have been a significant financial step up from our current status. Hell, so would a bed. But for some reason we were convinced (at least, I was) that we would be able to continue this blissfully bohemian romance story without anything so bourgeois as furniture... or long term commitment. I was wrong.

Neither of us slept more than a couple of hours that night - as soon as we stayed in one position for more than fifteen minutes, muscles would start to cramp or limbs would fall asleep. If one of us did manage to drift off, the other would have to shift position, and we would wake up again. It was the worst.

After sunrise, coffee, and a serious debate about whether we should drive back to the nearest town to buy an air mattress (still deemed too expensive), we walked down to the main climbing area, and I saw some people working on a climb I had tried a few weeks before. We stopped, and I asked if one of them would mind belaying me on it before they took down their equipment. After two attempts, I finished the climb, cleaned it, and thanked them. They suggested I climb with them for the rest of the day. I glanced at David.

"Would it be ok if we hung out with these guys today so I can climb?"
"Yeah, that's fine. I'll just watch."
He didn't seem thrilled, but he had said it would be fine if I climbed, so climb I did. I have to admit, I was showing off a bit: I wanted David to be impressed with how well I climbed, to think I was graceful, athletic, strong, etc, etc. Unfortunately, it was hard to tell whether he was impressed or bored. He became monosyllabic, and didn't seem interested in talking to the other climbers in the group. When they suggested moving on to another area, I asked him if he wanted to go.
"How much longer are you going to climb for?" he asked.
"I don't know... maybe two more climbs? An hour? Maybe an hour and a half. Are you bored?"
"I'll just meet you back at the campsite."
"Are you sure? I can come with you now if you like."
"It's fine, you keep climbing. I'll read in the hammock. I'll see you later."
He strode back up the trail without saying goodbye to the rest of the group. I felt uncomfortable, like I had done something wrong, but couldn't figure out what. I told myself that I'd made it clear I was coming here to climb, so he couldn't be mad at me about that. I wondered if he had just changed his mind about coming here, and had realized he was going to be bored. I decided to put it out of mind, and talk to him about it at the end of the day.

We moved on to an area beside the river: a steep, featured wall with a wide roof at the finish. Each of the routes began in a mess of limestone tufas (misshapen stalactites which protruded from the wall, and were great for wedging in a knee or forearm for a rest), which took two or three attempts to figure out. The routes were difficult to see, because there seemed to be infinite holds on the wall, but in fact only a few were solid enough to hang from. As the wall sloped steeply backwards, it became more and more important to grab the exact right hold with the correct hand the first time, as the lactic acid began to build up in my forearms, and my endurance started to fail. I spent three attempts on a climb that had taken one of the others one, but finally topped out, after a particularly strenuous move which required me to hook my heel into one hold, pull with my leg, hang my full body weight from my right hand, and reach to my full extension over my head, blind, to a huge hold which was totally invisible from below. All this while I was three meters above the last bolt, meaning that if I fell, or couldn't reach the hold, I would fall at least six meters before the rope caught me. I clipped the anchor and came down, elated, and wanting more, even though I'd already been climbing for nearly four hours.

Egged on by the enthusiasm of the group, I jumped on a route no-one had tried yet - a thin, winding line up the right hand face of the cliff - and much to my surprise, on-sighted it. It had been one of my best days climbing on the trip so far, and I was feeling euphoric (and sore, and exhausted) as I made my way back to the campsite. David was reading in the hammock, and didn't look up at me until I was standing next to him, sweaty from climbing the trail with all my climbing gear on my back.

It turned out we had run the clock out on "not talking about stuff". It turned out that David had seen my decision to climb with the group rather that hang out with just him as symbolic of my decision not to commit to him in a relationship. My brilliant defence to this was "you *said* it was fine!" (as if I wasn't a member of the sex who *invented* 'fine' to mean just the opposite).

What followed was the first, proper, all-out fight I had ever had with a boyfriend (or whatever the hell we were calling one another) - including the relationship where I had found out that the boy had cheated on me in the same week I'd been evicted from my apartment. That time I had just thrown his phone off a balcony (the giveaway had been a dirty text message) and called him an asshole bastard son-of-a-bitch, before storming out. I avoided romantic conflict at all costs, even if it meant physically running away, but this time, there was no storming out. We were in a campsite in the middle of nowhere. Neither of us could drive off, because the other one would be stranded. We couldn't shout or scream or cry, because, well, we were in a very public space. But boy, did we have that fight. All the unresolved emotions from the original break up, the issue of living in two different countries, the undefined feelings we had for one another, the resentment that neither one of us would concede to what the other wanted, all of it, came bubbling to the surface, and boiled over. It was getting dark before we settled into simmering silence, having resolved absolutely nothing. David slept in the hammock, and made it clear the next morning that he was ignoring me by pulling the blanket over his head when I asked how he had slept. Fine. Let him be that way. I grabbed by climbing bag and stalked off towards the trail, resolving that I didn't need this kind of drama, and that this was exactly the kind of shit that I'd had in mind when I told myself I didn't need to get involved with some tattooed, full-of-himself American guy, no matter how much I liked his abs. Or how much I looked forward to spending time with him. Or whatever.

It took me ages to find someone to climb with, and then I climbed like absolute crap, and stormed back to the campsite after only two hours, ready to pick up with David where we left off, and tell him to go to hell.

There was no one in the hammock or the tent, but there was a piece of paper on my sleeping bag. My heart sank. He must have hitched a ride out of here. I sat back on the ground and tried to talk myself out of crying, still holding the folded paper in my hand. I told myself I was just bummed because I hadn't had a chance to get the last word in, but in reality, I was crushed that he would have just left (even though the fight had been so shitty). After a second, my eyes focused, and I realized that his clothes were still folded in the corner of the tent. I opened the paper, and saw that he had drawn a cartoon of an old, gypsy fortune teller, crouched over a crystal ball, a maniacal grin on her face. The picture was clear and stylized, and I wondered how it had never come up that he could draw. Under the image was the caption "If you had visited a fortune teller before coming to Rome..." and in the speech bubble from the fortune teller's cackling mouth were the words "You're so screwed!"

I laughed out loud, in spite of myself. It wasn't an apology, but I wasn't really sure I deserved one. It was, however, a peace offering. On the bottom of the paper he had written "I've gone for a hike, to take some photos. I'll see you later. Never have I ever..."

The next three days went like this. We would have a blissful few hours in one another's company, then something would come up to remind us of our "situation" and we would start fighting again. One or other of us would storm off, and then later we would make up. One day, we fought over a Canadian girl we had both met in Costa Rica, who I found out David had dated on and off when he returned home. In my defence, he was using her to make me jealous, hinting that he had plenty of options back home. In his defence, I had repeatedly said that I wasn't going to be going back home with him, which logically meant that he was free to do whatever he wanted. Another time, he went on an hour long rant about how Eli and I were still in touch, and how I was just stringing him along until I could go home and get back together with my ex. This was a tricky one. I was realizing that I missed Eli differently the longer I travelled. I had had my reasons for breaking up with him, and even though I missed spending time with him, I wasn't planning to start back up where we left off when I got home (whenever that would be). It was impossible to convince David of this: it made no sense to him that I would stay "friends" with my ex, even when I explained that we had been friends to begin with. It didn't matter - we were both being irrational, blaming these innocent people, thousands of miles away, when in reality, we were angry at ourselves, and at geography, and *the situation* (I refused to use the word fate).

I obsessed over how amazing this *could* have been, if only we had met while living in the same city. We could have flirted, and gone on normal dates, and gotten to know one another without this ridiculous ultimatum hanging over our heads: one of you needs to move to the other side of the world; or you need to break up. Neither of us was delusional to think that an American-Australian long-distance relationship could survive long, particularly since it was becoming obvious that we were both prone to being a bit childish and irrational when it came to the other person (to put it mildly).

Even though a large part of my brain was rebelling against this level of ongoing, irreconcilable conflict, and begging me to just cut and run, I found myself noticing more and more how sweet and considerate David could be (when he wasn't deliberately being an asshole). One day, we had our clothes hanging on a string beside the tent, and a strong gust of wind blew some of my shirts (ok, all of my shirts... I had three shirts) over a stone wall and into an impenetrable thicket of brambles. I made a half hearted attempt to retrieve them, then gave up, and decided I would just wear the tank top I had on until it fell apart. David spent ten minutes splayed on his stomach on the stone wall, using a long stick to coax the shirts away from the brambles, cursing and muttering to himself, and getting a fair amount of thorns in his fingers in the process. For some reason, I found this slapstick act of chivalry so touching.

Somehow, we made it up to the day that David was due to fly and meet Carly. I hadn't asked to come, and he hadn't invited me. Despite what he had said back in Madrid, I was still feeling prickly and defensive about Carly's existence, and I wasn't ready to meet her yet. I told David I was going to climb for a few more days, then catch the train down to Valencia and meet them before the festival.

I drove him to the tiny, rural airport for his flight to France, pulling over into a field at one point for one last "one for the road" (this part had survived the fighting), and saying goodbye without having resolved a single thing.

The next time we saw one another, we would have a third wheel, a girl who was, by all accounts, *much* more available than me; and David would be flying home after the festival, effectively ending whatever the hell this thing was between us.

Or at least, that's what I thought.

*****

I left Rodellar a few days later, and drove back to Madrid. I hadn't finished my project. I didn't know if it was my headspace, or whether I had just been aiming too high (no pun intended). Climbing is as much a mental sport as a physical one, maybe even more so. You are trying to overcome the natural fear of gravity which is instinctive to all flightless animals: I mean, you die if you fall off a high thing. Convincing yourself that the equipment will catch you, and that it's safe to take risks, takes a *lot* of concentrated mental energy. The people who are best at climbing are those for whom height is not a factor, and those who thrive on adrenaline. I am not one of those people. If my head wasn't in it, I climbed like shit.

I dropped my car off and made my way to the train station, headed for Valencia, and David, and Carly.

CHAPTER 15:
BENICASSIM

__The Crux:__ the most difficult and dangerous section of a climbing route. Some climbs are fairly consistent the whole way in terms of difficulty, but the climbs you remember are the ones which lull you into a false confidence, and then unceremoniously throw you off with a series of seemingly impossible moves that you didn't see coming. Getting through the crux can be a bitch.

D avid and Carly had spent three days in the South of France in a beach campsite, hanging out with a bunch of surfers and getting tanned. I knew this from Facebook. Not that I'd been paying attention or anything. I also knew that this was Carly's first ever overseas trip, and under the still simmering trepidation and petty competition that was tying my stomach in knots, I wondered vaguely how she was feeling. Luckily for me, Carly was neither unobservant, nor competitive. It had taken her all of ten minutes to size up the situation, and realize that whatever was going on between David and I, it wasn't something she wanted to get mixed up in. Whatever her intentions may have been with David when she planned her trip, she never said a word; and was nothing but sweet to me the entire time we spent together. Besides, she was a sexy, single redhead traveling in Europe. She was already getting plenty of attention when I turned up at the hostel where we had agreed to meet in Valencia.

Once I got over the guilt of having seen her as a threat (though to what, I had no idea), I allowed myself to get swept up in the fun of what I realized I'd been missing: a girlfriend. Having spent most of my time climbing in Spain, I had been branded as "one of the boys", and, with the exception of Crystal, I hadn't really spent any time with girls since I'd left home. I was so relieved about putting the jealousy to bed, and Carly was so giddy about being in a new country; we all decided that the first order of business at the hostel should be to get really, properly, drunk. Luckily, the bar downstairs had a special on Jäger bombs (a beverage which I now cannot so much as sniff without feeling sick). Carly, undeterred by the fact that her (perhaps) preferred partner was unavailable, soon got the hang of a fundamental aspect of backpacking as a single girl: being hit on by absolutely everyone at the bar. This particular bar was full of people heading to the festival, and by the time David and I crept upstairs at one am for some "catching up", the party was still going full-swing.

The next day, after we had managed to locate and wake Carly (who hadn't gone to bed until the sun came up), we spent three hours and about 150 euros in Decathlon, and emerged with a very unwieldy collection of blow up mattresses, tents, blankets, deck chairs, a cooler, and rope for the hammock. We were ready. No more sleeping on the ground for us!

The campsite at the festival looked promising - there were shade cloths, and orderly rows of tents, and a few trees dotted about. The toilets were clean, the showers were hot and there was a bar and a cafe in the campground. By the end of the week however, there were broken tents, bodies, rubbish and blow up mattresses strewn over every inch of ground, there was never any paper in the toilets and the hot water only worked at midday, when the thought of a hot shower was enough to make your sweaty, clammy skin crawl. Thank god for the beach, just ten minutes away. The water was bliss - the perfect hangover cure, and there was a cafe on the boardwalk, which served the most amazing fruit shakes. I don't think anyone can truly appreciate how much of a big deal it was to find those shakes, or how many we consumed in a day, as the temperatures soared, and the sun shone down on us.

As the campsite filled up over the next three days, we noticed a distinct demographic trend: our neighbours were almost exclusively loud, brightly dressed, grossly drunk, horrendously sunburned British people. It was a veritable invasion! The little town was crawling with bleary-eyed twenty-somethings, moving slowly through the alcohol aisle in the *supermercado*, slouched in cafe chairs staring into space or bragging to their friends back home about how hot and sunny it was in beautiful Benicassim.

On our second night at the campsite, David and I were lying in the hammock and Carly was reading in her tent. We were listening to music, and whispering sweet nothings to one another, and they were starting to turn into sweet somethings.
"Do you know, I realized something." David murmured, as I stroked his hair.
"What's that?"
"I realized that if you came back to America with me, you would be the last girl I ever kissed." he said, displaying a flagrant disregard for the fact that recent history had proven this would not be a conversation which went well.
I was instantly assailed with a cascade of conflicting emotions. It was both the most romantic and the most terrifying thing anyone had ever said to me. I'd said "I love you" to almost all the people I'd been in relationships with, and none had hesitated in saying it back to me. Those words to me didn't imply a promise: they merely expressed how I felt at the time. Maybe

that was fickle, maybe it was naïve: maybe none of them had really meant it, or even knew what it meant. I'd never thought about the future of my relationships, only the present, and I'd never had someone so clearly express the future that could be had, if I agreed to be a part of it. This should have been the moment when the heroine realizes that all will be well in her life, because her man has declared his intention to make her his one and only, and they could now live happily ever after. For me, all I could feel was the conviction that I was, at that time, utterly ill equipped to take on such a responsibility. I knew that for this relationship to work, one of us would have to uproot our life completely, which put a tremendous amount of pressure on it being "a big deal". There was no way to do this by halves, no way to be cautious – it was all or nothing. I remembered the feeling of clinging to the rock, hundreds of meters above solid ground, paralyzed with fear of falling, unable to make the next move. The analogy was not lost on me.

David could feel my response even before I gave it, and I could tell he was angry. I tried to explain how I was feeling, but again, I lacked the words, and after I had mumbled a few inadequate, pathetic excuses, David had had enough. He climbed out of the hammock and turned to face me.

"Fuck this," he said coldly, and then climbed inside the tent and zipped it closed. I lay in the hammock, crying in frustration, trying to be as quiet as possible, aware that Carly had probably heard the whole thing, feeling embarrassed and angry and helpless. After what seemed like hours, he came back out again.

"I'll leave in the morning." I said, avoiding his gaze, and sniffing in the least attractive way possible.

He scowled. "Why is your solution to everything to just leave?"

"What's the point in staying here? We're just going to fight! Just like we did in Rodellar. We aren't going to work this out. One of us needs to leave, and you need to stay here with Carly ."

He sighed, and ran his hand through his hair, dropping his head in frustration.

"I know all this. But I also know that if you leave, I'll just chase after you. I can't help it, for some fucking reason. So, come inside, and let's just go to sleep, and we can pretend this didn't happen. I'm leaving in a few days anyway, so you can do whatever you want after that."
Even though this was exactly what I had been saying the whole time, hearing him say it for the first time made me cold. We crawled into the tent and lay as far away from one another as possible, and I thought that I had never been so sad in my life to get what I wanted.

*****

We spent the next day at the beach, and by the evening, to my utter disbelief, it really was like nothing had happened. We got ready to go into the festival as the sun was setting, drinking and talking around our little table, Carly drawing crazy patterns on all our faces with her eyeliner, which she insisted was necessary for us to "blend in". The conversation drifted onto relationships, with Carly telling us about a guy she had been dating back home, who she had dumped because he had no ambitions in life.
"It's not like I wanted to be the one to change him." She explained. "Being with someone shouldn't be about you wanting them to be different. But he just had no passion – nothing he was striving for."
"The person you're with should love you as you are; but you should always want to be better for them." David said. I glanced up at him, surprised.
"Is that a quote from something?"
"No, I don't think so. It just makes sense to me."

Eventually we made our way into the festival, and as we pushed through the crowd at the gates, we heard a voice shouting at us.
"David? David!"
We looked around and saw a small, blonde, tanned figure hurtling towards us, before flinging himself at David.

"Holy shit – Simon! What the hell are you doing here?"
Simon's friends caught up with him, and they all started chatting excitedly. Carly and I were completely out of the loop.
"Simon and I met in Costa Rica last year! Simon, this is Sophie and Carly – Sophie and I met on that same trip - this is so crazy!"
After a little while, Carly and I left David to catch up with his friends, and went off to explore. We wandered from stage to stage, dancing with whoever was next to us, allowing ourselves to be jostled and lifted up in the mosh pit, our feet dusty and sore, our arms raised, our faces shining with sweat. Around one am we saw David and Simon in the distance, and the four of us, along with Simon's two friends, went inside the huge tent labelled "Silent Disco". Wearing huge headphones, sometimes tuned into the same song, sometimes not, we all danced and danced, pulling the most ridiculous moves we could think of, lurching wildly around the dance floor until everyone else in the tent was laughing at us. At one point, David picked me up off my feet, and spun me around in his arms, and I was laughing so hard I could barely breathe, gazing down at his grinning, happy face. I thought, how am I ever going to forget this boy, who looks at me like this, and makes me feel this way?

*****

The rest of the festival passed in a hazy blur of sunshine, music, dancing and swimming in the warm, blue ocean. We woke up on Monday morning after an hour's sleep, and piled our bags and barely conscious bodies onto a train to Barcelona, having managed to cheat/squeeze/luck our way through the ticket queue, to spend the next three hours curled up like pretzels on the floor amongst bags, legs and smelly feet, dead to the world. We arrived at our hostel and stumbled into proper beds for the first time in a week, and slept. Poor Carly suffered from the fact that both David and I had already been in the city, and had little interest in sightseeing the next day. Valiantly, she strode off

SOPHIE SMITH

(well, she got a taxi) into the city alone in search of culture and history and, perhaps most importantly, *Port d'Angel*, the "best shopping in Spain". When she returned, we all made a big dinner in the hostel's large, poorly stocked kitchen, and then said good-bye – her flight was leaving that night.

The last few days with David were sweet, and sad. Somehow, we managed not to fight, although I often caught him staring at me with a look on his face that could have been frustration, or anger, or just sadness. I found it more and more difficult to re-member the reasons I had given him when he had asked me to come with him the last time, and not to get caught up in the excitement of it all, this clandestine international romance we had built up in a matter of a handful of days together. On the day of his flight home, David woke me up early, looked into my eyes and asked me, again, to come with him.

"Come with me to the airport and see if there are seats left on the flight."

"No," I said. "I can't do that."

"Why not? Just come and see."

And in this moment, my inner romantic, whom I had been struggling to contain for the past couple of months, broke out and, with my better judgment fighting to hold her back, nodded my head.

"Ok."

"What?"

"Ok." I repeated, pushing myself out of bed. "Let's do it".

A huge grin spread across his face.

"If it's possible, I just became even more crazy about you!"

"Think of what a great story it will make!" I laughed, and for the moment, the adrenaline pushed aside the feeling of foreboding, which crept under my skin.

I shoved my things together and we ran down the hill to the train station, chattering and laughing nervous laughter like lit-tle kids who've stolen some cake and think they've gotten away with it.

"I mean, how full can a plane from Barcelona to the U.S. be?"
Completely, as it turned out: the only seats left were in business class, and so far out of my budget it was laughable. Although we rushed off to the nearest computer and looked up the price of flights for the next two weeks, I could feel my common sense slowly beating my romanticism into reluctant submission. The spontaneity was gone. All my old reasons came rushing back to crush my little inner romantic and squash her flat.

"It's gone. The moment's gone. You are going to get on that plane, and I'm going to keep traveling."

"No. You are going to get on a flight as soon as we can afford it, and you are going to come to America, and be mine."

"How can I be yours? How can I say yes to a commitment like that when I'm still trying to figure out how to be myself?"

"Why are you so afraid of saying yes to me? I'm not trying to lock you away from the world – I want to see the world just as much as you do – I just want us to see it together!"

"But that's just it! If I come back with you now, you will be going back to university in a few weeks, and then what will I do? My options will be to stay in one spot and wait for you, or travel without you! If you let me just finish what I started – once I figure out what that is – then I could come and meet you, or you could come and meet me. Maybe when I've had that time to myself I will be ready to handle all of this!"

"That's not enough."

"Why not? We both get what we want..."

"You have to choose me!" he shouted, throwing his hands up, and causing people sitting at the nearby coffee bar to stare and whisper. "You have to make a decision to be with me – you can't just ask me to wait for you because "maybe" you'll be ready to be with me in three months! It doesn't work that way! You are either mine, or you aren't."

Right there: that was the problem. He didn't want us to be "with" each other, he wanted us to "belong" to each other. When he spoke about what was happening between us, he referred to it as a state of me being 'his', and this language made me feel like I was being trapped in a very small space. Shaking my head, I took a step backwards, unable to form the words to express what I was thinking.

"Well. That's it then."

He looked at me furiously, but when he spoke his voice was even.

"Yeah. You've made yourself pretty clear. Stupid really, I should have listened. I guess I'll see you in another life."

He turned away but I couldn't help myself: I reached out and grabbed his arm.

"Just so you know: I do love you."

He gave a short, sharp laugh and for a moment I thought he was going to shake me off, but instead he hugged me tightly, and growled:

"Oh, you are just the fucking worst."

And he was right. I was being the absolute worst person to him in that moment, but I couldn't help it.

He pulled away.

"I love you too. Call me if you ever figure out what it is you want."

And as he walked away, I truly believed that would be the last I saw of him.

*****

I got back to the hostel in tears, feeling pulled in a million directions, not least of them heading west across a significant volume of water. Even though I knew it was a terrible idea, I Skyped Dad.

"I just tried to get on a plane to America"

"You WHAT?!?!"

Needless to say, talking to Dad didn't make me feel any better about my decisions, or my situation. My brother was more sympathetic, but since I hadn't been keeping him up to date on the whole "me and David" saga, he was a little confused that it had escalated from "we aren't going to sleep together" to, well, me crying in a hostel after not getting on a plane. He wasn't alone: I couldn't fathom how things had gotten so spectacularly complicated.

I spent the next few days in a state of nervous panic: one minute sure I'd made the right decision; then furious at myself for being so stupid; and a moment later crying and wishing I could go home. I skyped with Dad and Gavin multiple times a day, but they had no solutions to offer. Dad suggested that I needed some kind of direction, or destination to work towards, which seemed both painfully obvious, and unfathomably difficult. I spent another week in Barcelona, barely leaving the hostel, at my emotional rock bottom. I thought about going home. I thought about going to America. I thought about my Mum. I felt utterly, heartbreakingly alone for the first time since I had left Sydney... for the first time since Mum had died. It was a feeling made worse by the fact that it had been my decisions to be where I was. I only talked to three of my closest friends, and their reactions varied from romantic encouragement that I should "follow my heart" (code for "follow that boy"), to outright dismay that I was such a mess. I was embarrassed that I'd gone out into the world intending to discover myself as this strong, independent, competent woman, and had ended up curled up on a bottom bunk, unable to make a decision because of a boy. No, that wasn't right. It wasn't *because* of David. I had the horrible feeling that this meltdown had been inevitable.

At this point, I feel it is necessary to offer a disclaimer of sorts: at no point was I actually *stuck* or in any actual danger. I had a loving family who wouldn't hesitate to buy me a ticket home, even though I had, in fact, enough money left to get myself home. I was incredibly lucky to have had the freedom to have gone on this trip in the first place, and I felt like I was wasting that privilege by feeling this way, so that added guilt to the bundle of emotions I'd tied myself up in. Needless to say, I wasn't doing well. I felt like I was reaching for a hold that was just beyond my grasp, and falling, and falling, and falling. The prospect of the next few months stretched out before me in a bewildering, unknowable haze, and I just wanted something familiar to curl myself around, cling to and be comforted by.

Given my yearning for the familiar and comforting, I was surprised at the strength of my reaction when Eli suggested that I come home. He and I had stayed in contact since I had left Australia, but we had both kept a respectful, wary distance from the topic of one another's love lives. I knew that he was aware of how much time I had spent with David - there had been plenty of pictures of us together - and I had heard from my other friends that Eli had been having plenty of fun himself. The fight David and I had had about Eli in Rodellar had been a symptom of David's distrust of our supposedly platonic friendship. Whatever it looked like from the outside, I hadn't been thinking of Eli as someone I was going to "go home to". Part of the reason I'd been fighting David's plans so hard was that I didn't want to be *anyone's* girlfriend - I felt like I had too much to deal with in my own head and my own heart. I'd gotten used to speaking with Eli as friends - chatting about what we had both been up to, our plans, how we were feeling - and I was sure he saw it the same way.

I have a self defence mechanism that kicks in, and makes me very blunt and unemotional, when I'm discussing things that in fact affect me very deeply; and I have a complementary coping mechanism that compels me to talk about whatever is on my mind with whoever will listen, until I've worked it out in my own head. Because of this, I may have been somewhat insensitive when I skyped my ex-boyfriend back in Australia to vent about the fact that I'd been this close to getting on a plane to America with another man.

"What the hell am I doing here?" I wailed. "I wanted to go off on this big adventure to figure things out, but I've been away for months and I feel more confused than ever!"

"Come home." Eli suggested gently, concern etched on his face.

"I can't come home. Or maybe I should come home. Shit, I don't even know. It's like I'm trying to figure out who I am, but I don't know if I'm the same person I was before."

"Listen to me. You're amazing, and you are going to figure this out, but you can do that from home, where there are people who love you. You can come back to Sydney, and no one will judge you for not "finishing" - they'll just be glad you're back..."

I listened. What he was saying sounded so tempting, so easy. But then he said, hopefully, "and, you and I can pick up where we left off, and everything will be back to normal."

I knew in that moment that I couldn't just go home. Whatever I'd come halfway around the world to achieve, I hadn't achieved it yet, and my life wasn't magically going to go back to "normal" if I went home. It wasn't even going to become a new normal if I went to America. It became clear to me in that moment that I wouldn't find a solution to how I was feeling if I waited for someone else to give it to me. I wasn't myself - at least, not yet. I needed to keep going until I felt that I was. We talked for a while longer, and I missed him, and the easiness of what we'd had, but I knew it wasn't going to fix me.

A friend had given me a collection of famous quotes when I turned sixteen, and I memorized several of them. This was one of my favorites:

"The risk of making a wrong decision is preferable to the terror of in-decision." - Maimonides

I'd made the decision to keep traveling, but I still didn't know where I was going to go. I didn't suddenly spring from my bunk and stride out into the world, full of purpose. I stayed in that hostel room in Barcelona for five more days. Occasionally I made an effort to go out into the city, and a couple of times other travellers would include me in their plans, but for the most part I stayed in bed.

I didn't know it at the time, but this was the first of a series of bouts of depression, which were most likely part of the grieving process. I'd unintentionally been holding them at bay with all my adventures, but they had finally caught up with me. At the time, all I knew was that I was in one of the most exciting, beautiful cities in the world, but I just wanted to sleep.

CHAPTER 16: PICOS DE EUROPA

Multi Pitching: Like trad versus lead, multi pitch versus single pitch climbing separates the hobby climbers (me) from the true adrenaline junkies, who don't feel the need to stop after just one pitch, but keep climbing, one after the other, leap-frog style, until they reach the summit. Multi pitching removes the height limitations that single pitch climbing is bound by (ie, half the length of a rope), which makes it both exhilarating and terrifying.

A few months before I had left Australia, a girl I worked with at the climbing gym had introduced me to a Spanish guy, whom she had recently met and befriended, who'd come to Sydney to learn English. Alejandro was exceedingly good looking: quite stocky for a climber, with olive skin and dark brown hair that flopped over his smouldering, Mediterranean eyes. I had been more than a little smitten, as had my friend, and when the three of us went climbing in the Blue Mountains for a weekend; we found that the language barrier was no barrier at all to a fair bit of shameless flirting.

My friend (a much stronger climber than me) took the opportunity to show off her skills on the rock, and I (not averse to a bit of healthy competition) was determined to keep up. The result was a twisted ankle, a thrilling bit of chivalry when Alejandro carried me over on his back to the car, and the nickname "crazy-girl", which was about as creative as Alejandro' English would allow. He had arrived back in Spain a few weeks ago, and had issued a standing offer to go climbing. I started chatting with him while I was trying to pull myself out of my Barcelona-funk, and he suggested we go climbing in the Picos de Europa.

Note: for those of you flipping back through the pages right now, wondering if you missed a chapter, you didn't. I really did try to pull myself out of a break-up induced coma by going climbing with a cute guy from another foreign country. What could possibly go wrong?

Picos de Europa was like the mountain version of a playground: a national park in the North of Spain, with world famous climbing, just inland from some beautiful coastline. Apparently, the local delicacy was a kind of cheese sauce and there was a town with (I couldn't really believe this) the word "poo" in the name. One other important detail caught my attention: all the climbing was multi-pitch.

This didn't sound like anything I wanted to do, but I did want a reason to get myself out of bed. So, I agreed, telling myself that I could always back out when we got there, and it couldn't have been that hard, really.

Besides, the idea of doing scary climbs was much more exciting than the prospect of more moping around in a hostel after breaking up with a boy I had maybe been in love with, who lived halfway around the world. I remembered my long-ago conversation with Liz about having a torrid affair with a sexy Spanish guy, and quickly gave myself a mental slap on the face. *No romance!* You can ogle him all you want, but you do NOT need to be getting caught up in anything beyond that. Besides, he probably sees you as "one of the guys". And you literally *just* finished crying over the mess with David. And so, after leaving behind the nest of my hostel bunk-bed, and taking an incredibly quick train ride, I stepped out into the oppressive heat of Madrid in summer, and saw Alejandro waiting over by his tiny car (large cars being apparently illegal in Spain), which was stuffed to the roof with ropes, bags, shoes, and boxes of food.

I did a (probably noticeable) double take at how unreasonably attractive he was, and simultaneously, David's face flashed in my mind, and I reminded myself that I was just here for the climbing, thank you very much.

"Hey crazy girl!" He called, in his lilting, accented English. "Are you ready to have an adventure?"

After an unsuccessful and embarrassing attempt to converse in Spanish (it turns out that the word for "language" – as in, "We should practice the language", can be translated as the word for "tongue" – as in, "we should practice..." you get the idea), we lapsed into English, as we headed north. Another of my grand plans which I'd failed to realize - my Spanish was still far from fluent.

Driving out of Madrid, we passed through endless fields of sunflowers, millions upon millions of bright golden heads uniformly bowed in their beds of green. I remember being told that sunflowers rotate their stems to follow the sun with their heads, hence the name. Apparently, Mao Zedong used sunflowers as symbols of loyalty - he being the sun and the people being the flowers. However, as we drove through this infinite green and gold landscape, I noticed that without exception, every flower was bowed away from the sun. A more superstitious girl may have taken this as a sign, but I had decided to ignore any signs from the universe by that point. It was clear that I had very little control over what was going to be thrown at me, and that I was just going to have to take things as they came.

Alejandro had asked if I would mind spending the first night at his sister's house. She and her husband lived in Gijon, about two hours drive from Picos, and apparently they had an open house policy when it came to Alejandro and his climbing partners.

"She might be a *little* surprised to see you," Alejandro explained, without a hint of embarrassment, "I bring lots of friends to her house, but I have never climbed with a girl before. Most of the women who climb in Spain have climber boyfriends." Then he brightened, and said cheerfully, "maybe I will be your climber boyfriend!"

I choked on the coffee I'd been drinking, and tried to mop it up with a wad of toilet paper (the car really was decked out for serious camping). I wondered if his sister would assume we were together, or would she believe that we were just friends? Were single men and women able to be friends in Spain? I had been here for months, but I had had shockingly few interactions with actual Spaniards. Would his sister think I was some loose-moraled, scarlet woman, here from Australia to draw her brother into sin? I admit, I may have let my imagination get the better of me.

I fell asleep while we were driving through the rocky desert of central Spain, and awoke an hour later to find the landscape completely changed: we were in Asturias. Steep green hills flashed by, dotted with tiny towns, sporting identical, brick church spires. The roadside was forested by eucalyptus trees and thick, tangled vines. It was like driving through coastal New South Wales. The familiarity in this strange place made me smile. Gijon, I saw, bore a striking resemblance to Newcastle, a town just north of Sydney: originally an industrial settlement, now populated by young people and a thriving surf culture, with beaches packed to bursting on sunny summer days, just like the one we drove in on.

Alejandro' sister and her husband were lovely - good-naturedly teasing Alejandro about his habit of turning up at their house with two hours' notice, and asking how he had managed to get himself an Australian girlfriend (so there was my answer).

"We're just friends" I explained (a little too quickly) to his sister as we walked down to the beach from their little apartment. "I don't date anyone who is better looking than me!"

She laughed and nodded.

"You be careful though – make sure he doesn't try anything when you are out alone in the mountains!"

It occurred to me that to some people, going off into the mountains with a man I'd only met a handful of times, who had already made a joke about becoming romantically involved, and to whom I was attracted, was an example of poor decision making. Unfortunately, none of those people were at that time in my immediate vicinity to give me advice, so I ignored the idea, and set about ingratiating myself with these total strangers who were letting me sleep in their house for the night.

The water of the Bay of Biscay was shocking and refreshing and wonderful. It reminded me of swimming in Sydney in October, when the sunny days make people think of summer, but the water still stubbornly clings to the memory of July. After our swim, we wandered up onto the hill above the old church and saw something extraordinary. Perched on the cliff edge was a massive concrete sculpture, shaped like a cut out cylinder, and about ten meters high. "Elogio del Horizonte" was designed by Eduardo Chillida, and constructed in 1989 (the same year I was born) and has a truly remarkable architectural quirk. From outside the cylinder, you can hear the noise of the cars on the road, the seagulls calling, and the families on the beach. Standing exactly in the centre of the cylinder, however, all the other noises stop, and you are inexplicably enveloped with the sound of the waves crashing below. The shape of the sculpture somehow amplifies the sound of the sea, and cuts out the noises from behind and either side. Walk forward two steps and all other noises rush back, and the sea can no longer be clearly heard. The experience was wonderful – like the discoveries you make when you are a child, and everything you find is new, and interesting, and unexplained.

Alejandro's sister's husband (whose name I had instantly forgotten and been too embarrassed to ask about after the first
five minutes) took us to his friend's restaurant for dinner. Although they were probably only in their early thirties, to me,
Alejandro's sister and her husband seemed very "grown up".
They were getting ready to move to the UK to work, and they
were planning to have children once they were settled there.
They seemed so confident and comfortable with one another -
the opposite to how I had been feeling for the past few weeks...
really since I'd left Australia, if I was honest with myself. For the
thousandth time, I imagined my exasperated inner-self, rolling
her eyes and asking my great, bumbling, external self what the
hell I was doing.

Gijon, and the region in general, is famous for its cider, or 'sidra'.
When I confidently announced at dinner that night that we
drank cider in Australia, I was told I must be mistaken.
"I never saw cider the whole time I was there." Alejandro as-
serted.
Alejandro and his brother in law had ordered various tapas for
the table, most of which I had not seen before, and the waiter
brought out a bottle of sidra. We were a table of five, but they
only brought us three glasses. Alejandro poured me a tiny measure of sidra, which I presumed was for me to taste, so I took a sip,
and found it bitter, and much stronger than the sweet, bottled
drink I was used to.
Alejandro was laughing at me.
"You don't know how to drink sidra do you?"
He demonstrated the correct protocol, knocking back his measure of sidra straight from the glass like a shot of liquor.
"You have to drink it right after it has been poured," he explained.
When I told them that in Australia, we drink cider from a bottle
like a beer, all assembled were horrified at this barbarism. A few

days later I saw that the real tradition of sidra consumption is even more involved: they actually have a contraption similar to a spirits dispenser, which holds the bottle and the glass, and has a button which, when pushed, forces two high pressure jets of sidra into the glass, which must then be drunk immediately. How boring are bottles?

The food that night was a crash course in flavour. There were chunks of chorizo sausage cooked in sidra, still sizzling hot and bursting with oil; a 'torta' of fish, with the consistency of cheesecake, which was eaten with tiny pieces of toasted bread; and fried chunks of potato, which everywhere else in Spain are served with spicy sauce or aioli, but in Galicia come drenched in 'cabrales' sauce, made from the local cheese. Everything was rich, new and delicious, and we stayed at the restaurant until the wee hours of the morning.

Alejandro' sister made me a bed in their guest room, and ordered Alejandro to sleep on the couch, so there was no risk of blurring the lines around our friendship – at least, not yet.

"You hussy," I scolded myself. "You need to find yourself a bloody convent. You are NOT falling for the first boy who comes along, immediately after the last boy whose heart you broke. No rebounds!"

I felt very strong and saintly in my convictions, as I drifted off to the distant sound of the ocean.

Despite asserting that he was "desperate" to get to the mountains and climb, it was nearly impossible to get Alejandro off the couch the next morning. His sister and brother in law emerged at around ten am, and pottered around making coffee and reading the paper, while I fidgeted and flipped back and forth through the guide book. Eventually, and with very little enthusiasm, Alejandro dragged himself as far as the car, and we set off at about 1pm. The Spanish have a weird relationship with sleep, almost completely separate from their relationship to nighttime. Dinner happens sometime before midnight, usually, and if there's no work the next day, it seems unreasonable to get out of bed before noon. Then, in the afternoon, perhaps a nap. I found it impossible to get in sync with this schedule, so it was probably good that this was my first time actually traveling with a Spaniard.

After winding our way through the impressive mountain roads of Picos de Europa national park; which were dotted with tiny, stone villages, seventeenth century churches, and cascading waterfalls; and up a particularly nerve wracking dirt track, we arrived at mouth of the trail which would take us to our destination: the refuge at the base of Naranjo de Bulnes. The slopes around us were impossibly green, and the air was full of a strange melody, which turned out to be the chorus of hundreds of cowbells, slung about the necks of the hundreds of cows that had, for all intents and purposes, been left to their own devices of the hillsides It was, of course, raining. The north of Spain was green and lush for a reason: it was almost always raining. The forecast had assured us that it would stop during the night, and Alejandro had assured me that the rock would be dry enough for climbing, so I wasn't unduly concerned. It was then he discovered that he had left his hiking boots in Gijon. Disaster. One cannot traverse the peaks of Europe in flip-flops.

After a frantic phone call to his sister, who did indeed find the boots (under the couch), we had a decision to make: a four hour round trip to collect the expensive footwear; or try to find a shop which was open and sold boots in his size. There was no reception on the mountain, so we bundled ourselves and our stuff back into the car and drove back to the last village, where there was, indeed, a gear shop. It was not, however, open. We had already driven forty minutes, and the next shop was another thirty, so we decided to just go back for the boots. The next four hours, as we retraced our steps, grabbed the boots, and turned immediately back on ourselves, were a little tense.

By the time we arrived back at the trailhead, it was almost eight pm, and far from clearing up, the weather had taken a turn for the worse. As we unloaded the car for a second time, thunder rolled around the dark hills above us, lightning cracked, and fat raindrops fell with surprising force, into our faces.

Alejandro had said that the trail would be easy to follow, and not too challenging. Since we had already lost an entire day, I was all for hiking up in the dark. If we started now, and took it slowly, we could be there by midnight, and get a few hours sleep before getting up to climb the next day. Embarrassed by the whole "boot-forgetting-fiasco", Alejandro tried to save face, by manfully agreeing that it would probably be fine, just as an enormous clap of thunder sounded overhead, and the entire hillside was lit up by lightning.

At that point, driving back down the mountain to find a place to sleep was just as unappealing as walking up in the storm and darkness. Suddenly, Alejandro brightened.

"There is a lower refugio - just up the trail! Nobody stays there, but it should be open."
"Will we be able to climb tomorrow if we have to do the hike as well?" I asked. I knew the climbs were long and we would need an early start, so we wouldn't still be climbing in the hottest part of the day.
"Why don't we sleep until the rain stops, and then walk up before sunrise."
I blinked at him.
"You're going to wake up at," quick calculation, "three am??"
"Sure! It is no problem when there is a mountain to climb."
I was sceptical, but we didn't really have any other options. We walked the little way to the lower refugio, and settled in for a few hour's sleep. The building was utterly empty, save for the two, slightly odd men running it, both of whom smoked foul, pungent cigars and completely ignored us, except to take our money and point us to our bunks. We cooked a can of vaguely edible mush, and ate it with a handful of bland biscuits. The

beds were narrow as ships' bunks, and stacked one on top of the other as if we were in a boarding school dormitory.

After a few hours of fitful sleep, we rolled blearily out of our warm sleeping bags, shouldered our packs full of climbing gear, and began plodding up the mountain into the retreating darkness. The pathway was frosty, shrouded in mist, and utterly silent. The cows and their musical jewellery were nowhere to be seen, and all that could be heard was the crunch of our boots. It was impossible to tell if it was getting light or not, because we had risen into a dense blanket of grey clouds. We had been walking for about two hours, when Alejandro stopped and pointed up ahead, grinning. Rising out of the fog, catching the blazing, golden rays of the sunrise, was the distant, impossible monolith of rock. As we continued to climb, we kept catching glimpses of the pale orange shape through the clouds, lumpy and irregular and enormous, like a giant's thumb poking out between the mountain peaks. We finally broke through the cloud cover, and I turned to gaze out onto a new and fantastic world: the blanket of clouds made the valley below us invisible, and the peaks rose up around us, breaking through the clouds like icebergs floating in a sea of white and grey. The sunrise tinted everything with gold and orange, and we walked on towards the little stone hut at the base of Naranjo, which grew more and more massive as we approached.

We arrived at the refugio, and, without pausing for breath, tea, or breakfast, re-packed our bags and headed for the wall. I had done two multi-pitch climbs in my life before this: both in Thailand in 2008, both of which had scared me silly, even though they'd been under 100m long. For the most part, I had been emphatically against this sort of nonsensical endangerment of mind and body, but on Naranjo de Bulnes - against all my better judgment - I joined the noble ranks of "real" climbers.

Alejandro had shown me the route he wanted to take - the East Face - in the guidebook the day before, and I hadn't paid much attention. The route was slabby rather than steep - nothing like the vertical to overhanging faces of rodellar or (heaven forbid) Riglos, and this meant that it would feel less exposed. That feeling of vertigo you get in your head and stomach when you look down from somewhere high, is what climbers refer to as "exposure" - it's worse the higher you go, the more vertical or overhanging the face, and the narrower the climb. Nevertheless, it was going to be challenging, not only because of the technical difficulty of the climb (which was higher than I was comfortable on-sighting) but because the protection, rather than being orderly and regularly bolted like the climbs in Rodellar, was a mish-mash of bolts, slings, and well, nothing at all, with some pitches run out to six or eight meters. I was not prepared for the lack of conformity, or the impact it would have on our ascent. The rope we had was shorter than I would have liked. At one point, I was belaying from an anchor around 180m off the ground, shouting at the top of my lungs against the wind, as Alejandro, some 30m above me, and well out of earshot, seemed to be doing his best to yank me off the cliff.

"There's! No! More! Sodding! Rope!" I screamed, praying he would figure it out, knowing there was nothing I could do but sit and wait.

After about ten minutes, I heard a distant bellow: "Safe!" and breathed a sigh of relief. When I finally reached him, he was jerry-rigged into the cliff face on a single bolt (you should always be attached by at least two points of contact when belaying) with the anchor taunting us from two meters above. He seemed utterly unfazed that our rope, one of the main factors in our continued existence, was not long enough.

"Let's bring walkie-talkies next time." I suggested.

By the time we reached the final anchor, I was exhausted, drained, and starving. All we had had to eat since our early morning wake-up call was a few chocolate biscuits, and my sugar levels were down to my socks. The Spanish ability to go without breakfast was not one that I possessed, nor appreciated! Alejandro didn't seem the slightest bit bothered by the lack of sustenance, and insisted that we scramble the last 100 meters up the gently sloping peak to the very top. The gently sloping peak in which no ropes could be anchored. He was essentially asking me to go for a stroll up a hill, with a 200m drop on all sides. We scrambled up the last section of rock, sans protection (sorry Dad, if you're reading this), and clambered onto the flat rock at the top, kings in the world above the clouds. The peaks and valleys of Picos de Europa stretched out below us in a breathtaking tapestry of white, grey and blue.

There was something magical about being in a place that only climbers have ever seen. Unlike some multi-pitch climbs, this summit could not be reached by hiking, or (without great difficulty) by helicopter. So, ruling out superpowers (which in these uncertain times is always unwise), the only people who have walked that platform of rock are those who have climbed up there from the ground. I felt a new sense of perspective, knowing that somewhere under that blanket of cloud below me, people were going about their day, perhaps grumbling about the weather, whilst above them, there was calm, there was sun, there was infinite space.

We took silly photographs of one another, posing against the impossible backdrop, and I tried not to look too terrified as we crawled back down the slope to the anchors. After we made our long and slow descent, and I had devoured more than my share of our lunch (ladylike manners being low on my list of priorities at that point), we spent most of the rest of the day sleeping in the sun and mooching around the refugio, until another impressive storm rolled in, and we huddled inside, listening to the thunder, and watching the peaks light up against the sky. Thank god the rain had held off while we were climbing!

We played cards, and chatted with the other guests at the refuge, and read in silence while the storm raged outside. I was mostly enjoying Alejandro' company, although I felt at times that he wasn't really listening to what I was saying – perhaps it was because of the language barrier, but my instincts told me he wasn't always that interested. He would bring up topics or ideas that we had discussed only a few days before, and propose them anew. He would question me about aspects of my life that we had already covered in some detail. It was somewhat unnerving, and off-putting, but harmless.

Other than this, he was pleasant, easy company, and to some small extent, his devastating looks had ceased to be quite so devastating. He had teased me on several occasions that I would have to be careful, or I would fall in love with him, but his arrogance was too contrived and self-deprecating to be unpleasant, and I was fairly confident that he was joking. We were staying in a room with around fifteen other climbers and hikers – all rather malodorous, older men (although one man had his small son with him – who was already a better climber than I could ever hope to be), so there was no danger of my succumbing to his charms. I meditated once again on the notion of spending the rest of the year in celibacy; taking time to appreciate beauty, without becoming involved in romance. A year of moral clarity and wisdom. I fell asleep feeling sure I had stumbled upon my *true* purpose.

The next day, we had to accept that the bad weather wasn't going anywhere, and one good day of climbing might be all we could hope for. Unfortunately, Alejandro's back-up plan was about as appealing as the idea of climbing in the rain.
"Let's go climb Riglos!"
I protested, almost as a reflex. "No way. I will quite literally wet myself if I try to climb those things. I will simply curl up and die of vertigo."
"Don't be silly, Crazy Girl! You climbed Naranjo, that's almost the same thing. I will make sure nothing happens to you."
I thought about it. I had climbed Naranjo de Bulnes. I had stood

on top of that giant's thumb and gazed out over the clouds. I hadn't died. I hadn't even fallen.

I realised that when I'd be researching my trip with Stuart, I had built Riglos up in my mind as this impossible, unassailable challenge, when really I'd just been assuming that it would be too hard or too scary. I hadn't been afraid of falling to my death, or hurting myself: I'd been afraid of feeling fear. But then I thought of the fear I had felt about leaving home; the fear of the uncertainty of traveling alone; the fear of my feelings for David, and what they might mean; and most of all, the fear that like my Mum, I would run out of time. I was afraid of so many things. I thought back to the letter Mum had written me eighteen months ago in Buenos Aires, where she had called me brave. So much had changed in that eighteen months. I didn't feel brave any more. I felt like I had spent that time skirting the edges of my fears, never really jumping in. I was pretty sure she would have been horrified at the idea of me climbing a 300m cliff face with a boy who was essentially a total stranger; but I also felt like she would have been a little bit disappointed in me, if the reason I didn't do it was because I was too scared.

Fuck it, I decided. If I'm going to be scared, it had better be of something real. And so, two days later, as the frost glinted on the jagged shrubs and rocks at the base of Riglos, and the sun was a whisper on the horizon, I set off to scare the hell out of myself.

CHAPTER 17: RIGLOS

Topping out: climber slang for reaching the top of the climb. When you've worked on a route for a long time, and it has tested your strength, your nerves, and your endurance, there is literally nothing like the elation of grabbing that final hold, clipping the anchors, and knowing that you have conquered the rock.

Alejandro wanted to climb a route called Mosquitos, which zigzagged up one of the tallest pillars in Riglos. Stamping my feet against the morning chill, I watched him struggle up the first pitch, bleary eyed, and thought that it looked ok. It was taking all my self-control not to look past the first pitch, to the vast rock face above.

"One pitch at a time." I kept telling myself. "That's how I will get through this."

I'd insisted that we bring more water and food this time, since it was going to take us all morning (at least) to get to the top, and that had seemed like a good idea, until it was my turn to climb, and I tried to get off the ground with an 8 kg pack on my back and an overhanging start.

I fell off. Swore. Audibly smacked my knee on the rocks. Swore some more. And eventually hauled myself, most inelegantly, up the first pitch. This wasn't exactly the redemptive, life-changing ascent I had pictured, but I was in it now. Only six more pitches to go.

The second and third pitches were much easier, although I was still getting used to the pack on my back. The rock was lumpy and difficult to read, but the holds were big and the moves weren't too strenuous. I focused on watching Alejandro climb, and trying to follow his sequence

Halfway up the fourth pitch, I started to get really scared. We had to traverse horizontally across a section of the cliff, at around 200 high, to reach the next ledge. Until that point, I had managed not to look down. When I did, it was like I was standing on top of a 40-story building, except without the comfort of concrete beneath my feet. I forced myself through the traverse, which, had it been at ground level, wouldn't have been worth sneezing at, but with the prospect of swinging out over all those meters of nothingness, might as well have been impossible.

Safely secured at the anchors on the next ledge, I found myself taking stock of the situation and concurring that never again would I let myself be talked into something so insane as this, no matter how alluringly dark and handsome my climbing partner was. I would finish what I started, but then I would go home and take up knitting, or some such activity where my feet need never leave the ground. I felt a hard and vicious ball of ice in my stomach every time I looked down, and my vision creased and blurred when I glanced up, so instead, I stared ferociously at the rock directly in front of me, and climbed higher.

Alejandro had been surprisingly patient throughout the climb, even though it was probably taking us way longer than it should have (and by that I mean it was taking *me* way longer), and hadn't mentioned the fact that I had clearly been on the brink of a pretty disastrous meltdown for the past few hours. I realized he was probably desperate to get off the wall and as far away as possible from the crazy chick who had said she was a climber but was clearly more of a mole person. The humiliation wasn't helping my mood.

It became a mind game. If I allowed myself to focus on the evidence of my physical sense, I would panic. The rope linking me to the rock looked impossibly thin, straining against the flimsy looking titanium carabiner: a quarter-inch of metal holding my vulnerable body 300 meters above the dry, dusty slope below me. The rock face stretched up from the plain, towering above me for another eighty meters, pockmarked, wrinkled and ancient. The only sound I could hear was the blood pounding in my ears, and my own slow, deliberate breathing – count to three in, hold, count to three out – the rhythm the only thing separating me from total panic. As I reached for each hold, the void behind me stretched infinitesimally.

The next pitch was the worst. This was where the wall of the cliff sloped backwards into an overhang, which got more extreme to the left, thankfully on the routes we weren't climbing. From the ground, it had looked like a tiny change in gradient, but from the start of the 30m pitch, it looked like a horizontal roof. We had been climbing for nearly three hours at this point, and I was exhausted. About four moves into the pitch, I grabbed for a hold which should have been good, and found my fingers scrambling on smooth rock. Before I could readjust, I was falling.
"Well", I thought, "this is it. I'm going to die."

Actually, I didn't have time to think that. What I really thought was "Fuckfuckfuckfuckfuck!!"

Since Alejandro was above me on this pitch, I didn't fall as far as I would have had I been leading, but when the rope caught me, I swung out in a wide, unstoppable arc, and the shock and adrenaline caused my breath to catch in my throat and my heart to beat so hard I could hear it. I hung from the rope over hundreds of meters of air, trying to slow my breathing, reminding myself that these ropes could hold the weight of a bus, and the bolts in the wall were *not* going to break. I forced myself to stare directly ahead at the wall, and reached out for the holds once more. I could not understand how anyone could overcome this instinctive terror I was feeling, to the extent that they would actually *enjoy* this kind of climbing. For me, it was going to be a case of taking it one move at a time, and climbing in spite of the fear... so that's what I did. At several points as I climbed that pitch, my tired arms gave out, or I reached for the wrong hold, and I was left dangling from the rope, trying not to swing, or think, or whimper, but just to breathe. I focused on the rock in front of me so hard that I'm surprised I didn't burn a hole in it. I made it to the next anchors, but there was still one pitch remaining.

Alejandro was smiling broadly at me as I hauled myself up to the last set of anchors, where he was waiting.
"Congratulations! You fell! You're a real climber now."
I glared at him, unable to muster the energy to respond.
"The last pitch is the easiest, and then we will be finished. You should lead it!"
I'd been seconding (following Alejandro's lead) since the second pitch, and hadn't led when we had climbed in Picos. Now, facing the highest climb I'd ever done, with arms that were essentially jelly, I was being asked to lead. If I fell while leading, I would fall twice as far as the last bolt I'd clipped. I didn't think I could comprehend what that would do to me.
I was about to tell Alejandro "I'd rather poke my own eyes out than lead this climb", when something in my brain clicked. I realized that unless I lead this last pitch, Alejandro would have essentially pulled me up this cliff, and I wouldn't be able to truly claim that I had done it. And I was damned if I was going to let the last few hours of torture be for nothing.

I looped the rope up behind me, checked my gear, and, ignoring the trembling in my muscles, started out on the final pitch. In sport climbing, if the route is too difficult, you ask your belayer to let you down. On this pitch, it would have been very difficult for me to return to the anchor, since the climb sloped outwards. I would have had to swing on the rope and catch Alejandro's hand, then he would have had to pull me in, and we would have had to spend ages rearranging the gear so he could lead. By starting this pitch, I was essentially committing to finishing it, one way or another.

I forced myself up that rock, my usual mental excuses surfacing with every meter, but somehow I kept going.
Third bolt: "Fuck, it's like five meters to the next bolt! There's no way I can make that without falling. Oh, God, I don't want to fall, I should have asked Alejandro to climb first..."
Keep going.
Fourth bolt: "These rocks look loose. What if one of them breaks off and hits Alejandro and knocks him unconscious through his helmet and then I fall to my death?"
Keep going.
Fifth bolt: "I swear my arms are going to fall off. Even if I make it, I'm going to have to go through life without arms."
Keep going.
Sixth bolt: "You can do it, put your back into it, uh-huh... oh God I'm losing my mind."
Seventh, eighth, ninth, tenth bolts: "I'm scared I'm scared I'm scared I'm scared..."
I reached the anchor.
It was 35 metres of sketchy, scary, reachy, wind-swept, unfamiliar rock... and I climbed every step of it.

The feeling of ecstacy when I reached the top was indescribable. I had felt excited when we topped out on Naranjo, but nothing like this. I was dirty and smiling and sore and tired and it felt amazing. Safely anchored into the miraculously flat rock at the summit, belaying Alejandro up the last pitch, I looked down on 300 meters of terror to the stones and shrubs and village far below, and mentally high-fived myself for the fact that I was still standing. Just.

We had climbed for seven hours without a break, and when I removed my shoes (which were very comfortable as far as climbing shoes go) the pain was unbelievable. I sat on the flat rocks as the adrenaline which had been keeping me going began to ebb away, sweating, trying not to cry, as arrows of pain shot through my poor, crushed feet. Imagine holding your toes in a vice, and then using this vice to support your weight for seven hours. I seriously thought I had crippled myself, but the pain eventually subsided. Why did I keep doing these crazy things to myself? As I carefully tended to my poor feet, the answer came to me. I had just conquered fear itself. I had faced the impossible, and I had come out on top - literally! What was left to stop me?

*****

We hiked down the back of the spire and went in search of a swimming hole. We found a perfect spot by the road, where a large, shallow pool was flanked by eucalyptus trees, with a waterfall at the far end. There was something about the smell of the Aragon mountains. Interspersed amongst the spiky, evil mountain roses and thorny brambles were wild rosemary bushes, and thyme, and lavender. In the middle of the day, the heat fermented their aromas, and it was warm and rich. Mingled with the faint tang of the eucalypts by the river and pools, it somehow smelled like home, and it was comforting.

I was still flying high after my triumph on the cliff earlier, and it was wonderful to soak my sore muscles and stinging, bruised skin in the shallow, clear water. We munched our way through a bag of apples, and Alejandro tried teaching me a few random Spanish words. He turned out to be a good teacher, having been so recently a student himself. Every time he taught me a new word, I tried to match it to English words to remember it. The first one he taught me was the word for eagles – *agilas* – (like the word agile, and angular, and angel) because there are hundreds of them soaring around the cliff faces. You could see them gliding in elegant spirals on the hot air currents, in contrast with the tiny, acrobatic swallows which dip and somersault as though pulled by opposing magnets. My favourite new word was *libelula* - dragonfly. We moved on from wildlife after a while, and ended up swapping idiomatic jokes, toasts and pick-up lines we had heard in bars on our travels, laughing at how little sense they made in each other's language.

"Is there a line in Australia that people use when they want to kiss someone?" Alejandro asked.
That's an odd question. "I can't think of any. Why?"
"Because I have been thinking that I want to kiss you."
Oh my.
Before I could form a coherent thought in response to this, he leaned over and kissed me lightly on my cheek, then my nose, then my mouth. He kissed me slowly, intensely, and he tasted of salt and the apples we'd eaten.

"Oh my gosh," (he used this phrase unironically - I think it was from one of his English classes - and in his accent it sounded like "Oh my ghash"), "you are so beautiful. From the moment I saw you, all I can think is how beautiful you are."

I practically melted into the water. Here was this gorgeous Spaniard, kissing me in this gorgeous swimming pool, telling me how beautiful I was, hours after we had just conquered a mountain together (well, more or less).

We made out for what felt like forever, and then drove back to Riglos to find some food. As we made our way back to our campsite, the wind began to pick up and slate grey clouds began to roll over the horizon. The weather had followed us from the mountains. By nightfall the wind was accompanied by threatening booms of thunder, and there was no sense putting the tent up, so we slept in the car – he stretched out in the back seat, and me curled up in the front. This meant there was no possibility of any further... activities.

The next day, Alejandro needed to head back to Madrid, and I realized that, once again, I needed to make a plan.
"You can come and stay with me at my parents' house" Alejandro told me, with his characteristic cheerfulness. "There are so many climbing spots around Madrid. You will love it."
"Won't your parents think it's weird that you're bringing a random girl home?" I asked, half teasing, but also really needing to know.
He thought for a moment, his brow furrowed.
"Yes. They will think that it is weird. But we are friends." Friends who make out. "And you are Australian, so they will think that it has something to do with your culture."
So his whole family was going to see me as the wild Australian girl who was running around the country, seducing unsuspecting young Spanish men. Great.

I consoled myself that at least we had only kissed, and perhaps it was a one-off thing, sort of like a reflex. We had, after all, spent the last week together. He himself had categorized us as "friends", so maybe I would be able to meet his mother's eye without having to worry about being judged for scampering sinfully around the countryside with her son. This was all well and good, until we pulled into the dark street outside his parents' house after driving through the desert for five hours, and he leaned over the seat, took my face in his hands and kissed me. Just like the first time, I was not prepared, and had no appropriate response but to kiss him back.

When I shook hands with his perfectly made-up, coiffed, and glamorous mother fifteen minutes later, I felt painfully aware of my flushed cheeks and swollen lips. Damn that boy! He had set me up. I cringed inwardly, while admiring his mother's impeccable taste in décor, and accepting a glass of heady red wine from his amiable, towering father, who asked me an endless stream of questions about climbing, and traveling, and what my plans were, and on and on...

Finally, at around one am, his mother noticed my poorly stifled yawns, and bustled me off to the guest bedroom, fussing over towels and bedding as if I were a long-awaited guest, rather than some scruffy, unexpected foreigner who had turned up on her doorstep at midnight, minutes after making out in a car with her son.

I took ages to fall asleep - the situation was very bizarre. Here I was, in Madrid, in the spare room of the house of the parents of a Spanish boy I had met in Australia, having just broken up with another, American boy (for the second time), on a trip where I was ostensibly trying *not* to get involved with anyone. I thanked my stars that the guest room was right next to his parents' bedroom, so I wouldn't have to worry about anything *happening*. Or did I want something to happen? I didn't know.

When I emerged for breakfast the next morning, I'm sure I looked terrible. His sainted mother treated me with the same exaggerated courtesy as she had the night before, brightly enquiring about our plans for the next few days, and offering me coffee and toast. Alejandro' father suggested that we should go and visit the museums and art galleries, since it was too late in the morning to go climbing. So, we spent the afternoon exploring the endless corridors and galleries of the Museo Nacional, at first in awe of the artworks, and then increasingly amused by how closely the figures in the paintings resembled people pulling bad dance moves. Alejandro frequently grabbed me by the waist and told me how beautiful I looked. We kissed in the Museum gardens, only coming up for air when it was time to go back for the dinner his mother was preparing.

It was very weird. I was acutely aware of the last time I had been in Madrid, only a few weeks earlier, and felt more than a little conflicted about this kind of slutty déjâ vu I was acting out in the same setting, with a different man.

Over the next two days, Alejandro showed me some of the amazing climbing around Madrid: from the beautiful little town of Cuenca, built on the side of a gorge, whose houses clung precariously onto the cliff faces; to the fairy tale crag of La Pedreza, where a fault line had left a slanting, 100m long, 20m deep fissure in the hillside, shaded from the scalding summer heat: the locals' best kept secret. We were having fun, and his parents were very hospitable and friendly, but I was *living* in this boy's house. *With his parents.* I only knew two people my age who lived with their parents: one actually owned the house and their parents rented from them, and the other was in the seventh year of "completing" his three year undergraduate degree.

On the weekend, we met up with some of Alejandro' friends, who thought the fact that I was Australian was "hilarious". They found my accent when speaking Spanish "hilarious". The fact that Alejandro kept kissing my neck was "hilarious". I decided these people just had a very low standard for comedy. They announced that they were going to show me just how the Spanish can party, which, I quickly deduced, is exactly how the Australians can party. And the Americans. And pretty much how everyone in every city in the world parties. They drink. They go out to a club, which is crowded and loud, and to which it is difficult to gain entry. They dance. They spend the next day bemoaning the pain of lost brain cells, liver function and cash.
Alejandro's friends were *very* interested in the exact nature of our "friendship", and delightedly commented on what an impact Alejandro's "novia Australiana" (Australian girlfriend) was having on him.
"What have you done to Alé?" they teased me, "he never used to dance!"
As far as I could tell, he still didn't - he had spent most of the night leaning up against the bar, bobbing his head to the music

with studied nonchalance. I really didn't get the jokes with these people.

We had still done nothing more than make out (compulsively) and flirt (constantly), which I assumed was due to his good, Catholic upbringing... and the fact that his parents were sleeping in the next room from me, but nevertheless, all the "girlfriend" comments were starting to make me feel suffocated.

At around five in the morning, Alejandro and I left the club, and wandered unsteadily through the streets of Madrid towards his parents' house. The sun was just starting to rise, and as we walked along, we sang bits and pieces of the songs that had played in the blurry hours before. When we were almost back at the house, Alejandro put his arm around my shoulders.

"You'll have to be careful," he said, his speech slightly slurred, "or else I might fall in love with you."

I smiled tightly, and said nothing, but I felt suddenly sober. He kissed me affectionately on the cheek, and clumsily unlocked the door.

I knew then that it was time for me to move on.

For someone who was supposedly in danger of falling in love with me, Alejandro was surprisingly chipper when I told him that I was leaving for Seville the next morning.

"Oh my ghash", he said excitedly, "you must visit El Chorro, near Granada. The climbing there is superb! SO many amazing crags. Maybe I will come meet you there next weekend!"

I had thought about it. I enjoyed kissing him, and looking at him, and climbing with him, and I most definitely did *not* want him to come and meet up with me. I needed to do something on my own for a change.

Of course, I couldn't actually give a straight answer (well he had been letting me stay in his house, and he had basically saved me from myself in Barcelona) so I hedged.

"Sure, maybe, yeah... if you get time off."

He yawned, seeming utterly satisfied with my answer. "You'll have to wait for me then, crazy girl. It's been so much fun. Maybe you will decide to stay in Spain!"

At the bus terminal, he hugged me enthusiastically and called "hasta luego" out the window as he swerved into the crazy morning traffic. To this day, I have no idea if he was serious when he said he would fall in love with me, or if he was just caught up in the moment, kissing the nearest pretty girl, optimistic as he always was about what could happen. I never saw him again.

I turned to cross the road to the bus terminal with my bag and my hangover, and no one beside me to catch me if I fell.

CHAPTER 18:
ANDALUCIA

Free Soloing: free climbing is the trad climber term for sport climbing, that is, climbing using only the rock, rather than assisting yourself by inserting steps and slings into the cliffs, but still protected by bolts, quickdraws and a rope (this is the type of climbing I had been doing). Free solo climbing is a whole different ball game. Free soloing (recently made extremely famous by the legendary Alex Honnold) means no equipment but a chalk bag and a pair of climbing shoes. No rope. No belayer. No safety net whatsoever. If you fall, you hit the ground.

T he bus trip from Madrid to Granada was ridiculously long, which was awesome, since I wasn't at all having an existential crisis or freaking out about my remaining money or lack of plans. I was stuck next to a conversationally challenged Spanish guy, who seemed to be surgically attached to his iPhone (ah, a simpler time; when this was considered rude), furiously texting ten people at once. There were no movies, and the only in-bus entertainment was the small child sitting two rows up, busily engaged in the absorbing task of transferring all the snot from his left nostril to his mouth with his right forefinger.

Occasionally he paused to inspect his findings intently, before continuing in his endeavour. I couldn't help staring, horrified, wondering how it was physically possible for such a small child to contain such a mountainous volume of mucus. Despite the company, I must have subconsciously enjoyed the bus trip (or at least decided to dabble in masochism), because I spent a significant amount of the next two weeks on buses very similar to the first. This was my first stint of 'proper', solo backpacking: staying in hostels, meeting other travellers (a large number of them Australian) spending a couple of days in various cities in succession, wandering the streets, seeing the sights, and lugging all my worldly possessions around on my back. It was stressful, expensive and exhausting, but unforgettable, and I finally figured out how I was going to get home.

Each region of Spain glows with the influence of some ancient culture, in the language, the food and the architecture: in Barcelona it is the Catalans, in the north it is the Basques, and in Andalucia, and some of the centre, it is the Moors. Spain and Portugal were part of the Umayyad Caliphate for 700 years - from the early eighth century to the fifteenth. Islam was the dominant religion during that time, and the Arabic influence can still be seen in the language, the food, and most of all the architecture of the region. Cordoba was, at one time, the largest and most important city in Europe. The Catholic monarchs slowly reclaimed the Iberian Peninsula from the top down, in a slow but relentless *reconquista*, until finally, only the city of Granada remained, and was taken in 1492, just two months before a certain Cristóbal Colón was granted the money to sail off in search of a "new world", and proceeded to wreak havoc across the Atlantic.

I may, or may not have written an unnecessarily long and detailed research paper about the Muslim rule in Spain and the *reconquista* in my third year of studying European History at university. During this time, I *may* have bored my friends and family to death with "interesting facts" about the history of Spain. It may, or may not have been, a large part of the reason I'd thought of traveling to Spain in the first place.

I *may* be a giant nerd.

Moving on.

I arrived in Granada tired, sore, and in *desperate* need of a shower after my autobus ordeal. Of all the southern cities, Granada was the one that had received the most glowing reviews by backpackers. According to my guide book, the Alhambra, the giant, ancient palace I'd read about in my history class, was "the most visited tourist attraction in Spain", and only just missed out on being nominated one of the 7 man made wonders of the world, which seemed unfair.

However, as the bus pulled into the station, I felt a little apprehensive. This was not a pretty town. My *pension* (amazingly cheap and clean) was in a dirty, deserted, dark neighbourhood, with ugly apartment blocks and road works in the next street. It was oppressively hot, and the streets seemed to be unnaturally empty. "This can't be IT", I thought to myself, dumping my bag on the floor and gazing dejectedly out of the tiny window. I decided that I was simply in one of the less picturesque neighbourhoods, and so I laced up my boots and set off to be entranced and charmed by the city everyone talked about. About twenty minutes later, I was still not impressed.

"Excuse me, how far are we from the city centre?" I asked, with childlike hope in my eyes.

"This IS the city centre", came the somewhat sneering reply.

I wandered around a little longer in the soporific heat, and concluded that people must have been exaggerating when they raved about how unique and beautiful the city was. I made my way back to the hotel, feeling disappointed. My big, spontaneous, solo trip to the South suddenly seemed rash and naïve.

I spent the rest of the afternoon and evening reading travel websites and Lonely Planet guides online, and getting unnecessarily frustrated with the slow wifi. Around 9.30, I forced myself to go out in search of food. In the dimly lit bars and cobbled streets; in the jostling crowds spilling from narrow doorways and alleys; in the fairy-tale lights of the Alhambra on the hill above the city: I finally saw the magic of Granada I spent six hours taking in the beauty of that tiny city. I went from one bar to another, sampling the small, free plates of tapas they served with each drink, sometimes chatting with other patrons, sometimes just sitting alone and watching. When I finally made my way back to my room, I was buzzing and happy, and I slept more soundly than I had in weeks.

The next day, I woke up late (how very Spanish), and went off in search of breakfast, and somewhere quiet to sit. I found a miniscule terraced café overlooking the main square, and ordered eggs and coffee. On the wall opposite me was a huge map of the world, and I amused myself by comparing the sizes of the different European countries to the vast, unpopulated expanses of Australia. My mind wandered back to Trish and Tom's plan to visit Greece, and I located the tiny Island of Kalymnos on the map, realising that it was closer to the Turkish coast than to Greece. I drew an imaginary line from Granada to Kalymnos, and then, almost reluctantly, from Kalymnos back to Sydney. As I thought of the distance between myself and home, feelings of homesickness lingered at the edge of my consciousness, mingling with a reluctance to admit that my year abroad was already almost halfway over, and I had, in hindsight, moved very little. At some point, I would have to go back to Sydney, and that point was getting closer every day. Suddenly it dawned on me, looking at that imaginary line: there were a lot of countries that I had never visited, or even considered visiting, that fell roughly on that line. Who was to say that I had to make the trip home all in one go? Why didn't I make a few stops along the way?

I spent the rest of that day in a fury of planning, budgeting, researching and spending. By the evening I had four months, five thousand dollars, six countries, and seven plane tickets between me, and my arrival home. Very little logic or rationale had gone into this plan, besides my sense of "that place sounds interesting, and I'm sure someone has recommended it to me at some point". To stave off the inevitable traveller's panic at the enormity of the decisions I had just made, I shut my laptop, and took myself out into the city. I ended up a small, dark, underground bar, sipping over-sweet sangria, and watching an astonishing Flamenco performance, in which the woman was so beautiful it made my heart ache, and the singer was 84 years old, and needed to sit on a chair to make it through the show, but had a singing voice so strong and raspy and downright *sexy* that it was impossible not to develop a small grandpa-crush on him.

Over the next few days I managed to keep my anxiety in check, telling myself just to live in the moment, and finding comfort in the finality of non-refundable airline tickets. I joined a 'free' walking tour of the city, led by a hilarious British guy who ran a burger bar in the city, and who told us that the place to find a boyfriend with a dog and a van (we didn't ask, he just assumed every girl would want one) was to visit the gypsy caves up on the hill. His stories were side-splittingly funny, especially his re-enactment of the (scandalous) relationship between Columbus, Isabel and Ferdinand of Castile. Finally, I took myself up the hill to explore the magnificent Alhambra.

It was breathtaking. The gardens alone were gorgeous, with panoramic views of the city (I was lucky enough to be there at sunset), but the inside of the palace itself defied belief. Every wall, every beam, every ceiling, every floor was carved and painted and tiled with such amazing intricacy. Each room was its own carefully preserved masterpiece of Moorish decoration, and each courtyard contained long pools of water, which reflected the buildings in such a way as to make them appear to be floating. I wandered around for hours, fantasising about living there, in my own mosaic wonderland. Apparently, the Alhambra has only held its tourist trap status for a few decades. Earlier last century, artists like Federico Garcia Lorca lived in and around the deserted palace, lazing around the gardens and discussing great ideas and art. On the day that I visited, it was so crowded that I had to book a time to visit the palace. Don't ever go to Granada and miss out on the Alhambra.

*****

I'd given myself another week in Spain, and the next city on my list was Sevilla. After another long bus trip, I arrived late at night at the Garden Hostel, where the staff were friendly, the sangria was free, and the night was young. I quickly made friends with a large and loud group of Germans, who were already very drunk. They were horrified that I hadn't included Germany in my grand travel plan, and were admonishing me severely, when another Australian girl came over to our table. She had been on the same bus as the Germans the previous morning, and they greeted her with voices and glasses raised. Sarah was very pretty, with long dark hair, and a shy, sunny smile. We were by far the least drunk and noisy in the group, and we soon distanced ourselves at one end of the table, talking about our travels and what our lives had been like back in Australia. Like me, she had broken up with someone before leaving home, but her break up had been the reason for leaving, not a consequence.

Before long, two of the German boys (the two who had been most excited to see her, and friendliest to me when I had arrived) became offended that we were not taking proper part in their drinking game, and told us off us for being "boring", and demanded that we go out dancing with them, so the game was abandoned, and we tumbled out onto the streets in search of a dance floor. We found a bar whose music, and inhabitants, made very little distinction between the inside and outside of the building, and joined in the party. We had only been there for half an hour or so, when Sarah found me, and complained that the German boys from earlier had been getting a little too persistent, and it was no longer charming. I saw them on the other side of the room, making their way over to us, so I grabbed her hand and we pushed our way through the crowd, laughing as we bumped into people, ducking to avoid being hit as limbs flailed to the music. We hid in a corner, and watched as our two pursuers were waylaid by three of the girls from their group, until the five of them went to get more drinks. Flushed and laughing, I turned to her to ask whether she wanted to go dance, and without a word, she put her hand up to my face, and kissed me. I was surprised, not so much by the kiss, as by the realisation that I had been waiting for her to kiss me all night. We danced together for a while, and she asked if I wanted to go back to the hostel, but we lost our bearings, and eventually curled up to rest our eyes (it was three in the morning by this point) underneath a tree beside a fountain.

The heat woke us several hours later. As the sun rose it scorched the streets and buildings, and even though we were lying in the shade, it was oppressive. With the worst hangovers in living memory, we managed to find our way back to the hostel, where I stood in a cold shower for nearly half an hour, trying to get my head to stop pounding. We had hardly spoken after we woke up, navigating the streets in silence, and I wondered if she had regretted kissing me the night before. I realized that she hadn't specified if her break up had been with a boy or a girl, but I doubted whether it mattered.

This wasn't the first time I had been attracted to, or kissed a girl, but I didn't feel the need to analyze what it meant too closely. To me, the night before had shown me that I was open to anything. I'd fooled around with the sexy Spanish guy, and ruined things with the gorgeous American who made my heart beat like crazy. Now I was starting a new chapter, and it seemed like, from that moment on, I could make my own rules. This was the universe telling me to stop trying to predict what was going to happen, to stop trying to make a good "story" to prove something to other people, and just to experience things as they came. When I saw Sarah that afternoon, we smiled in shy acknowledgement, and said nothing about it.

Once the heat had subsided enough to be bearable in my fragile state, I went on the obligatory 'free' walking tour of the old Jewish quarter - the largest of any city in Europe, and I felt myself fall quietly in love, yet again, with Spain and its stories. I say 'free' because, for true Scrooges like me, there is a very awkward moment at the end of the tour when the guide, who has just spent two hours regaling you with stories, says "well folks, I make my living on tips, so if you enjoyed the tour, pay what you can". This was my cue to either reluctantly part with my lunch budget, or alternatively, do my uncanny impression of deaf person with somewhere very important to be. Our guide warned us that he would not distinguish between the stories which were fact and those which were legend, so I have no idea if what I repeat here is true or not, they are just the stories which piqued my imagination.

There is a street, for example, called *Calle Susona*. Here there lived a young Jewish girl who was in love with a Christian soldier. When she heard her father and his friends plotting one night to rise up against the Christians, she feared for her lover's life, and snuck out to warn him. The deceitful young soldier of course, passed the information on to his superiors, and the girl's father and his co-conspirators were killed, along with all Susona's family and friends. Distraught, the girl hung herself, and in her suicide note, requested that her skull be displayed outside her house as a warning to other love-sick girls. Today there is a wall tile with a depiction of the skull, which sat for years watching over the street.

The Sevillans were, it seems, fond of decorating their walls with heads of the deceased, real and depicted. In another street, *Calle de Cabeza del Rey*, there is a bust of the king Pedro. Apparently, the king was a nasty piece of work, and used to dress up in disguise and sneak out at night to murder unsuspecting citizens, when being king just wasn't enough of a buzz. One night he accidentally murdered a young nobleman, and the next day, the family called for justice. "I will find the killer", pronounced the wily king, "and when I do, his head shall be displayed on the street for all to see". Some days later, a wooden box was placed upon display, with instructions that it was not to be opened. When, years later, someone's curiosity got the better of them, they found a bust of the king himself who, true to his word, had displayed the killer's head for all to see.

My favourite (slightly less bloody) story appealed to my romantic imagination. When the caliphate ruled Gavin Andalus, the Caliphs were known not only as rulers, but as famous poets, and they would often challenge their advisors and courtiers to poetry competitions, where lines must be recited off the cuff, until one was unable to think of a rhyme. One day the Caliph was walking along the river with his *Visir*, and he challenged him to a poetry contest. The *Visir* was stumped, but much to the surprise of the two men, a young peasant girl making bricks beside the river answered the Caliph's challenge. She, being very beautiful, became his favourite wife. One day he asked her if she was happy in Sevilla, at that time a very great city. She replied that although she loved him, and his city, she was saddened that there was no snow. "Granada has snow", she opined, "and therefore Sevilla will always be second to Granada." The Caliph thought long and hard about this dilemma, and that autumn, he planted thousands of orange trees in the streets of the city. The people couldn't understand it: the oranges themselves were inedible. "Just wait", the Caliph told them. When spring came, the white blossoms of the trees covered the streets, mirroring the snow-capped peaks of Sierra Nevada. These days, these orange trees define Sevilla's streets, and the bitter fruits that grow there are used to make gin.

Sitting in a café the next morning, I finally found the courage to do something I had been avoiding for weeks: log onto the university website, and re-apply for my degree. It was a long and frustrating process, and it was terrifying, because there was no guarantee I would be accepted a second time, and I'd been spending quite a lot of energy not thinking about what I would do after I got home. I wouldn't find out if I was accepted or not for another three months.

The next three days were a blur of tapas, buses, mosques and palaces. The *Alcazar* palace in Seville was decadent and quiet, and the smaller palace in Cordoba gave a panoramic view of what must be said, is not a beautiful city. I visited the famous *Mesquita*, also in Cordoba, with its thousands of internal arches and columns, and its anomalous catholic artworks decorating the walls (the mosque was appropriated by the Catholic kings and rebranded as a cathedral in the 14th century).

In the delicate beauty of these ancient spaces, with their conflicting ideologies and icons, I saw flashes of the dry sage bushes and grey rocks of Riglos and Rodellar; the azure waters of the caves in Mallorca; and the bright colours of the markets in Barcelona. I'd seen so many sides to this country since first arriving, and I realized with surprise that I'd begun to see different sides to myself. It wasn't clear yet which side of myself would win the battle: maybe I would end up like Spain itself, a mosaic of different colours.

My Spanish summer had come to an end – it was time to head east.

CHAPTER 19:
KALYMNOS

Project: if you're climbing at or below your comfort level, you usually complete all climbs the first time you try them (this is called a flash, unless you've done the climb before). If you're reaching above your comfort level, it takes several tries to complete a climb "clean" (without falling or leaning on the rope). A project is a climb that forces you to work on it over and over again, until you can visualise every move and every hold, and you're just trying to get the sequence, or the endurance, or the balance, or the balls to put it all together.

I disembarked at the tiny pier in Kalymnos, Greece (although it's actually closer to the coast of Turkey), after flying from Spain, to Italy, to Athens, to the island of Cos, and then boarding a war-era ferry to cross the water to the Mediterranean climbing Mecca. As my taxi wound its way up the steep mountain side out of the little port town (endearingly referred to as 'the capital') I craned my neck to spot the fabled cliffs I'd come all this way to climb, but nothing caught my eye. The slopes around me were carpeted with shaven, yellowy brown grass and the same stunted, spiny shrubbery I'd seen in Spain. The narrow road wound its way along the coastline, dipping in and out of small clusters of white-washed stone buildings, with the luminous blue ocean to the left. We passed the occasional, forlorn-looking donkey, and four or five children playing beside the street. There were splashes of colour from gaudy bougainvillea flowers and blood red pomegranates growing on skeletal trees, and bursts of music coming from the open doors of the taverns as my driver whizzed us past at an unnecessary speed.

It took us about half an hour to drive to the little village where I had arranged to stay. I'd scoured the various facebook pages and forums for this island in my last few days in Spain, and had struck gold: a group of climbers were renting an apartment and had a spare bed. The rent for two weeks was about half what I would have paid for a hostel in Spain. There was a brief, linguistically challenged exchange with the driver (life was going to be a lot harder in a country where I didn't speak the language *at all*) as we tried to figure out where this place actually was. It turned out that the letters 'u', 'v', and 'y' are interchangeable in the Greek alphabet - which is why my repeated requests to be taken to *'Aura'* apartments fell on deaf ears: the driver knew them only as *Avra*, and his friend (with whom he conferred through the open window while parked in the middle of the street, after having screeched to a halt without warning) knew them as *Ayra*. I resolved to learn at least some basic Greek phrases while I was here.

After a good deal of driving in circles, we finally found the right place, and I saw a note taped to the door.
"Gone climbing - back this afternoon. Let yourself in! Your bed is on the left."
I paid my driver, and squeezed myself through the door (my backpack had been stuffed to the brim with souvenirs I'd acquired in Spain, and had meant to mail home, but had run out of time). The layout of the apartment was bizarre - half of the space was outdoors, a sort of low-walled balcony, overlooking

the ocean, with what I suppose you would call the kitchen: a table with a single, portable hotplate on one side and a miniscule sink on the other. The indoor space was all one room, except for the bathroom, which ran the width of the room but was only about half a meter wide, with the toilet facing the shower, and the sink in between. One could save time by sitting on the loo, brushing their teeth, and sticking their smelly feet in the shower. Backpacks were piled up precariously against the bathroom wall, next to a mirror which had been attached, for some reason, at waist height. It became clear why they had an extra bed - two of the inhabitants were clearly sleeping in their hammocks on the balcony.

I dropped my backpack on my bed and wandered outside to gaze out over the sea, then I turned and looked behind the apartment, and my jaw dropped. Stretching out behind the town as far as the eye could see in either direction, was a wall of flawless limestone, dotted with caves. My fingers twitched in a Pavlovian climber's response as I took in what must have been hundreds of potential projects. Two weeks suddenly seemed an absurdly short time.

*****

Sarah, Dean and Tom had been on Kalymnos for a week already, and were well and truly settled in by the time I arrived. The three of them came bounding through the door late in the afternoon, just when I was weighing up the idea of taking a nap. All three looked absurdly fit and strong (you may be noticing a pattern here, with yours truly as the exception), their skin was deeply tanned and their hands calloused. Sarah was Malaysian: she looked like a teenager, but in fact was a few years older than me, with the kind of arm definition that would make a bodybuilder jealous. Dean was Canadian, and Tom, Australian. Dean was short and muscular, with reddish blonde and brown eyes. He smiled a lot but rarely spoke. Tom was pale and skinny, wore rectangular glasses, and was there on summer break from studying in England.

The next morning Sarah woke me at 5.30, just as the sun was starting to show.
"Time to get up. It's too hot to climb in the afternoon so we need to get going."
I didn't want to take too much with me, since I'd need room in my pack for water, so I wolfed down a big bowl of oats and honey. I noticed that Sarah carefully measured out her oats, and counted her ration of almonds for the day into a bag. It seemed that I'd be back on the "climbing food" diet while I was here (at least it was better than the Spanish climbing diet). Twenty minutes later, I was seriously regretting my greediness. The walk up to the cliff base was long and brutally steep, and I could feel my breakfast churning in my stomach with every step. When we reached the top, I had to stand and belay the others for an hour before my food settled enough for me to climb.

The rock in Kalymnos was almost identical to Rodellar: overhanging, with large, protuberant stalactites and deep pockets. I'd built up a fair amount of strength in Spain (despite my inconsistent schedule), but these climbs were a new challenge. It always takes some time to adjust to the level of grading in each new climbing spot – sometimes the climbs seem overly tough for their grades, sometimes ludicrously soft. I cautiously tried out an easier climb, and found it relatively comfortable. I jumped on a more difficult one (one that would have tossed me to the ground when I first arrived in Rodellar), and flashed it. I was feeling good – the break I'd had since climbing with Alejandro had actually made me feel stronger rather than weaker. Breaks are always risky, because your endurance and power deteriorate so quickly, but sometimes they're just what your body needs in order to push even harder afterwards.

By the end of the first morning, I'd climbed five routes in a range that didn't make me look like a total beginner, and was feeling pretty good. Sarah had made five unsuccessful attempts at her project climb, but had taken it all in stride (whereas I would probably have thrown a tantrum), and Dean and Tom had been taking it easy. We headed back down the hill, this time in full sun, and retreated into the blissful shade of the balcony. I pulled out my sketchbook and started doodling, glancing back up at the cliffs, where you could still see the flashes of rope and brightly coloured clothing; and hear the faint shouts of the belayers. Tom lounged in his hammock next to me, reading, while Dean napped, and Sarah sent emails (she was working remotely while traveling). It was a companionable silence, and I felt like "one of the group". Well, at least until the next day.

The next day was a designated "rest day", but I soon discovered that there was only minimal resting involved. Everyone was up by 7am, and without so much as suggesting the idea of coffee, Sarah announced that they were going running.
"Rest days are for cardio", she told me, with perfect seriousness. The boys were already kitted out in running shoes and shorts, and were stretching in the doorway.
"Oh well", I thought, "in for a penny, in for a pound."
The only shoes I had with me were my leather walking sandals, my hiking boots, and the cheap, flimsy tennis shoes I'd worn for canyoning. I decided that these would be best, and told myself that it would be like running barefoot. I soon discovered what Sarah meant by "cardio". We jogged into the village, and down some steep, narrow steps towards the sand. I wondered if we would be beach running, but at the bottom, she turned around and started running back up the stairs again. Bloody hell.

There were 87 stone steps from the sand to the street, and we ran them 15 times. By the end I was a sweating, red-faced, breathless lump of jelly, and I collapsed, fully clothed, into the clear blue shallows. It was starting to look like my two weeks in Greece were going to be something of a boot camp...
I'd never considered running fun. At fifteen, I'd undergone a brief but intense stint of dieting, and had tried to accompany it with

regular jogging sessions up the hilly road above our property. I'd found it frustrating rather than fulfilling, but almost in spite of myself, I'd gotten quite good at it, and began placing first and second at school athletics events. Since high school, however, running had been a purely functional venture, a way to stay light enough and fit enough to climb.

As I lay in the warm, Aegean water, and watched Sarah and Dean doing sit ups in the sand, apparently unperturbed by the ordeal of the stairs, I was aware of a small, stubborn, competitive voice inside me, saying: "You could do that".

The good news was, that on rest days, the group ate out at one of the many restaurants lining the main street. As I remembered from my time in Greece with David, the food alone was enough to warrant a return visit. We ate whole calamari stuffed with feta cheese, huge bowls of fresh salad, moussaka, souvlaki, fresh fish, bread still hot from the oven, homemade fig jam, stuffed tomatoes, lamb cooked in local herbs, donut pastries swimming in honey, local goats cheese and yogurt, and drank fresh orange juice by the giant glass. I now appreciated the need for all the running.

On our second day climbing, I picked a climb called 'Spartacus' as my project: a steep, pumpy, 20m long, marathon, two grades above my best climb in Rodellar. It was ambitious for my level of endurance, but I felt like it was within the realm of possibility. After my third attempt, I sat down to give myself a break, and watch Sarah on her project. Tom sat with me. I hadn't talked to him much since my arrival - I had been caught up in getting to know Sarah.

"How long are you staying on Kalymnos?" I asked him.
"Just another three weeks," he replied. He had a curious habit of ducking his head when he spoke, as if trying to avoid eye contact, and I wondered if he was shy.
"I'm only here for two," I said, ruefully. "But after today it seems like no time at all!"

213

"Where are you headed after this? Home?" he asked.

"Not yet – I'm kind of taking the long way home – I have a few more stops along the way." I didn't really feel like going into detail about my plan, so I returned the question before he could probe me further.

"I'm heading back to England after this. I have a place at Cambridge – I'm starting my PhD."

"Wow! That sounds... very impressive! What's your area?"

"Particle physics."

Good lord.

"Oh dear. I'd love to ask you more about it but I'm afraid I wouldn't understand you. Physics isn't really my area beyond high school level."

"That's ok," he smiled. "It isn't most people's area."

He was, quite literally, a rocket scientist! I remembered when I had been in high school, my Dad had spent six months trying to figure out a way for me to do my A level exams in England, and then take the entrance exams for Oxford and Cambridge. I'd been a good student, but even I thought that this was probably unrealistic, and in the end, I'd stayed in Australia. But this guy had actually gone there. We chatted for ages about England, and what it was like to live there, and what he wanted to do with his PhD (he gave me what I'm sure was a heavily dumbed-down, abbreviated version). I'd always been in awe of highly intelligent people - I'd taken a class in Literary Criticism in uni, and had been drawn into a small, but intense, fan club of girls who hung on the professor's every word. She was one of the most blatantly intellectual people I'd ever met -you couldn't hear her order coffee without realizing that she was worlds smarter than you. Yet, somehow, she had never come across as pretentious or inaccessible. I had struggled to comprehend the ideas in that class, and in the end had come away with only a vague understanding of Derrida (on whom I'd written my final essay), but I'd loved listening to the professor speak - even when I couldn't quite wrap my brain around what she was saying. Tom reminded me a little bit of her.

The quality of the climbs in Kalymnos was outstanding, but, as is the fate of all popular areas, it is a victim of its own success - the best routes had become polished from the amount of traffic, and the limestone stalactites which make the walls so distinctive, had a nasty habit of breaking off in your hands, meaning that a climber may return to their project after some time away, only to find a crucial hold missing. The infrastructure and organisation in Kalymnos, as in the whole of Greece, was relaxed to say the least. Instead of a single, clearly marked trail leading up to the crag, there was a winding maze of approach paths which people followed in a vaguely upward direction, and which rendered the hill an eroded, dusty, gravelly mess.

At the end of the first week, after making a total of fifteen attempts, I topped out on *Spartacus.* I was ecstatic: as far as I was concerned, anything else I ticked on this trip was a bonus after that climb. It was the hardest route I'd ever climbed, and I briefly considered having tee shirts and bumper stickers made.

I demanded that we all go out to celebrate the fact that I'd just climbed the hardest outdoor route of my entire life, and so we broke from tradition, and went to the tavern on a non-rest day. I bought a round of *ouzo* for the table, and we ordered our usual: everything on the menu. As we tucked into our appetizers and waited for the mains, there was a loud burst of laughter from the door, and I caught a glimpse of a head of blonde hair and a snatch of conversation between low, male, American voices. I dropped the piece of calamari I had been about to devour. No way. It couldn't possibly be him. I began to panic as I wondered what the hell he was doing here and what I could say to broach the last few months of silence.

It wasn't him. Obviously.

It was a group of climbers from California, notable not only for their loudness and average level of attractiveness, but also for the brightly colored lycra leggings they were all wearing. Inevitably, our groups ended up drinking together, and we found out that they weren't, in fact, an 80s aerobics revival band, but that they had purchased the pants on a dare, and realized that they were the most comfortable thing to climb in.

"So we just decided to go with it," the tallest one explained, with a shrug.

They came climbing with us the next day on one of the smaller islands off the coast, and I ended up partnered with the blonde boy I'd momentarily mistaken for David. He told me they were all medical researchers, and went on to explain, in gruesome detail, the experiments they performed on chimpanzees in their lab, I was horrified - I thought that kind of thing only took place pre-animal welfare activism, but apparently it was still happening, and still legal. I had previously been considering whether I found the tall guy in their group attractive enough for some casual flirting... but this information put a stop to that pretty definitively.

On my next climbing project (which was far too ambitious) I found myself taking turns with a tiny woman called May, who told me that she had heard about me in Thailand when she had visited a few years ago – apparently, she had missed me by a day. Just like in Barcelona, I reflected on what a small world climbing could be. Even though she was half my size, she was a formidable climber, and I found myself wishing I could stay here longer, and become as strong as she was.

On some afternoons, our group took motorcycle tours around the island (and very nearly met our end when we encountered a flock of goats crossing the road on a hair-pin bend!) We swam every day in the impossibly warm water, which glowed with supernatural phosphorescence at night, and every rest day, we did our sit ups and stair runs. I could feel my stomach flattening and hardening, and the stairs became less tortuous. My hair was longer and lighter, and my skin was tanned (and scraped to shit from the rocks). I hadn't worn makeup in since my night out clubbing in Madrid, and my one "nice" outfit was crumpled at the very bottom of my backpack, under layers of tatty climbing clothes. I felt amazing.

All too soon, however, I had to leave, and after one last feast at the Aegean tavern, Sarah and I embarked on a long travel day to Athens, she to return to Australia, me to continue to Israel.

Although this was my second time in Greece, the full impact of the financial crisis didn't hit me until I arrived in Athens. There were boarded up shops on the main square, little kids selling packets of tissues on the street, people with stalls selling what can only be described as useless junk...and yet, a few streets away, there were stores selling fur coats for upwards of 400€. There was still money in Greece; it is just very sparingly distributed. I saw the Acropolis, and the ancient markets and the other various ruins and temples, but I must admit I was somewhat uninspired. Perhaps it is because the most beautiful pieces have been under the "care" of the British museum for the extent of living memory, and are nowhere to be found in the Greek capital.

Speaking of controversial ownership, I was about to make my first foray into the political and religious scrapbook that was the Middle East. The town I grew up in was shockingly "Anglo Saxon" and I doubt I had knowingly met more than two or three Jewish or Muslim people by until I moved to the city for university. Thus, I confess that I boarded my next flight with a negligible grasp on the politics, much less the history of the region I was about to explore, and scoffed at my friends who expressed concern about my next travel destination. As I soon discovered, the best way to start to understand a country is to go there.

So off I went, to Israel.

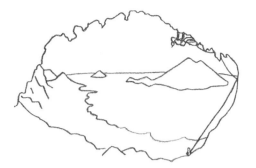

CHAPTER 20: ISRAEL

Onsighting: unlike projecting or "flashing" a climb, where you use someone's beta or practice the moves in order to top out, onsighting requires you to complete the climb blind. Purists will argue that a true onsight can only happen if you're the first person to climb the route, but most climbers allow a route to be considered an onsight, provided you haven't seen anyone else climb it, or asked anyone for help.

I have to say, that if you had asked me a year beforehand to name five places on earth I least expected to find myself, even if you had asked me when I was in a particularly whimsical and creative mood, "the near-empty dance floor of the only gay bar in Jerusalem on a Wednesday night" would probably have been pretty high on the list. And yet, on a Wednesday night, I found myself on the near-empty dance floor of the only gay bar in Jerusalem, marvelling at the fact that Britney Spears could still be played in public at high volume, balking at the price of drinks, but still enjoying myself immensely. It seemed a fitting culmination of the two weeks I spent in Israel, where everything had been, well, unexpected.

Israel was not pretty. Israel was not cheap. Israel was not convenient. I found Israel to be conflicted, confronting, ancient, new, harsh, beautiful, welcoming, dangerous, both challenged and challenging in its very existence as a nation. The brief research, many conversations, and two weeks I spent there, still put me in no position to comment on Israel's military history, or its relations with the rest of the Middle East. Luckily for me, most of the Israelis I encountered spoke pretty fluent English (especially my Couchsurfing hosts), so there was very little language barrier, and almost without exception, the people I met were friendly, intelligent and kind.

I arrived in Tel Aviv late at night, and paid an absurd amount to catch a taxi from the airport to my hosts' house. I couldn't have asked for more accommodating hosts than Ami, Liron and their little cat, referred to simply as "cat", or sometimes "OW, you little ****!", an animal in possession of a highly tempestuous nature.

My first order of business in Israel, after a couple of hours of sleep, was not sightseeing, but a panicked, and ultimately fruitless morning spent trying to organise my Indian tourist visa, which I had foolishly believed could be obtained online. Travelling around Europe on a British passport has softened me to the harsh reality that it is not always so easy to pass from one country to another. I was told that it would be impossible to organise a visa in the two weeks I had before my flight, especially since these two weeks included two of the biggest Jewish holidays of the year.

I am proud to say that I processed and accepted this news sans emotional meltdown. Not even a little one. Not even when I found out that because my flight to India was with an Arabian airline, I had no way of contacting them from Israel to change my flight. An enormous amount of credit and gratitude goes here to my Auntie in England, who reorganised my flights from the UK. Where I would have ended up on this trip without the help of my extended, loving family, I shudder to think! In the end the only solution was to rebook my flights so that I went straight to Nepal, rather than trying to negotiate with the Indian immigration officers. I later discovered that most travellers get land passports and enter India via Nepal. At least I know for next time!

As soon as I had managed to negotiate one set of plans-gone-awry, I was faced with another: Jewish holidays. I had planned to spend a couple of days in Tel Aviv, then bus down to Eilat on the Red Sea for a couple of days of diving, then work my way back north toward Jerusalem. Unfortunately, nothing (and when I say nothing I specifically mean dive companies) operates during Yom Kippur - the Day of Atonement - where no one drives, works or eats, in the hope of righting past wrongs and ensuring a prosperous year ahead. Ami and Liron went above and beyond the call of couch duty helping me organise my week, and after a couple of hours of brainstorming, I had something vaguely resembling a plan. I had four priorities: dive the Red Sea, see the Dead Sea, explore Jerusalem, and make my way to Jordan to visit Petra.

First, I caught a bus to Jerusalem and took my first ever *paid* walking tour around the old centre of the Holy city, from the room of the last supper, to the western wall, the mosque on the hill, the church of Golgotha, the Via Dolorosa and the bustling Arabic quarter. I felt myself slipping back in time as our group was jostled down impossibly narrow alleyways, lined with tacky tourist stalls, and herded inside cavernous cathedrals with shrapnel holes in their outer walls. Standing in line to visit the mosque, I met a tall, striking, dark-skinned girl named Dina, who, after very little in the way of introduction, and minimal persuasion, agreed to hire a car with me so we could visit the Dead Sea and Masada.

We hired a car and drove east to Jericho, then south through the desert, along the shores of the Dead Sea to *Ein Gedi*. It was dark by the time we got there, but honestly, what better time to go swimming in the desert? The car park was deserted and silent, and the sky was bright and unclouded. We stripped off our clothes and flung them over the rocks, closing our eyes tightly against the stinging salty water as we splashed into the depths of the Dead Sea. Floating in that water is a sensation that defies logic. The water was warmer than any sea I had ever experienced – even the balmy Mediterranean, and the density of the salt buoyed our bodies to the surface as if they were weightless. We lay, floating, gazing up at the stars, with no sensations of temperature, light or sound, the only living beings left on this silent, sleeping earth. The sensory deprivation could have been unnerving, but I felt soothed and serene. When we eventually emerged from the heavenly waters, we rinsed off in the showers and set up camp. We had stopped in Jericho and bought ourselves a pipe and a supply of fragrant shisha tobacco – the only kind I had ever smoked – and a bottle of whisky. Dina told me stories of her mother, who had moved to Holland from Eritrea, and married her Dutch father. She was on her way to visit her relatives there, who lived in a gated community in one of the cities. She told me that whenever she visited her cousins, they would tease her about her "pale" skin, and inability to speak in their native language. She intrigued me, with her husky voice, and her way of looking at you as if you were a puzzle she was trying to figure out. I caught myself wondering if she found me as interesting. The memory of dancing with Sarah in Seville was still fresh in my mind, but I pushed it away.

We had planned to get up by four thirty to make the trek up to the ancient fort of Masada, to watch the sunrise from the top. Unfortunately, the combination of the shisha smoke, whisky, and stories meant that we stayed up talking and swimming until 3am, falling rather untidily asleep in and around the car. We woke just as the horizon was beginning to glow, and with record speed, stuffed ourselves into the car and raced the few kilometres to the base of the mountain we intended to climb. It was a LOT steeper, longer and more daunting than pictures had led me to believe, and it took all my touristic integrity not to say 'sod the view' and go back to sleep.

The reward, when we finally made it to the top, was worth it. The desert stretched out beneath and around us, the sun drenching the mountain peaks beyond the shimmering sea where we had floated beneath the stars just hours before. After we explored the ruins on top of the mountain, and the sun had come up in full force, we made the long descent back to the car. We spent the rest of the day swimming in the clear, fresh water of the Ein Gedi spring, before returning the car and driving back to Jerusalem. Dina was going to stay with a friend of hers, and I returned to Ami and Liron's house in Tel Aviv, but we agreed to meet up and travel south to Eilat together in a few days.

That Tuesday was the eve of Yom Kippur, and from five pm, nobody drove save for policemen, ambulances, Muslims, and people whose wives were giving birth that instant in the back seat, for fear of being stoned by Orthodox Jews. I'm not exaggerating, that was how the situation was explained to me. It is not illegal to drive, but it isn't advised: instead, everyone rides, rollerblades or walks. Ami had organised bicycles for everyone ('everyone' being me, Liron, and two other German couch surfers) and we all caught the bus back to Jerusalem to wait for dark. As the evening fell, the city changed. The traffic slowed to a trickle, and the traffic lights began to blink yellow. The streets emptied of people wearing day-to-day attire, and began to bustle with long cloaked, behatted, ringleted Orthodox Jews, who averted their eyes at the sight of four women in cycling gear. At a small petrol station on the highway leading to Tel Aviv, a group of cyclists eagerly awaited the night. In the gathering dark, we set off down the first long steep descent with head torches, laughter, and a very optimistic idea of just how far seventy kilometres was.

We arrived back in Tel Aviv some five hours later (having stopped for a picnic on the way) and fell into bed complaining of aching legs and sore backsides. Wednesday was a blissful day of doing nothing much whatsoever, which, as any traveller will tell you, is an essential part of retaining one's sanity. Besides, it was Yom Kippur, and it was one's religious imperative to do nothing whatsoever. When in Rome, do as the Romans do.

The next day I met up with Dina once again, and we spent five hours on an early bus to Eilat, Israel's gateway to the northernmost tip of the Red Sea, threw our bags down at the stingy little hostel, and shopped around for a diving school. After a brief refresher course, during which I realised just how long it had been since I'd breathed through a regulator, I signed up for four more dives.

The water was colder than Greece, and the visibility was average, but oh! The colours! The coral! The fish! There were giant parrot fish munching on coral; schools of tiny jewel-bright fish darted amongst giant skeletal fans, watched by beady-eyed moray eels and a chameleonic octopus; gardens of thin, waving eels which darted down into the sand as we floated over them; and, unnervingly, a menacing looking barracuda, which floated unmoving until we had almost passed it, then nonchalantly glided between us, staring each of us down through our masks before disappearing into the blue. Everyone on the dive staff seemed intent on assuring me that Eilat waters were far inferior to those in the south Sinai Peninsula, or in Jordan, but I was happy to have seen as much as I did.

Over the next three days, Dina and I made friends with the dive instructors, who taught us to play backgammon over a shisha pipe and miniature cups of ridiculously sweet tea. One of them, a young Israeli man named Ariel, took us out to a club that looked like it had been built on the set of *Pirates of the Caribbean*: it was essentially a huge tree house, with multiple levels, built of wood, with trees growing through the floors in some rooms, and other jutting out over the ocean. Descending to the basement, you came across five or six deep pools, shrouded by long hanging curtains, where those patrons less inclined to party lay floating in warm water, in the arms of silent, sarong-wearing men and women. It was the artificial version of the Dead Sea we had swum in a few days before Ariel told me that this was supposed to simulate the experience of being in the womb: suspended in the quiet and the dark. I remembered the surreal sensation of floating in the Dead Sea under the stars, feeling totally alone, and thought it would be very difficult to achieve the same peace and tranquillity while being held by a total stranger, while a few hundred people milled above and around you. We went back upstairs where the live band was in full blast, inviting members of the audience up on stage in a kind of pseudo karaoke performance. I made the mistake of telling my new friends that I liked to sing, and they pushed and pulled and cajoled me onto the stage.

"What do you want to sing?" asked the guitarist.

"I have no idea!" I replied in a panicked whisper. "Help me!"

He sighed in exasperation.

"*Can* you sing?"

My injured pride and indignation suddenly overtook my embarrassment.

"Yes, I can sing. Can you play..." I frantically searched for a song that my unpractised voice could handle at such short notice, and my mind flashed back to the hammock in Greece, lying next to David with one headphone each, sharing our music ... "Fast Car" I finished triumphantly.

They did, and I sang, remembering how it had felt to be lying beside David in our hammock, as Tracy Chapman crooned about her deadbeat boyfriend and his unsafe driving.

When the song finished, I moved to step down from the stage, but the guitarist grabbed my arm.

"You can stay for another one," he said, grinning.

I sang with them for three more songs, and then re-joined Dina and Ariel, and danced till our feet hurt, and we could barely keep our eyes open.

For our third day of diving, we went across the border to Sinai for a day of boat diving (Oh! The colours! etc...). When crossing from Sinai back into Israel, there was an actual threat alert in the immigration queue, and the hundred or so people waiting to cross were ushered unceremoniously out onto Israeli soil to watch thirty or forty military personnel pour into the building. All was silent for five minutes, until they re-emerged and, without any explanation; we were all herded back inside into our queues. It was a tense experience; mostly because it brought home the reality that these land borders served to separate such volatile differences of ideology with only a few meters of sand and buildings.

When we'd had our fill of the underwater treasures of Eilat (or rather, when we could no longer afford to pay for the equipment necessary to breath while viewing them), Dina and I decided to cross another border, this time into Jordan. We drove for two hours through the tangerine coloured desert to Wadi Musa, the dusty town on the outskirts of the ancient city of Petra – the reason for our visit. Petra is an archaeologist's wet dream: over 2000 years old, massive and astonishingly well preserved. Despite its age, it was recently named one of the 'new' world wonders (whatever that means), and was declared a UNESCO world heritage site in 1985. What was once the burial city of the Nabataeans, is now an impressive collection of tombs and temples carved from the ochre sides of the ravine, crowned by a truly massive monastery at the top of a steep hill. The Nabataeans who worked on the tombs lived in caves in the surrounding mountains. Walking through Petra is eerily like being on a movie set (they shot one of the Indiana Jones movies here) because each site presents a massive facade, carved with infinite precision from the rock, but the actual rooms and tombs are small, some only a couple of metres across.

Dina and I wandered through the canyon, guided part of the way by a beautiful little Bedouin girl who explained the importance of each monument with in hushed, reverential tones. We gave her some of our food, and bought her a bottle of coca cola, and then huffed and puffed our way up the hill to the monastery, where we took in the amazing desert vista, then clambered up onto the monastery roof and looked back on the ancient city. We ran back down the hill and rode donkeys part of the way back, arriving at the hostel in time for one of the best dinners I had ever had (according to my completely empty stomach).

After dinner, a tour guide came around, trying to recruit people for a 'desert camp experience' tour, which was supposed to leave that afternoon, but needed more people. Dina and I refused, since I was on a tight budget, and we spent the evening watching old films in the recreation room with the chef and the other backpackers. The next day we hiked through a small canyon flanked by olive trees and sat for a while in a quiet, green oasis, fed by a small spring, until a large, clamouring herd of goats arrived and rather spoiled the tranquillity. Back at the hostel that night, there was a commotion: some of the other backpackers looked distressed and the owners were talking in violent whispers to one of the tour operators in the office.
"What happened?" I asked one of the girls.
"That group that went out last night got attacked in the desert!"
"What? Who attacked them?"
"They are pretty sure it was some of the local villagers. They said that they came to the camp and threatened them with knives, then they stole all their backpacks and money and everything! They were lucky that the tour guide had a spare set of keys to the truck or they would have been stranded out there!"
I'd heard several stories like this on my trip, about tourists being targeted by unfriendly locals, and I felt shaken, but also supremely lucky, because it could so easily have been me. I hadn't had many close calls on this trip (which was shocking, given the number of times I'd put my safety in the hands of total strangers), but the knowledge that "the world is a dangerous place, especially for a young woman traveling alone" had been

drummed into me growing up (although interestingly, never by my parents), and was never far from my mind.

Dina and I had fallen into an easy, companionable partnership, but nothing of the Seville persuasion had transpired, and I was fairly sure I was ok with that. We returned once more to Jerusalem for the last two days of my trip, staying with another couch host, her small daughter, and her unbelievably evil cat. There must be something in the water to explain the horrid disposition of every cat that I encountered in that part of the world: studies should be done. I left sporting some impressive physical and emotional scarring from sharing space with this menacing creature, but Adi and her young daughter were lovely. We all visited the archaeological exhibit in the Israel Museum and the markets in the old city. There was yet another Jewish holiday, and we joined in on a street party near Adi's house, took salsa lessons, ate pita bread and drank delicious pomegranate wine, before deciding to hit the town, thus leading us to the point where I found myself swaying to Britney's dulcet tones at 2am, watching two skinny guys try to outdo each other's flamboyance on the dance floor, and realised that this was not what I had envisioned when I bought my ticket to the Holy Land.

CHAPTER 21: NEPAL

High Point: pretty self explanatory, the highest point you've reached on a climb, usually the highest hold you've "controlled" or held onto. Every time you attempt a climb, you're trying to beat your high point.

To get from Israel to Nepal I had to stop over in Greece and change airlines (from an Israeli airline to Etihad). Bored, I sat in the airport for my five-hour layover, listlessly trawling the internet, my mind wandering back to the first time I'd been in an airport on my way to Greece, when David had been with me. As I was picturing his face, a message popped up on my screen.

"Hey."

It had been six weeks since I'd told him that I wasn't going to get on a plane to American, and I'd heard nothing from him in all that time.

I felt a jolt of "fight or flight" adrenaline rush through me at the sight of that one word on my screen, loaded with so much potential and conflict, even though at last count, we had only spent about three weeks in each other's company.

"How are you?" I replied.

"Drunk. I'm sitting in a bar, and my friends are all having a good time, and I'm miserable, because you aren't here. Where are you?"

"About to get on a plane to Nepal."

"Wow. You are covering a lot of ground."

I was silent. I didn't really have a response.

"So, I was talking to this girl tonight. She was really cute."

"Uh huh. Do I really need to hear this?" I asked, scowling.

"Shut up. Yes, you do. I was talking to her about my trip, and out of nowhere she suddenly asks me if I'm still in love with you. She said, 'You're still in love with her, and you are no use to anyone till you've gotten over her'. So, there you are – you've left me useless."

I felt equal parts jealousy at any girl who felt the need to enquire into his love life, and elation at the fact that he had said he was still in love with me. With only the briefest of preambles, we fell back into our old bantering flirtation, tight-rope walking the line between fantasy and making actual plans. Inevitably, we lost our balance, and swung wildly down on the side of danger

"I will give you my credit card number if you fly here right now. I'm serious, just come for the weekend."

"Don't you dare! You and I both know it would never be just for the weekend. You'd never let me get back on a plane, so stop it."

"What if I won't stop?"

"I'll ignore you and just sit here making a list of all the places we had sex to torture you."

"You can't ignore me. That's a standing offer on my credit card. Just a quick.... Long.... Weekend.... Ish"

"When I have the rest of my life free I'll take you up on the offer."

"46555557847296. Expiry 05/13. Next time I see you, I'm never letting you go."

"I know. That's what scares me."

"Why?"

Why? That was the million dollar question wasn't it? He kept throwing these grand, romantic gestures at me, and I kept ducking them (this had always been my strategy when forced to play volleyball). It scared me because before I met David, I had never even considered that anyone I met in the next few years – or the foreseeable future - would want me to make a commitment I couldn't make. I had loved Eli, and been faithful to him, but I had, in the back of my mind, expected it to come to a natural end. I expected to have a few more relationships after that, that didn't go anywhere, and I was fine with that. I wasn't looking for "the one", and so I had never expected someone to tell me it was "all or nothing".

I thought about trying to be flippant, but decided to be honest.

"I'm just not ready to be someone's everything. I'm not even sure I can look after myself, let alone be responsible for someone else's happiness."

He didn't reply for a while and I thought he may have given up, but eventually he wrote back.

"Why do we always end up here? Sophie, some day we will end up together, because no one has ever been as good as us together. I will always be ready to drop everything to spend my life with you. My heart still belongs to you. No matter what I do. And I will get you back one day."

Wow. In a movie it would have made me cringe, but reading those words from him made me melt a little bit.

"Well, maybe one day..."

"Cool. So what kind of underwear are you wearing?"

We talked for three more hours, me curled up in a hard airport chair, oblivious to the world around me, only saying goodbye when my flight was called for the third time, and I had to get on a plane that would take me closer to home, but further away from him.

*****

Coming from Israel to Nepal was a massive culture shock: not least because of the Nepali airport security. In Israel, security is tight: at the airport, at the land borders, at every public building, there are scans and interrogations and suspicious checking of passports. You feel guilty and nervous, even if your answers are legitimate, probably due to the large and prominent semi-automatic weapons sported uniformly by every public official, as well as the knowledge that every citizen was, at the age of seventeen, trained to kill you. Holding my precious passport in one hand and scrutinising my face for traces of wayward political leanings, the Israeli border control officers would fire off seemingly ridiculous questions, hoping to catch me out.

"What did you have for breakfast on the first Tuesday in January last year?"
"What is your opinion of Kant's theory of ethics?"
"What is the average flying velocity of an unladen swallow?"

In Nepal on the other hand, I stepped off the plane with no cash to pay the visa fee, which could only be purchased at the airport. The security guard directed me to an ATM that turned out to be broken. When I pointed out that it was not working, they told me to go to the other one outside the terminal; on the other side of security; which I walked through without a visa, and without showing anyone my passport; which I then walked back through with equally little hassle, to stand in line for my visa. Nobody batted an eye at the fact that I could have just carried on my merry way without having my passport stamped, or my bags checked, and been loose in Nepal without a visa. I should have had an inkling at that point that this was going to be a country where nothing worked as it was supposed to.

I had read up on several of the Nepali treks while I was in Greece and Israel, and I'd decided that I didn't want to do the two most popular (Everest base camp or the Annapurna circuit), since all the information suggested that these would be very crowded at that time of year. I'd settled on the less popular, easier to get to Lang Tang - Gosainkunda trek, which according to the guide, took twelve to fifteen days, and allowed one to see a variety of landscapes up to 4610m above sea level. My original plan had been to hike the trek alone, since it was reported to be very safe (i.e. low risk of avalanche or ambush), and popular enough that there would be a huts for me to sleep in every night, and other hikers to meet along the way. I discovered however, that the government had recently issued a ban on people hiking the route without a guide, perhaps in an effort to support struggling trekking companies, so this plan was moot. After my experience with trekking and guiding companies in Central America with Gav, I had decided not to book ahead, and instead to shop around for a guide when I got to Kathmandu. This presented two problems: firstly, I had to try and ascertain what a fair price was from scratch (and, as any young, white, solo female traveller with a somewhat gullible look about her will tell you, this can be a minefield); and secondly I had to find people who would go on the trek with me (I didn't want to spend two weeks alone with a guide, and they wouldn't let me hike the trail without one).

One of my dad's cousins from England had heard about my trip to Nepal, and, by stroke of good luck, had told me she would be there at roughly the same time. Although I had only met her once, I was somewhat in awe of her: she was a very direct, frighteningly intelligent woman, who had had a tragic marriage, which had ended, leaving her with no children; something she had always wanted. Not one to be put off by such a set-back, she began involving herself with orphanages in different countries. Every six months she would travel to these places and work in the orphanages, playing with the kids and helping with construction, cooking and gardening. She had just heard of a new school that was being opened by one of the companies she was involved with, a school in a very remote area of the Himalayas, specifically for the children of the farmers and herders who lived too far from the cities for their children to attend schools there. She had come to Nepal with a group of other volunteers to bring supplies to this school and make sure that the money was being well spent. Unfortunately, our paths only overlapped by a day, but she kindly offered to put me up in her hotel room for my first few nights in Kathmandu. I quickly realised that this gesture, while very kind, was detrimental to my plan. To make this trek, I had to find people to join me, and there were no other people my age staying at this hotel, save for those there with their families, all of whom already had their trips booked.

The hotel was right in the centre of Thamel, the main tourist area of the city, packed with bars, restaurants, and stores selling the most beautiful jewellery, art, and handmade goods, so there was plenty for me to see (and tell myself I couldn't afford to buy). On my second night in the city, after my Dad's cousin and her group had left, I wandered into a bar and attached myself to a laughing, drinking group of English speakers, who turned out to be students from Delhi who had come to Nepal on holiday who were "with the band". They quickly adopted me into their group, and we followed the band around as they played two or three gigs in one night, before crashing a gig being played by their friends. Unfortunately, none of my new friends were at all interested in trekking, so I was still at square one.

That night, when I went off in search of Wi-Fi, I had another message from David.

"What's your schedule look like in November/December?"

"Climbing in Thailand last week of November, home 8th December. Why?"

"Interesting. And if someone wanted to go climbing in Thailand, where would they fly into?"

It took me a second to realize what he was saying.

"You can't be serious..."

"What if I were?"

"Because, you coming to Thailand is exactly what I suggested two months ago, and you said no, you said that to see me again you needed me to prove to you that I was yours, and commit to you. I said I wasn't ready to make a commitment like that, and that's where it ended. Badly."

Not only that, but how I felt at the possibility of seeing him again scared me. I told myself, I still couldn't go to America - I had to start my degree in February!

"That was two months ago. This is now. Now I'm saying I want to go. Don't you want to spend a couple of weeks on a beach, eating mango off one another, and sleeping in a hammock?"

God damn him. Obviously I wanted that.

"And what happens when we have to go home?"

"Listen Aussie, this is just an idea right now. It would take some work and figuring out on my end to make it happen, but it is possible. And I know that the last time we went through our little dance it ended about as badly as it could have. It'll never be easy for us to say goodbye. If it were, then this thing between us wouldn't be worth all the trouble."

I started to type a reply, but he wasn't finished.

"I wouldn't trade the time we spent together for anything. And I can't stop thinking about the day I saw you standing in the doorway in that hotel in Madrid. I want to kiss you again. I want to hold your hand, touch your face, and wake up with you wrapped around me.... I also really want a Thai bamboo tattoo."

That made me laugh - I couldn't help it.

"You *would* go to Thailand just to get a tattoo."

He delivered his closing argument with the finality of a barrister in court.

"I just know if I don't come see you I'll regret it. So, I'll make you a deal: I won't bring up the future if you don't, and we will just enjoy one another's... company... one last time. Let's do it."

All the reasons to say no were lined up, ready and waiting in my brain, but I couldn't wipe the grin off my face at the thought of seeing him. Not for the first time, I decided, what the hell?

"Ok. Let's do it!"

Two hours later, he sent me a screenshot of his purchase confirmation: LAX - Phuket. I would be seeing him again in less than six weeks.

Later that night I had a message from Carly, who had been made privy to our plans and was, I realized, the only person I was in contact with who had actually spent time with us together and might have some kind of perspective. She had this to say about the situation:

"The reason the two of you keep going back and forth and can never reach any kind of resolution is because of your zodiac signs. You're both fire signs. David's bossy, you're arrogant (not in a bad way) and both of you are stubborn as hell. But your passion and love for all things in life mesh well. Also, you guys are crazy."

I didn't know about all that, but there certainly seemed to be something that kept throwing us back together.

*****

Still unable to wipe the grin off my face, and by some miracle managing to stave off the inevitable panic attack that should have followed my conversation with David, I set about trying to organize my Himalayan hiking adventure. After two days, I had talked to eight different trekking companies, none of whom had any treks with room for me to join in the next few days, I was starting to think that my "take things as they come" attitude was going to cost me this experience (or else cost me a large chunk of my remaining money to go on one of the more organised, expensive trips). On the evening of the second day I sat despondently in a cafe, accosting random strangers and asking them if they were going trekking. One girl, sitting alone, re-

sponded that she had just come back from a trek, but that she was staying at a hostel not far from there, where I might find some interested parties. "It's only a twenty-minute walk" she told me, why don't you come and ask around?
I had planned to meet up with my musical friends from the night before, but I figured I had time to do both, so off we went.

Twenty minutes turned into thirty, which turned into the two of us wandering down dark, unnamed streets, far outside the tourist center of town.
As we walked down yet another unlit street, I heard a noise behind us, and turned to see a small dog following us. I have always loved dogs, and this one looked cute and harmless, but my companion grabbed my arm and started walking faster. The next time I looked back, two more dogs, bigger ones, had joined the first. Suddenly I felt a little unnerved. I heard a howling off to my left, and suddenly we were being pursued down the alley by a growing pack of dogs, many of whom were growling and snapping, and all of whom were picking up pace. Just as I was getting ready to scream, or look for a weapon of some kind, the girl pushed me through a lit doorway, and we sprawled on the floor of the warm hostel lobby, an hour after leaving the cafe. Twenty minutes my ass.
I resigned myself to the fact that it would be cheaper (and safer) to stay the night there than catch a taxi back, and settled in to grill every resident about his or her travel plans.
I had no luck that night, but, undeterred, I resolved to start again at breakfast.
Still no luck, but there were more possible trekking partners here than I'd seen in two days at my hotel, so I walked back, collected my bags, and returned to the hostel for another night. Just as I was about to give up, I found someone; and that night, we found someone else, which gave us three people to share the cost of a guide, ready to leave in two days.

Kelly was Canadian: nineteen years old, sassy, funny and fresh into Nepal after spending two months living barefoot in a beachside hippie commune in Turkey. Heidi had the most amazing white-blonde hair, and had come to Nepal on her winter holiday from Norway. Although Heidi was well equipped, having set out with trekking in mind, both Kelly and I were much less well organised, and needed to stock up on supplies. We all headed back into the city, returning with water purifiers, chocolate bars, camel packs, extra socks, extra hiking pants, hats, gloves, sunscreen and, for Kelly, a pair of hiking boots (the first proper pair of shoes she had owned on this entire trip).

Organising a guide for our trek turned out to be something of a disaster. The hostel where we were all staying recommended two different companies to us, and we negotiated a reasonable price with one of them, who introduced us to a very nice looking, well-spoken local guy, who was to be our guide. After going to sleep the night before we were to set off, feeling excited and nervous about the days ahead, we woke at five to meet our guide, only to discover that he had been replaced! The trekking company representative told us that our guide had been taken ill the night before, and would be unable to accompany us. Instead he presented us with a skinny, gangly man who couldn't have been over eighteen, and who, it transpired, spoke very little English. We later learned that this was a common trick played by some of the smaller trekking companies, who would employ a 'poster boy' to reel in customers, and then replace him with one of their inexpensive, inexperienced guides on the day. Luckily the hike was not so demanding that neither our guide's lack of English nor his morose, unfriendly attitude, caused too big of a problem.

We set off on the longest, scariest, bumpiest bus trip I had experienced since South America, where the road clung to the crumbling cliff face, and landslides were negotiated with terrifying nonchalance. To distract ourselves from the 100-foot drop just outside our windows, Kelly and I spent the trip comparing opinions of everything from literature to boys. I told her the story of my "clandestine international love affair" with David, and she in turn told me about the boy she had met in Turkey, who had offered to come and visit her in Canada that Summer. We found out later that Heidi was involved with a man back in Norway, who she had only recently met, and who she wasn't sure about. The three of us bonded over our collective states of romantic insecurity, and I wondered if this way of living – partially committed to someone far away – was ubiquitous for women traveling alone, or if we were the ones who were doing it wrong.

When we finally staggered off the death-trap-on-wheels bus, we were already high in the mountains. The air was crisp and chilly, the opposite of the polluted fog of Kathmandu. We spent the night in a tiny room in a tiny hotel in a tiny village at the beginning of the trail, and woke as the sun was rising to begin our walk. The first week would be spent going up the Lang Tang Valley, rising from 1500 meters to 4,200 meters at Kyanjingri, then back along the valley to a turn off that would take us to the Gossainkund Pass, which would take us another three days. Depending on our endurance, we could then walk back to Kathmandu through the jungle, or catch a ride from one of the small villages on the other side. On that first day, it all felt very large and unknowable. The cold mountain air seemed full of ancient secrets, drowned out by the crunching of our boots on the gravel, the calls of strange birds in the trees, and the thundering river, whose voice became so familiar to us that we barely heard it after the first day. The mountains towered around and ahead of us as we made our slow ascent up the valley - slower than our guide would have liked – he took to making snide remarks about my friends' levels of fitness and our tendency to stop and gaze at the ever-changing landscapes around us, and take hundreds of photographs as we walked. Initially we were horrified at his rudeness, but after a while, we ignored him, and settled into a comfortable pace, letting him stride on ahead, disappearing for hours on end.

The first day was spent negotiating thick, green jungle, with vines the size of my arm hanging from the tall trees. We stopped for lunch at the first of the picturesque little tea houses that dotted the trail, all of which provided food, tea and beds (provided you got there early enough). We soon realised that the chocolate bars we had brought with us were worth their weight in gold! Food, toilet paper, and other luxuries increased in price, in accordance with the altitude, as the trail wound its way up through the mountains. Every single thing that was to be sold had to first be carried up there on someone's back, and chocolate bars especially fetched a high price. Even though my shoulders were already aching from carrying my fifteen-kilo pack, I wished I had brought a larger supply.

On our first night on the trail, we bunked down in a large, lodge-like tea house in a small clearing, surrounded by goat sheds and bordered by small streams. As we ate our dinner of dahl, pickles and *momo* dumplings (the same meal we would be eating twice a day for the next two weeks), we got talking to another group of girls at the next table. Jen and Kate were Americans and Carrie was Danish, and all three of them were working as research fellows in Kathmandu: Kate was researching the causes and extent of suicide amongst young Nepali males for her Masters in social sciences in America. The six of us quickly became friends, bonding over our unpreparedness for the trek ahead, and a mutual awe at the scenery. Much to the dismay of our guide, we decided to walk as a group, which further slowed our progress.

The next morning a light mist shrouded the valley. By the time we had eaten our breakfast and shouldered our packs, it had developed into a downpour, and water filled out boots and drenched our socks as we trudged onwards along the slippery, treacherous path. The trees on either side of us and the river were strewn with brown, feathery lichen, and the undergrowth was woven through with neon-green ferns and delicate orchids.

Tiny monkeys played and screeched above our heads, and we craned our necks back, to try to catch a glimpse of them, occasionally getting drenched by the raindrops they shook from the branches.

I was fascinated by the changing ecosystems we passed through as we rose higher and higher above sea level. It took us two more days to reach the end of the valley, and in that time, the landscape changed dramatically. The jungle thinned out on the second day to alpine woods, where we walked beneath towering pines, catching glimpses of snow covered peaks through the branches. This is turn gave way to bright red grasslands, with stony slopes rising on either side, scarred by avalanches, with cascading waterfalls tumbling towards the river by our side. At intervals, we would pass large boulders which had been painted with brightly-coloured Tibetan prayer symbols, and as we climbed higher, we noticed more and more fluttering strings of yellow, red, green and blue prayer flags on the hillsides.

I have always been a walker, and up there I was in my element. I inherited "strong Welsh legs" (which makes me sound like a pony) from my mother's side of the family, making me an excellent endurance hiker. When my mum and dad had been trekking in Patagonia, Derek and his brother had been amazed that this tiny woman, with a pack on her back almost as big as her, had powered up near-vertical trails without pausing for breath or break, seemingly boundless with energy. Although I could have covered more miles in a day by myself, I soon realised that I would have missed out on some of the little, beautiful things we saw each day that made the trail so special. Things like the tiny yellow butterflies that sometimes landed on our hats and packs. Things like the herd of shaggy cattle that we passed, staring at us from under their fringes as they chewed the tough mountain grass. Things like the elusive, silver-furred, black-faced monkeys (much quieter and harder to spot than those in the jungle canopy) that perched in the privet trees along the trail, delicately picking the bright red berries one by one, like prim old ladies selecting from a box of fine pastry. My feet and calves ached at the end of each day, but it felt good to be walking *to* somewhere - a different sort of accomplishment than topping out on a climb. It was calmer, more meditative, without the nagging fear I felt while leading.

When we arrived at the lodge at the base of Kyanjing Gumba at the end of the third day, we encountered our first major set-back. Kelly had been stopping more and more often throughout the day, and complaining of a headache. When we arrived at the lodge, she took to her bed and didn't emerge for eighteen hours, racked with altitude sickness. The second half of the trek, where we would be ascending twice as high as we already were, was out of the question for her. She decided she would make her way back to Kathmandu when we left the valley to begin the second part of the hike. We were sad that she couldn't complete the trek, but we could see she was ill. The next morning, Heidi and I dragged ourselves out of bed at four thirty to climb Kyan-jingri peak and watch the sunrise over the glaciers. The steep path and the thin, cold air made the climb pretty tortuous, but the view was breath-taking. We reached the peak just as the first sun beams spilled over the icy peak, catching the fluttering strings of prayer flags which crackled around us.

Our guide decided he had been too soft on us, and insisted that we make the trek back to our first camp (two days' worth of walking) by that evening. Kate, Jen and Carrie (who had booked with a much friendlier, more reasonable guide) elected to stop half way, and we stumbled into our camp that night, absolutely exhausted, coughing and sniffling and generally aching from head to toe. The next morning, we staged a mutiny, telling our guide that he could return to Kathmandu with Kelly if he wasn't prepared to go at our pace. I felt absolutely shattered, and my sore throat had developed into a fever. I demanded a rest day, and our guide, realising he wasn't going to win this particular argument, acquiesced. The three of us spent the day drinking tea, laying out in the sun, and reading aloud to one another from Kelly's copy of "Fifty Shades of Grey", dissolving hysterical fits of giggles, groaning in disbelief at the florid prose. The girls were surprised to find us still there when they arrived that afternoon, but happy that we would be continuing the trek together.

The next day, we shed a tear and entrusted Kelly to some twinkly-eyed Irish lasses who were heading back to Kathmandu. Heidi and I fell into step with the other girls, much to the annoyance of our guide, who huffed and sulked and snidely observed to anyone who would listen that we were "very very slow". We told jokes and riddles as we climbed the step path up the other side of the valley, and at one point, slightly delirious from endorphins, Kate laughed so hard that she had to sit down on a log. Her giggling fit lasted nearly forty-five minutes, and she was absolutely powerless to stop it. Of course, we did little to help her, trying our best to make her laugh harder every time she managed to get a little control back. That evening the five of us played cards while the two guides caught up with their friends who ran the lodge. I was interested to learn that both Jen and Kate had men in their lives back home, in varying states of monogamy and certitude, giving weight to my theory that every girl I met traveling solo had some level of commitment to a man who was currently somewhere else. Jen was expecting to get engaged when she returned, but Kate had been involved in an on again-off again, exciting yet unstable affair with a man she had met at university. After we had all shared our relationship Cliff's notes, Jen and Carrie berated me for having told David that I loved him at the last minute at the airport, saying it hadn't been fair and that I should have just let him leave, even if he had been angry with me. Kate, on the other hand, was on my side.
"I think you should always be honest about how you feel, even if it is inconvenient, or inappropriate."
"I agree with you to some extent," I said, not wanting to lean too far to the left, "I don't think you should fling yourself at some-

one if either of you are in a committed relationship, or if they're your boss or something."

"Basically, if they're unavailable?" Jen interjected.

"Yeah I guess."

"But haven't you been saying that you felt unavailable for the kind of relationship David was looking for? So, by your own standards, shouldn't you have kept quiet?"

I had no response to this, but Kate fired up in my defence.

"It's completely different, and for the record, I think that no matter WHAT the situation, you should be true to how you feel."

"You're only saying that because it justifies your own relationship, since he's ten years older than you, and hasn't said he wants anything serious!"

I got the impression that this was an argument they had hashed out between them many times before, and something of a sore spot.

This discussion made me question whether agreeing to meet up with David again had been a bad idea, despite our promises that we wouldn't let it 'mean anything'. Wasn't I being irresponsible and leading him on? I had been clear with him, but I'd been just as clear both times before, and now I was worried, and afraid of both of us getting hurt once again.

Even though I'd told him that I wouldn't be able to contact him while I was trekking, I sat at the ancient computer they kept in the lodge office, and waited half an hour for a connection, before my message box popped up on the screen. There were a few "how's Nepal?" and "where are you?" notes from friends, but I only had eyes for the message that I'd received three days ago from David.

"Five weeks to go."

*****

After a week of hiking, I had settled into a comfortable rhythm and routine. I could pack my bag in ten minutes in the morning, after brushing my teeth and braiding my hair to stop it getting too tangled (I hadn't been brave enough to take a cold shower, so it was already greasy and dirty). The girls and I chatted comfortably as we drank the hot chai masala, and ate the watery porridge that the huts all served for breakfast, slathered on sunscreen, applied a macrame of bandaids and strapping tape, and laced up our dusty boots on our poor, battered feet. Once we started walking, we would drift into different formations depending on everyone's speed and energy - sometimes walking as a group, chattering and telling jokes and swapping snacks; other days splitting off into pairs or walking alone, listening to music or just watching the landscape as it inched by. I couldn't remember the last time I had allowed myself to work towards such a simple goal with so few distractions: wake up, start walking, make it to the next hut, stop walking. No one was asking anything else of me, I wasn't asking anything more of myself, but to keep going. It felt primal, and raw, and good.

I began to notice that small memories were starting to creep back, unbidden, into my mind, as the days passed with so much space and silence.

When I sipped my cup of chai masala in the early morning, I saw my mother, leaning against our kitchen sink, clutching one of her favorite mugs (the ones with the native birds painted on them, steaming with the same spicy tea (a splash of skim milk, no sugar), as the early morning sunlight streamed into the room.

When I was the first person to wake up, unable to sleep because of the altitude, and I wandered out to watch the sunrise stain the mountains, I heard her footsteps padding down the staircase in the early morning, always the first to get up. She would read the newspaper in the kitchen with her chai until it was time for my brother and I to get up for school, and then she would put her head in through my bedroom door and call softly, melodically, "time to get up". Always the same, lilting scale of notes to that phrase, with two syllables to the word "up".

When I tried in vain to scrub some of the mud off my boots after the rain, I glimpsed her in her garden, covered in dirt, digging and pruning and picking, rarely bothering with gloves. She somehow managed to grow flowers and vegetables and fruit trees in the impossible red clay and steep slopes around our house, and our garden was a vibrant patchwork of color.

Nothing anyone says makes you feel better when you're grieving (even though you pretend it does, for their sake), but the one which I hated most after Mum died was "she'll always be with you" or sometimes "she's still alive in you". I had found it creepy and morbid and decidedly untrue, and yet I felt closer to her in these mountains than I had done in months, maybe even since before she died. I had no idea if it was the place, or the walking, or if it was just that the right amount of time had passed, but for some reason, I felt her there with me.

*****

For the next three days, we climbed "up, up, up", from 2,200m to 4,400m and over the Gosaikunda pass. We battled food poisoning (Kate), inadequate clothing for the drop in temperature (Jen and I), and blisters (Carrie), consoling ourselves with the last of our expensive chocolate, infinite, heavenly views, and photographs to make all our friends at home wild with jealousy.

On the second day of our climb, we stopped for tea (and, oddly enough, cinnamon rolls), and as we were stretched out in the sun, a little shaggy black shape came wandering up to us. We assumed that he was the tea-house owner's dog, but when we asked its name, they said they had never seen it before. On closer inspection, we realised that it was just a puppy, probably only four months old, and had no collar or tag. Kate felt for a microchip in its leg and couldn't find one. Their guide said that sometimes the goat-herds kept dogs, and when they had pup-pies they would occasionally just let them roam off around the mountains. Kate decided then and there, that she wasn't going to leave the pup to its fate. She called the animal rescue shelter in Kathmandu where Catherine was working, and asked them about animal adoption and transportation to the states. They told her it was expensive, but possible, and just like that, she made up her mind to keep him. We spent the next two days trying to decide on a name, before settling on Shadow, in tribute to the loyal old dog in the poorly dubbed children's movie from the 90s, "The Incredible Journey". We learned from one of our fellow trekkers that Shadow was a Black Mustang, a rare Nepali breed of dog that looked like a large, black border collie, and he was absolutely beautiful.

Our next stop was at the apex of the Gossainkund pass, where 108 mirror-smooth lakes sit nestled amongst the peaks, perfectly reflecting the sky. Thousands of Hindus make a pilgrimage trek to these sacred lakes every August, to honour the god Shiva. The night we spent at the top of the pass was uncomfortable to say the least. The altitude made sleep impossible and it was freezing cold. I awoke with painful stomach cramps which may have been due to the altitude, or to the questionable quality of my water purifier, or the cocktail of anti-malaria /anti-inflammatory /anti-altitude-sickness drugs I was taking, or may just have been because I hadn't pooped properly since Kathmandu (existing on an all porridge and lentil diet was messing with me in some unpleasant ways). I couldn't buckle my pack across my stomach, and so had to take the full weight on my shoulders, huffing and groaning my way through the pass. When we got to the highest point, and looked back, I managed to forget the pain, as we were rewarded by the most astonishing view of the lakes, which seemed to melt into the fluffy sea of clouds stretched below us... into which we then had to descent, following the wet and dripping pathway down near-vertical slopes, our knees and calves begging us to stop with every slippery step. The clouds obscured our view for the next two days, as we trekked through dripping green forest, past waterfalls and cliffs, willing the trail gods to have mercy on us when we were faced with yet another up-down-up section of path. Shadow kept up with us every step of the way, and although Kate kept him on a leash, it was clear that his loyalty already belonged to her.

On the evening of day ten, when we felt like our calves were going to crack and break off after walking down hill for two days straight, we huddled around a tiny fire in the freezing kitchen of a tea house which supposedly belonged to a musician of some repute, who was unfortunately on holiday in Malaysia. As we shivered and tried to get warm, we drank watery hot chocolate and noodle soup, and comforted ourselves with the fact that we only had two more days to walk.

The trail had thinned out and for the last two nights we were the only ones staying in our teahouses. We debated our final move: the guides voted for us to press on to a further village - a six hour walk - in time to catch the last bus back to Kathmandu, meaning we needed to get up at five am. However, we were tempted to stay at the village: we had just been told that there was to be a local religious festival the next day, and we were curious, but we had timed our walk to finish on the last day of the Dashain festival, after which, all the buses stopped. No, the guides insisted, we had to catch the last bus. We haggled a little longer, but none of us really wanted to walk all the way back to Kathmandu. So, after enjoying some very cosy hospitality crammed into the tiny kitchen (crouching room only) of our last teahouse, watching our food being cooked over the fire, we dragged ourselves up before the dawn to walk to the next village. We walked through fields of millet and stopped for tea beside a massive, brightly painted stupa on a deserted hillside, then continued, weaving in and out of emerald jungle, vibrating with cicadas and perfumed with flowers, and always down, down, down, our knees and calves screaming for mercy, our packs feeling heavier with every step. Finally, we collapsed into the sparse restaurant next to the bus shelter, with an hour and a half to spare, and fell upon ice-cold bottles of coke and bars of chocolate.

Our victory however, was short lived. There had been a bus earlier that day, but there would not be another. Not that afternoon. Not the next day, nor the day after that. We had effectively missed the last bus.

"We could have stayed at the freaking festival" I growled morosely. "What are we going to do now?"

Our options were: stay in this village and go stir crazy for three days; walk back to Kathmandu ("NO!" butted in Kate); or order a jeep to pick us up for about a hundred dollars. After three hours, four mars bars, five plates of food which were devoured in extremely bad grace, several very angry calls to our guiding offices, and a huge argument about who had/hadn't paid, we bumped our way off down the road, eleven of us crammed into a six-seat jeep, which took us back to Kathmandu.

Jen, and Kate invited Heidi and I to stay with them, and we spent the three days after the trek recovering in Kathmandu and playing with Shadow, who, despite teething, had to be one of the most loveable stray rescues I'd ever seen. We watched "The Incredible Journey" and bawled our eyes out at the end, when Shadow's namesake came limping over the horizon. We made chocolate filled *momo* dumplings and mulled wine, and we read and relaxed.

At the end of the week, Heidi and I caught the bus from Kathmandu to Pokhara, bouncing our way across the countryside crammed in with the usual array of chicken crates, families and unbelievable uncomfortable seats. We took morning yoga classes, braved the bandits to hike up to the world peace stupa and looked out over the Annapurnas and the lake far below. Heidi went skydiving and I got Nepali Belly (the projectile vomiting kind) for a day, after telling myself that it would be perfectly safe to eat a salad, which, for the record, it was not.

After two days we caught another bumpy, uncomfortable bus to Chitwan national park, where we were lucky enough to glimpse a rhino on our first day, walking through the park in the swelter-ing afternoon heat. The next morning, we took an elephant ride at dawn through the forest, spying deer, eagles, pigs and birds amongst the dappled shadows. The elephants were surprisingly quiet when they moved through the jungle, and as far as we could see, very well treated. Later that day we had a slightly more unorthodox pachyderm experience: we wandered down to the river and found two elephants being bathed amongst a crowd of Indian tourists - and so we joined in, clambering up on the elephants' backs and letting them shower us with water from their trunks. Buddhists believe that laughter heals the soul, and I think after that hour in the river, being splashed by elephants and giggling children, my soul was singing. That even-ing we rode our rickety bicycles down the dirt road out to the elephant breeding centre, and saw the young elephants who had been bred in captivity, who would later be trained by the centre to carry tourists and rangers on their backs. Once again, the in-formation we were given and the evidence we saw, pointed only to humane treatment of these beautiful creatures, although it was hard to see them chained up as they fed.

Having ticked elephants and rhinos off our list (although sadly, not tigers), we boarded our third and final bus of the week, and it was by far the worst: a tortuous, seven-hour drive along dusty, bumpy, steep roads with unexplained stops for an hour or more in the middle of nowhere. Nevertheless, we made it back to Kathmandu, where we made a beeline for an Israeli cafe serving large, fresh (parasite and bacteria-free) salads and mint lemon-ade, because delicious though the food may be, the Nepali diet is significantly lacking in anything green or crunchy.

The next day we shopped until we very nearly dropped, buy-ing Christmas gifts and trinkets in Kathmandu's bustling tourist hub. Anyone who has visited a major tourist city in the world will be familiar with the *deja vu* one encounters walking down the street or around the market. You'll spot some unique, hand-crafted piece of artisanry, and marvel at its uniqueness and beauty. Maybe you buy it, maybe you don't. Maybe you have a go at haggling with the stall owner, who will no doubt tell you that he made it himself, just the other day, and that it is one of a kind. Regardless, as soon as you go five steps down the road, you'll see a different stall, manned by a different agent of consumerism, selling the exact same thing, which you'll eventually discovered is not made lovingly by "local artisans", but is in fact mass produced by child laborers in a factory in China. It rather ruins the magic of the whole thing, but on the plus side, no one back home would know (unless they'd been to Nepal... or the factory in China...or any other tourist city in Asia).

Shopping in Nepal is no simple matter. You don't get to walk into a stall, look around, point to what you want, pay and leave. Oh, no. You have to haggle. You have to bargain. And more likely than not, the store-owner will not be happy unless you've spent at least an hour under his roof. We learned pretty quickly to scan the place from the doorway, and only step over the threshold if we *really* liked it. At one point, we were sitting on the floor behind the counter in a jeweller's store, drinking tea that the proprietor had brewed on a hot plate behind the curtain at the back of the shop, and, having already thoroughly covered the topic of one another's family trees, had moved on to discussing the concept of destiny, and how one would realize their, according to the different Hindu and Buddhist teachings.

In the end, I was lucky that "the man" (AKA India's Immigration Policy) forced me to stay in Nepal, rather than trying to hop around the entire subcontinent. The time in the mountains had brought back memories of my Mum that I thought I might have lost, and the past month spent entirely in the company of women had been both calming and refreshing after so much masculine energy in Greece and Spain. I was happy, and grateful, and pleased with myself for choosing this path, rather than flying home, or trying to stay longer in Spain. I even felt good about my plans with David (for the moment at least). Was I finally getting the hang of traveling? Was it supposed to feel like *this*, rather than like the black hole of anxiety I'd experienced in Barcelona?

I hoped so.

CHAPTER 22:
CAMBODIA

Barn door: when the climber loses their balance, and swings away from the rock, trying to keep a hold with one hand, but usually falling off.

Heidi had decided to come to South East Asia with me, and after spending one more night with Jen, Kate, and a much plumper-looking Shadow; we flew to Bangkok and caught an extortionately expensive taxi to the infamous Khao San road: "The Gateway to Asia."

South East Asia has always been a favourite of backpackers the world over: my Dad travelled there on his way to Australia in the 1970s, and its price and location make it a convenient Gap Year alternative for broke Australians (although you'll never be short on Brits or Americans either). Like South and Central America, there is a very clearly defined 'Gringo Trail' through South East Asia, which has been immortalised in guides, blogs, and movies like "The Beach". According to my Dad, Thailand was much dirtier, cheaper, and even less convenient than it was when Heidi and I arrived We soon realised that it was a point of pride amongst backpackers to speak wistfully of their desire to experience that rustic authenticity denied to them by the last forty odd years of cheerful western commercialisation.

Note, that I say backpackers, not tourists. Calling a twenty-something, backpack-toting, pot-smoking, backpacker a 'tourist' will make you about as popular as lumping Canadians in with North Americans. Or Australians and New Zealanders. Or English and Irish. They take great pride in distinguishing themselves, but when it comes down to it, the differences are unremarkable. Backpackers complain that a place is "too touristic", unbearably "inauthentic", and long to stumble upon those undiscovered, untainted, untouched areas... but only if the Lonely Planet guide says they'll enjoy them. Backpackers are the hipsters of the global community, wearing their torn, hand-made-in-India tunics and carrying worn, Deuter backpacks, wide eyed and earnest, travelling vast distances in search of the "authentic, local experience", only to find themselves in the company of other backpackers. This was still prior to the phenomenon of "instagram influencers", which is how backpackers now manage to travel the world for free. I must hasten to add that I was as guilty as anyone of this vagrant snobbery (although my desire to avoid tours and resorts was usually motivated more by my budget than my integrity). As such, my travels in Asia followed a very well-marked route, advised by my peers and my trusty guide-book.

The first time I went to Thailand was in 2008, right after my final (disastrous) climbing World Cup, just after I turned 19. I had spent a blissful four and a half weeks on Tonsai beach in Krabi; rock climbing, swimming and watching my new friends smoke a truly astonishing amount of pot before breakfast. The extent of my 'travelling' on that trip had been a one-day motorcycle ride to some hot springs, and a day spent exploring the Krabi markets. The only people I encountered were other climbers, or backpackers who had wandered onto Tonsai beach by mistake, while staying in the much more popular (and much more expensive) neighbouring beach of Railay. Safe to say that this was not the experience most people sought when they came here. This time around, I realised just how much more there was to see...

Bangkok was everything I thought it would be, and more. We had thought that Kathmandu was hectic, but it was nothing compared to the hedonism of Khao San Road on a Friday night, or, as we discovered, any night. It was a whirlwind of distorted noise, whirling colours, lights, and a crush of weaving, shouting, laughing people. The street has been given over entirely to backpackers: to stalls selling singlets and shorts emblazoned with beer logos; to cheap cocktails served in buckets that cause you to go temporarily blind; to massage parlours and beauty treatments involving skin-eating fish; to *tuktuk* drivers hassling bleary-eyed victims of the harsh morning humidity, and a myriad of street vendors selling fruit shakes and Pad Thai for one dollar.

After a month of relative abstinence, high in the Himalayas, Heidi and I dived into the madding crowd, eager to get nice and drunk and make new friends. We accomplished both tasks admirably, and Heidi spent the entire next day in bed, groaning and exclaiming at intervals "but I NEVER get hangovers!" I was fine. Fine, that is, until around four o'clock, when my hangover struck with ruthless precision, in the hottest part of the day, just as Heidi had decided she was well enough to emerge and do something fun. I should have known better than to spend five hours drinking fifty cent liquor mixed with red bull and coke from a child's sand bucket in a Tiki-themed bar with a bunch of strangers, but, clearly, I hadn't.

We spent the weekend exploring the markets and going to see the new "James Bond" film, where I was reminded of how disorienting it can be to see a Hollywood movie in a strange country. When Gavin and I had been in Ecuador, we had gone to see a sci-fi film in a huge multiplex, and when we can come out, had been utterly unable to find our way back to our little hostel. It is so easy to get sucked into the world of the movie, in the familiar cinema space, but then you are expelled into the unfamiliarity of wherever you happen to be, and it feels like waking up from a dream.

Realizing that we could no longer be trusted with the kind of freely-available alcohol in Kao San road, Heidi and I boarded a mini-van with about eight other tourists Realizing that we could no longer be trusted with the kind of freely-available alcohol in Kao San road, Heidi and I boarded a mini-van with about eight other tourists and, in some significant discomfort, made our way across the border into Cambodia, to the town of Siem Reap. As the site of Cambodia's main tourist attraction, Siem Reap was a bizarre oasis of casinos, resorts, tuk tuks and 'westeraunts' serving food for delicate tourist stomachs. It was a very different vibe to Nepal, to say the least.

We stayed in Siem Reap for four days - longer than intended, because poor Heidi got food poisoning, she swears from merely walking past the restaurant beside our hotel - and so I made friends with a gang of European backpackers, winding their way through South East Asia at their leisure, with very little money or time constraints, content to stay in one place until they hear dof somewhere new and exciting (or were run out of town by the locals). I became close with Tammy, a lovely English girl who had quit her job to travel indefinitely, but was thinking of making her way home at the end of the month. We sweet-talked our way into one of the fancier resorts and spent a day lolling about in the pool to try and escape the heat, although it must be said that the pool - located as it was in a luxury resort - was not in fact very cold. We got talking with an Australian couple who were staying there, who told us about their journey so far through Vietnam, and their plans for the next two weeks, which included an earnest wish to finish their trip with a stay in "somewhere nice".

"Because this place is a dump!" I said, indicating the waiter serving drinks to a woman lying beside the pool, trying to keep a straight face. To his credit, the man looked sheepish.
"Sorry, that must have sounded a bit precious".
We all laughed it off, but it was a bizarre conversation.
It was odd to think that we, scruffy backpackers with very few dollars to our names, were sharing the same tourist attractions as people who were on their resort get away.

Speaking of tourist attractions: we bought our tickets for Angkor Wat (the main reason we had come to Cambodia), without realizing just how massive a place it was. The ticket seller recommended the four day pass, but we opted for two days, thinking he was trying to rip us off. What a whirlwind! Even with a tuk tuk driver, we barely scratched the surface of this incredible historical site. At over 400 square kilometers (the largest religious - Hindu - monument in the world), the temples and pyramids of Angkor Wat sprawled through the jungle, jutting irregularly into the humid air, some leaning at odd angles, some seeming to crumble before our eyes. Described by one sixteenth century visitor as containing "all the refinements the human genius can conceive of", it was pretty damn incredible to behold. If I was honest, I had been starting to feel the length of my journey, seven months away from home, constantly on the move, overwhelmed with both beautiful places and powerful emotions... but this still took my breath away. In the cool, quiet chill of the mornings, the grey stones and moss of the temples seemed frozen, and the chattering of the monkeys gave the place an eerie feeling. We scrambled over ancient stones and crawled beneath gigantic banyan roots as we explored the labyrinth of temples, transported back to childhood. As the day warmed, and the air began to shimmer with humidity, the jagged outlines of the roofs seemed to blur against the sky, and the cool, dungeon-like rooms became crammed with people trying to escape the heat. But, most magical of all, was sunset.

Tammie and I settled ourselves against a tree by the reflection pools, and waited for the sun to sink behind the eponymous Angkor Wat temple, outlined against the twilight sky. Even though the crowds soon became obnoxiously big and bustling, the scene remained calm and serene. The sky turned a brilliant crimson, outlining the dark buildings so dramatically that we gave up trying to take photographs, and just sat, letting the image imprint itself in our memories.

Years later, my friend Kate from Nepal would go to work for an NGO in Cambodia, and through her I would learn more about the country's devastating history that I cared to understand from my four days there as a traveller. It was sobering to me that I could have been so moved by a place, yet so utterly ignorant of the way its people lived, or what they had survived. I told myself that in future, I would always try to learn the history of a country before I visited, and for the most part, I've stuck to that rule.

*****

After Heidi had sufficiently recovered and was able to stand upright for more than an hour without vomiting, we planned to return to Bangkok and catch a night bus north to a Chiang Mai. We were told that under any circumstances, the bus should get us across the border and back to the capital within eight hours. Ha.

We arrived at the Thai/Cambodian border at eleven in the morning, the same as all the other tourist buses, and proceeded to stand in an unmoving line of sweaty people in the baking midday sun for two and a half hours. For the first time in my life, I was grateful to see a cold can of beer, when the man in front of us pulled a six-pack out of his bag. When the line eventually ground into motion, it took us a further hour to reach the front, where we discovered that the cause of the delay had been that the border officials were all on their lunch hour from midday to one. One hundred hot, stinking, pissed off tourists waited in the sun while six government officials took a simultaneous hour off from stamping passports. I couldn't help but feel that we were being punished for the existence of dickheads like the man we had met the night before. When we arrived at the desks we were stamped and rushed through post haste, with no instructions or questions. Needless to say, we missed the night bus, and discovered that our options were to wait in Bangkok one more day, or to catch the night train, leaving in half an hour.

We sped to the station, bought the only remaining tickets, and boarded the train in third class. As we sat in the hard, square seats, and surveyed the hard, square carriage with its wheezing fans and dirty floor, a feeling of apprehension began to creep into my bones.
"What does it say our arrival time is on the ticket?"
When Heidi told me, I must confess, I may have reacted badly.
Fifteen hours. The train journey was going to take fifteen hours. I had no book, no music, and no films. No pillow. No blanket. No space to stretch out. No food or water.
It took all of Heidi's considerable optimism to prevent me taking a flying leap back onto the platform and refusing to get back on the train.
"Just think of it as an adventure" she coaxed "this is how everyone travelled thirty years ago. This is how the locals travel."
She was right. A few carriages away, backpackers were dozing off in sleeper compartments, or curling up in second-class reclining seats. In our carriage, a five-year-old Thai girl was making increasingly bold dashes down the aisle to gawp at Heidi's blonde hair, before giggling wildly and running back to her mother.
I begrudgingly tried to look on the bright side – I was a real traveller now, just like my Dad had been forty years before me – and managed to fall asleep for a while, propped up on my backpack with my scarf draped over my face.

Fifteen hours on a train with no books, movies, or games gives one an inordinate amount of time to think over – and over think – one's life. My greatest fear on this trip had been that other people would consider me to have wasted my time. Being confronted by my mother's death, with the reality of how suddenly our time can be cut short, made me fearful of missing out on things, of choosing one path at the expense of another. With my Mum no longer there to reassure me that I was doing the right thing, it had been hard to let go of what I thought other people expected of me, and asking myself what it was that I really wanted. I realized that I had needed to prove to myself that I was able to deal with things, even when they happened out of the blue. The reason I had fought so hard against the "all or nothing" prospect of whatever it was that David and I had, was that I felt like I had to be ok on my own before I could commit to being with someone else. My mum was gone, my family had fundamentally changed, and I had come to understand that my friends, even though they did everything they could, couldn't make me ok. My boyfriend couldn't make me ok. I needed to make myself ok. And I knew, in the rare moments in which I allowed myself to be honest, that the reason I fought so hard against being with David was because I knew that if I let it happen, it could be something great, and something that could last the rest of our lives, and I would never again be truly alone. This was my last chance to prove that I could make myself ok.

In her letter to me in Argentina, Mum had called me brave, and so, sitting there on that train, I pictured my journey as two halves: the parts where I had been fearful, and those where I had been brave. Despite what other people may have thought, leaving Australia had not been brave. Impulsive maybe, but I had known that I had people waiting for me at the other end, people who would take care of me and make sure I had somewhere to stay and something to do. I had not been brave when I had tagged along with whoever I met, allowing them to make the decisions and plans. I had had some amazing experiences, met some beautiful people, and seen new and exciting places, but it had been at someone else's whim. I had been brave when I had faced my fears by climbing those crazy cliffs. I had been brave when I had jumped on that bus alone, and booked my flights without asking anyone if what I was doing was the right thing. I had been brave by visiting places where I knew no-one, where I had nothing but a map and a guide book. I had been brave in giving myself a direction, a goal, and working towards it rather than just floating in circles, and I had discovered that not only was I capable of making decisions and handling the consequences, but that even when things went horribly wrong, I was able to pick myself up again. And finally, I had been brave when I had not jumped off that train, but had forced myself to spend hours on end sitting with nothing but my thoughts and insecurities to entertain me.

The one puzzle I couldn't solve on that train was this: had I been brave or afraid when I told David I wasn't getting on that plane? Had I been brave or afraid when I told him I loved him? And did that mean that I was being brave or cowardly by agreeing to meet him for one last encounter, in only a few days? The times that I felt had been the easiest had been those when I had been drifting, relying on other people to make my decisions for me, allowing myself to be pulled in circles. David had given me the option to embrace that, and go with him and insert myself into his life, and let all my future decisions be made by that one choice. Had I been brave to choose to go off on my own instead? Or had I just been afraid of what people would have thought if, after telling them I was going off on my own, I ended up in America as somebody's girlfriend? Was that really the loss of independence I imagined it to be? Or had I just let myself get carried away in my own melodrama?

Meeting other travellers means you constantly compare your experiences to theirs, which can be very humbling, satisfying, frustrating or inspiring, depending on who you meet and how you are feeling on any given day. I'm sure there are people (I've met one or two) who just get it right. They know where they want to be. They accomplish things they dreamed of accomplishing. They spend their time and money well. *They* always have exactly the right equipment packed. They read the guidebook BEFORE they got on their plane. *They* never have to change their flights at the last minute because they underestimated the unattainability of any given visa.

I am not, and will never be, one of those people. My trip, both halves of it, had been dictated by luck, coincidence and thinking on my feet.

There was always the possibility I might get it right next time.

CHAPTER 23:
THAILAND

*Crimping: a crimp is a type of hold that is only big enough
to grip with your fingertips. Crimping is all about balance:
you have to position your weight very carefully, generally
keeping your body as close to the rock as possible. Typic-
ally, the type of rock you need to crimp on, has very little in
the way of decent footholds, so you need to trust the friction of your shoes and proceed delicately.*

We finally, finally arrived in Chiang Mai and took all of
five seconds to decide that it was a medical necessity
for us to have a room with a pool. Luckily, accommodation in
the north turned out to be far cheaper than in Bangkok or the
beaches in the South, and we managed to find a beautiful lodge
with a huge swimming pool. That night we wandered out to explore the famous night markets. Even though my pack was fit
to bursting, I bought a few final Christmas presents. We dared
one another to try the fried insects (I sampled a spider's leg, but
couldn't bring myself to take a proper bite. Heidi had a wedding
to go to when she returned to Norway, and so she decided to
get fitted for a tailored dress. We spent three days in Chiang Mai,
wandering around the night markets, sampling delicious and

curious foods, buying far too many trinkets and generally amusing ourselves by doing very little. We hired motorcycles for a day and went in search of waterfalls and caves in the hills, escaping the crowds for a while at least. The highlight of the trip was the cooking course we took in the back room of a local woman's house, where we learned that ALL Thai recipes require sugar, fish sauce, oyster sauce, and chilli. We were enjoying ourselves, but we felt like we were just killing time. I was itching to climb, and we were both running out of money, and patience. We decided to head south.

Even though we took the bus, and not the horrendous train, back to Bangkok, we still lost a day and a lot of money (and gained a few grey hairs) trying to coordinate ourselves. The bus dropped us off in Khao San road at four in the morning, when nothing was open except for the MacDonald's and the dodgier massage places. We were forced to get a room just so we could sit down, and after we had both fallen asleep, we awoke to find we had missed the bus going south for that day. *C'est la vie* – at least for backpackers. It was all immaterial in the end, because two days later we were stepping out onto the sandy beach of Ton Sai, and as we looked at the cliffs and the beach and the jungle before us, the city and the buses and the madness we had left behind melted away, and we both heaved a sigh of relief. Walking up to find somewhere to stay, we ran into Jamie, the English guy who had shared his beer with us in line at the Cambodian border, and the next day I saw May, the Australian girl I'd from Kalymnos.

One night, drinking cheap beers under the cliffs, May asked about my parents, and I opened up about what had happened to my mum. She listened as I recounted the story of her illness and death, and my trip, and how much I missed her. I realized that I had only talked about her a handful of times since I'd left home, and whenever I did it tended to come off stilted and rehearsed, becuase that was the only way I could get through it. I noticed that I was sounding like less of a robot as I talked about what she was like as we sat on the sand and listened to the waves lapping against he wooden fishing boats pulled up on the shore. When I finished, May put her arm around me.

"She'd be so proud of you."

It was the kind of platitude that had made me grind my teeth when people said it a year ago, and now, here was this person who I'd only met twice, who had never met my mum, probably saying it just to be nice. But, for some reason, instead of feeling irritated and dismissive, I felt relief. Maybe it was true. Maybe it was just time. I wasn't sure.

*****

Over the next week, we established quite the climbing crew with us, May's friends, and Jamie. Heidi hadn't climbed much, but she was fit and eager; and even though I hadn't climbed since Greece, I felt strong and confident. I'd now faced my fears so many times, and in so many ways, that I felt sure I could hold my own; and in the first week, I deliberately jumped on climbs which I knew were well above my range. Every day I threw myself at those limestone cliffs, but not becuase I had something to prove: quite the opposite. I no longer cared to prove anything. I'd made it this far - half way around the world and back - and I'd survived. I had no idea if I had "found myself" or if I had accomplished whatever it was I'd set out to do, but I felt so present, so at ease in this faintly familiar place, with these new friends, that it no longer seemed to matter. Even with my newfound steadiness, however, my mind kept returning to thoughts of the person who would be arriving from America in five days' time.

Since I'd been in Thailand, the emails between David and I had started to cool off. Both of us were nervous at seeing the other, neither of us knew what to expect, and the craziness of the whole situation was sinking in now that our plan was finally coming to fruition.

His flight didn't get into Phuket till eleven, and it was three hours from Ton Sai, so we'd agreed that I would get us a hotel room near the airport, meet him, and we would stay there for the first two nights before coming back. I couldn't eat at all on the day I went to the airport to meet him. I sat in the hotel room waiting until it was time to pick him up, unable to sleep or read or relax. I'd changed my clothes five times (even though at that point, I only had about six outfits left in my pack), I'd made a sign with his last name on it, and I couldn't decide whether he would find it funny or stupid, but when it was finally time to go, I grabbed it. As I waited at the arrivals gate, with clammy hands and the stupid sign flapping at my knees, in the worst outfit I could possibly have chosen, about to make what was possibly the stupidest mistake of my trip so far, I felt like I would faint... and then I saw him walking through the doors, looking travel-worn and grumpy, searching the faces around me until he saw mine, and as we looked at each other, suddenly the rest of the world ceased to matter, or even to exist.

*****

It was another 36 hours before either of us could keep our clothes on for long enough to catch the bus and ferry back to Ton Sai. Heidi and my climbing friends were waiting; eager to meet the mysterious guy they had been hearing about, and to my relief, everyone got along happily.

Since he left Europe (and perhaps after seeing the climbing in Rodellar), David had caught the climbing bug, and had treated himself to shoes, a harness, and a gym membership. He had told me all of this, and it may have been his desire to impress me, or my over-enthusiasm at the thought of us climbing together, or a combination of the both, but I threw him a little too far into the deep end on those first few days in Ton Sai. Climbing on real rocks is very different to climbing in a gym – it's a lot scarier for a start! David took it in his stride, but he soon got very frustrated with the 'easy' climbs I threw at him. To his credit, he refused to be beaten, and repeated the one (very difficult) climb every day we were there until he had conquered it.

On our second day, at the "easy" wall, David was getting frustrated with a particular move about halfway up his project climb. He'd been attempting and falling for about five minutes, when suddenly he let out a yell that wasn't frustration: about thirty monkeys of various sizes had appeared out of nowhere and had started clambering rapidly down the cliff directly above him. Small stones and twigs started raining down on me as I struggled to belay him back to the ground ahead of the advancing horde - it was like something out of The Jungle Book! He fumbled with the knot, trying to untie himself so we could run, but luckily the leader of the monkey army decided we were a bit scary ourselves, and they changed direction once they reached the ground, scampering off into the jungle beside the cliff.

"I didn't even get a rabies shot before I came" David told me, his hands shaking. It very quickly became hilarious that he had been chased off the wall by monkeys, and later that night at the bar, we discovered that this was not uncommon, and several "locals" (entrenched expats) bemoaned the fact that the monkeys were getting bolder every year, and were not afraid of climbers at all any more.

The potential need for rabies shots wasn't the only thing David had failed to consider - he also hadn't brought any proper hiking shoes, only flip flop sandals.

"Thongs" I explained to him, while he giggles like a twelve year old, "they're called thongs."

Unfortunately for him a lot of the best climbing in Ton Sai was only accessible by steep, muddy jungle trails, and on the third day, he gouged an impressive hole in his big toe when his thong slipped off his foot while he was trying to haul himself up a particularly treacherous bit of path. All credit to him for continuing to shove that foot into tiny climbing shoes for the rest of the trip.

We fell into a happy routine of waking early, going to the little hut-café-bookshop for coffee, tea and toast; climbing until the sun became too hot; having fruit smoothies for lunch; returning to our hut to lay in the hammock when the afternoon storms came in; and then meeting up with the group for dinner at one of the dusty, ill-lit little restaurants that lined the tracks to the beach. David managed to keep up with the climbing, even though he was frustrated most of the time by the fact that it was so much more difficult that the gym climbing he had trained on. We sometimes listened to music in the little cabana bars, where there were as many hammocks as there were chairs, and a couple of times, I allowed myself to be talked into getting up and singing with the band, whose guitar player climbed with us. One night there was a lamp-lighting ceremony on the beach, and the two of us lit a candle and sat on the sand watching as it floated up over the waves into the dark sky.

That night marked the end of our ability to avoid the reality of what lay ahead: both of us were leaving soon.

The next day, the moods started. The silences. The sentences that were started, and then cut short, with a muttered "never mind". It was horrible, because for the past two weeks, everything had been completely blissful between us...and that was part of the problem. This was the longest period of uninterrupted time we had spent in each other's physical presence, and it had been perfect: no fighting, no jealousy, and no fear. It was as if we had always been this way, and it was the easiest thing in the world. I didn't know what to do.

David was due to leave the day before me, and on his last night, we finally had the conversation.
"We could make this work you know." He was running his fingers through my hair, which had grown long and blonde from all

my time in the sun.

"How? How could we possibly make this work? The last few months have been so hard – we were barely excited to see one another by the time you arrived here. Long distance kills romance, it's just a fact."

"What if we lived in the same country?"

"Which one? We are both in the middle of our degrees, and it costs an arm and a leg to study in another country. We can't afford it."

"Stop saying no. Just hear me out: I only have one semester of my degree left, and I'm pretty sure it would be possible for me to do most of it online – and part of it is a thesis that I do alone anyway. If I could convince the rest of my professors that I had to be out of town for some reason, but handed all my assignments in and did the readings online, there's a chance I could still finish my degree, but be living in Australia. With you."

I said nothing, feeling the old fear of commitment washing over me. It was all or nothing, all over again.

"What if you come to Sydney and we hate each other after a month? I've never lived with anyone before. What if this is all just a holiday romance and we actually suck at this in real life?"

"You are just making excuses. I know this would be just as wonderful in 'real life' as it is here. But just to humour you: so what if it doesn't work? I'll go home. At least we will know for sure."

I wanted to believe him so badly, but I was still unconvinced. It was all too much to take in and agree to. I didn't trust myself enough to make a decision and stick to it, after I had spent most of the last year being so flaky. I was afraid that if I said yes, I would want to change my mind once I got home and reality hit once again. So I said no.

He didn't say anything for a long time, and I thought he had fallen asleep. Just as my eyes were closing, he said, very softly:

"I'm done. I'm done chasing you, I can't keep getting myself beaten up like this, so, you win. After I leave tomorrow, I'm done."

CHAPTER 24: HOME

Dyno: short for "dynamic move," is when you aren't able to reach the next hold, and so, quite simply, you jump for it. If this happens to be an onsight climb, you risk jumping for a crap hold, a sloper or a false pocket, and slipping and falling. You might not be able to jump far enough to reach the hold. Or maybe, you make the jump, and catch the hold, and keep going...

I woke up the next morning, feeling numb. We caught the ferry to the mainland and waited for the bus that would take David to the airport. I half expected myself to repeat the performance from Barcelona, and jump on the bus behind him, and I think he was thinking the same thing. When the bus came, he hugged me tightly, and then got on board without looking back. I watched the bus drive away, willing him to turn and look, to wave, anything, but he just kept staring straight ahead.

I told myself that this was for the best – we would both go home, and our lives would go on and everything would be simpler. I went to the ATM to get money out for my own trip the next day, but I felt so mixed up and strange that I couldn't remember my pin. I tried four times before the machine cut me off and told me to contact my bank, so I made my way back to the beach, cashless, and alone.

That night I drank more than I had since Seville. I felt wild and moody and nervous about going home. Heidi and May and most of my climbing friends had already left, so I sat alone in a hammock, and glared at the people around me. The next morning, I packed and boarded the ferry with a clanging hangover, my head spinning, not just from the booze, but with all the ways I felt different and new and old and alive and calm and open and optimistic and depressed, all at the same time.

This is it, I thought. I get on that plane and this chapter is over. But life had one more little surprise for me at the airport.

"You've overstayed your visa." The Thai immigration official glared at me over his spectacles.

"Sorry? I thought I had thirty days?"

"I'm afraid not Miss, the thirty day visa is for tourists entering through an airport: entering over a land border gives only fifteen days."

This was a small detail that, in the horrendous mess of the Cambodian border crossing, the lunch-hungry officials had neglected to mention: obviously, when you reentered the country from Cambodia, you were issued a new visa. Yes, I know that I should have checked for myself. I silently berated myself for making assumptions, for repeating the same mistake as India, steeled myself and asked how much I owed.

"$250."

Ouch.

Good thing I had budgeted for last minute emergencies – I still had $300 left in my bank account. There was just one problem: the bank had blocked my card the day before, and I only had about $30 in cash.

Calling the bank elicited assurances that all I needed do was try my card in five minutes and the problem would be fixed. I did. It wasn't. I called them again. Same response. Same result. I started to panic. My flight was due to leave in an hour, and I still wasn't checked in. Could the immigration officer take a credit card, since my pin wasn't working? Cash only. I proceeded to panic more enthusiastically. Crying hysterically, I went up to the last couple checking in for my flight and, throwing pride and caution to the wind, I begged. I explained my situation as best I could through tears and hiccoughs, trying to look simultaneously desperate and trustworthy.

To my utter astonishment and amazing good luck, they not only had the cash on them, but also handed it over to me after only minimal convincing. I thanked them profusely, offered to give them my credit card as collateral, and settled eventually for giving them my seat and phone number, and email address, and promising to pay them back as soon as we landed. An hour later I was in the air, on my final flight, the one that would take me home.

I sat in my seat, face red from crying and running around the airport, and realised that not only did I look a complete mess, but I didn't have any food. I hadn't eaten anything that day due to my hangover and nerves, and once I sat down I realised I was starving, and yet I had no money to buy food (here I cursed my past self for being so cheap and buying a flight without a free meal). To add to my anxiety, I was seated next to three massive Tongan guys, who looked as though they bashed heads together for a living. When they saw my obvious distress, they asked me kindly if I was ok, and, trying not to start crying again at the relief of a friendly face, I told them my story. They were impressed, and the guy next to me, turned out to be a nightclub bouncer in Sydney, and must have been at least three times my size, handed me a huge serving of chicken teriyaki that he had brought with him onto the plane, refusing to listen to my protestations, saying he had already eaten.

With a full belly, and a plane taking me closer to home every minute, I finally relaxed. Again, I had learned that people are, for the most part, fundamentally good. I hoped that one day, I could pay their acts of kindness forward to someone else in my situation.

*****

My brother met me at the airport in the early morning, and we both went for breakfast with my Dad, who was flying out that day to visit friends in New Zealand. It was so good to see their faces and hear their voices again – I told them stories of my trip, and my brother told me how he had finished his degree, and was now getting work, and loved it! He looked so much older than the last time I had seen him, I nearly cried to think of how much he had grown up while I'd been away.

I had a message waiting for me when I checked my phone after we said goodbye to dad.

"I made it home – the flight was murder. I miss you, and I love you. Let me know when you make it home. Never have I ever…"

I stared at the message for a long time.

I let myself back into my old house, and lay on my bed, gazing around the room, until my friends got off work of finished class, and mobbed me with kisses and questions and stories. We all went out for dinner, and Eli was there, warm and familiar, squeezing me in a hug that almost made up for all the ones I'd missed.

Everything was the same as when I'd left, but I wasn't.

"Never have I ever…"

It had taken me eight months, eight countries, and a very broken heart, but sitting there in that little dive bar with my old friends, and with my old life ready to sweep me back up, I finally made my decision.

*****

The Skype connection was infuriatingly slow, and I drummed my fingers on the desk as the little spinning wheel on my screen taunted me. Finally, I heard the familiar bleep, and David's face filled the screen.

"Yup." He was looking away at something, and there were lots of people around him.

"I just wanted to let you know I made it home safely."

"Uh Uh. I'm glad you made it." I could tell he was trying to make his voice as emotionless as possible.

"I was just wondering, if the offer is still there…how soon could you come to Australia? Because I just realized that all I want is to keep having adventures with you. Will you come?"

He didn't say anything for a minute, and I wondered if he had heard me, or if the connection had cut me off.

"Are you playing with me? Or is this for real?"

I laughed, although it felt like I was going to cry.

"This is for real. This is what I want. Will you get on one more plane for me?"

The familiar grin spread across his face.

"I hate to say I told you so… but I told you we would be together in the end!"

*****

Two months later, I was waiting at the arrivals gate at Sydney International Terminal. I had changed my outfit seventeen times (I had a few more clothes now that I owned a wardrobe instead of a backpack); I'd made (and then discarded) a welcome sign; and my hands were sweaty with nerves. I had gotten there way too early, and so my car was probably being towed at that very moment, and I had been double checking his flight arrival for the past twenty minutes, convinced I was waiting in the wrong spot… and then I saw him coming through the doors, with a pack on his back, and a smile on his face, and I knew, without a shadow of a doubt, that *this* was what I wanted.

ACKNOWLEDGEMENTS

To the friends, family, and strangers who gave me food, climbing equipment, or a place to sleep on my journey, thank you for your kindness.

To the wonderful people who read and re-read this manuscript "just one more time", and gave me feedback and encouragement, thank you for your patience.

To my dad and brother, thank you for always being there for me, even when I was far away.

To my husband, thank you for getting on all those planes for me.

To my mum, thank you for all that I am today.

Made in the USA
Monee, IL
30 May 2020

32195872R10163